50 Hikes in Kentucky

D0863721

50 *Hikes*

In Kentucky

From the Appalachian Mountains to the Land between the Lakes

First Edition

HIRAM ROGERS

Backcountry Guides

Woodstock, Vermont

AN INVITATION TO THE READER

Over time trails can be rerouted and signs and landmarks altered. If you find that changes have occurred on the routes described in this book, please let us know so that corrections may be made in future editions. The author and publisher also welcome other comments and suggestions. Address all correspondence to:

Editor
50 Hikes™ Series
Backcountry Guides
P.O. Box 748
Woodstock, Vermont 05091

LIBRARY OF CONGRESS CATALOGING-IN-PUBLICATION DATA

Rogers, Hiram.
  50 hikes in Kentucky : from the Appalachian Mountains to the land between the lakes / Hiram Rogers.—1st ed.
    p. cm.—(Fifty hikes series)
  Includes bibliographical references (p. 251) and index.
  ISBN 0-88150-551-X
  1. Hiking—Kentucky—Guidebooks. 2. Trails—Kentucky—Guidebooks. 3. Kentucky—Guidebooks. I. Title: Fifty hikes in Kentucky. II. Title. III. Series.
GV199.42.K4 R64 2002
917.6904'44—dc21   2001056648
                                        CIP

Maps by Mapping Specialists Ltd., Madison, WI
Interior photographs by the author unless otherwise noted
Cover photograph © Tom Till

Published by Backcountry Guides
A division of The Countryman Press
P.O. Box 748
Woodstock, Vermont 05091

Distributed by W. W. Norton & Company, Inc.
500 Fifth Avenue
New York, NY 10110

Printed in the United States of America

10 9 8 7 6 5 4 3 2 1

DEDICATION

I'd like to acknowledge the loving support of my wife, Jean, who scouted many of the hikes with me (including a steamy mid-August jaunt around the longest trail described in this book), provided many of the wildflower identifications, read very rough drafts of chapters, and put up with an absent husband for much of the last few months.

50 Hikes at a Glance

HIKE	AREA
1. Lakeshore–Moss Ridge Loop	Jenny Wiley SRP
2. Boardinghouse Hollow Trail	Robinson Forest
3. River–Geology–Overlook Loop	Breaks Interstate Park
4. Pine Mountain Trail–US 23 to Bryant Gap	Pine Mountain Trail
5. Bad Branch Trail	Bad Branch SNP
6. Sand Cave and White Rocks	Cumberland Gap NHP
7. Hensley Settlement	Cumberland Gap NHP
8. Chained Rock Trail	Pine Mountain SRP
9. Blue Heron Loop	Big South Fork
10. Yahoo Falls and Yahoo Arch	Big South Fork
11. Kentucky Trail–Ledbetter Trailhead to Troublesome Creek	Big South Fork
12. Koger-Yamacraw Loop	Big South Fork
13. Gobblers Arch and Mark Branch Falls	Stearns Ranger District
14. Natural Arch Scenic Area	Somerset Ranger District
15. Blue Bend Trail	Cumberland Falls SRP
16. Eagle Falls Trail	Cumberland Falls SRP
17. Cumberland River Trail	Cumberland Falls SRP
18. Bark Camp Trail	London Ranger District
19. Beaver Creek Wilderness	Somerset Ranger District
20. Bee Rock Loop	Somerset Ranger District
21. Rockcastle Narrows	London Ranger District
22. Indian Fort Mountain	Berea College Forest
23. The Original Trail	Natural Bridge SRP
24. Hood's Branch and Sand Gap Trails	Natural Bridge SRP
25. Whittleton Arch	Red River Gorge Geo. Area

Legend:

- E easy hiking rating
- M moderate hiking rating
- D difficult hiking rating

- * for non-members on weekends
- ** for overnight use
- *** for back country camping

RATING	DISTANCE (miles)	VIEWS	WATERFALL	ARCHES	CAMPING	BACKPACKING	KIDS	NOTES
E	3.0				★		★	part of loop circles Dewey Lake
M	1.8	★					★	great views from firetower
M	5.1	★			★		★	The Breaks, Russell Fork River
M/D	7.6	★	★		★	to Raven Rock		Raven Rock and Skyview Caves
M/D	7.4	★	★			to falls		Bad Branch Falls and High Rocks Overlook
M/D	8.7	★		near	★	★		White Rocks Overlook and Sand Cave
M/D	10.6	★		near	★	to falls		historic Hensley Settlement
E/M	3.4	★		★	★		★	unique Chained Rock & great views
M	6.4	★		★	★		★	river overlooks and Crack-in-rock
E/M	9.4	★	★	near	★	to arch		KY's highest waterfall and two arches
M/D	9.4				★			thru the wild core of the Big South Fork
D	11.1		★	near	★			challenging loop past Koger Arch
M	6.1	★	★	near	★		★	Gobblers Arch & Mark Branch Falls
E/M	6.1	★		★			★	fee; short hike to arch plus longer loop
M	4.7				★			Cumberland River and cliffs
E	1.5	★	★		★		★	two beautiful waterfalls
D	7.0	★	★		★	★		Cumberland River and falls
M	5.6		★		★		★	rockhouses and cascades
E/M	1.9	★			★		★	overlook above Three Forks
M	4.9	★			★	★	★	fee; cliffs and Rockcastle Narrows
D	9.4	★			★	to creek		fee; Rockcastle River and Cane Creek
E/M	3.0	★					★	great vistas & intricate rock formations
E/M	3.8	★		★			★	shortest route to Natural Bridge
D	10.4	★	★	★				Natural Bridge and Nature Preserve
E/M	4.4		★	★	★		★	fee**; Whittington Arch

50 Hikes at a Glance

HIKE	AREA
26. Courthouse Rock and Double Arch	Red River Gorge Geo. Area
27. Grays Arch–Rough Trail Loop	Red River Gorge Geo. Area
28. Swift Camp Creek–Wildcat Loop	Clifty Wilderness Area
29. Gladie Creek Loop	Clifty Wilderness Area
30. Sheltowee Trace and Tater Knob Loop	Cave Run Lake–Moorhead RD
31. Carter Caves Cross-Country Trail (4C's)	Carter Caves SRP
32. Michael Tygart Loop Trail	Greenbo Lake SRP
33. Main Trail	Boone County Cliffs SNP
34. Big Bone Creek and Bison Trace Trails	Big Bone Lick SP
35. Scotts Gap Loop Trail	Jefferson County Memorial Fores
36. Tioga Falls National Recreation Trail	Fort Knox Military Reservation
37. Otter Creek Trail	Otter Creek Park
38. Millennium Trail	Bernheim Forest
39. Lakeshore and Scenic Overlook Trails	Green River Lake SP
40. Echo River Loop	Mammoth Cave NP
41. White Oak Trail	Mammoth Cave NP
42. Raymer Hollow Loop	Mammoth Cave NP
43. First Creek–McCoy Hollow Loop	Mammoth Cave NP
44. Historic Cave Tour	Mammoth Cave NP
45. Grand Avenue Tour	Mammoth Cave NP
46. Backcountry Loop	Audubon State Park
47. Macedonia Trail	Pennyrile State Forest
48. Canal Loop B	Land between the Lakes
49. N/S Trail–Hillman Ferry Campground to Hatchery Hollow	Land between the Lakes
50. Honker Lake Trail	Land between the Lakes

RATING	DISTANCE (miles)	VIEWS	WATERFALL	ARCHES	CAMPING	BACKPACKING	KIDS	NOTES
M/D	8.1	★		★	near	to vistas		fee**; unusual Double Arch and vistas
D	9.4			★	near	to arch		fee**; the huge expanse of Grays Arch
M	5.5				near	★	★	fee**; wilderness and Swift Camp Creek
D	9.2				near	★		fee**; wilderness area around Galdie Creek
D	14.7	★			★	to tower		Tater Knob firetower
M/D	7.8	★	★	★	★	★		three arches and Smokey Valley Lake
D	10.1			★	★			wildlife and Pruitt Fork Creek
E	1.7						★	quiet nature preserve
E	0.9			★			★	fossil exhibits and bison herd
M	3.5						★	spring and summer wildflowers
E	2.0		★				★	Tioga Falls and historic railroad trestles
M/D	8.2	★		★			★	Morgan's Cave and Otter Creek
D	13.7							fee*; long loop through Research Forest
E	3.8	★		★			★	lake views
E/M	2.5	★		★			★	scenic front country trails
E/M	5.0				near	★	★	historic ferry route
M/D	8.5				near	★		two historic cemeteries
D	14.7				near	★		challenging backpacking loop
E	2.0			★			★	fee; original cave entrance & saltpeter mining
E/M	4.0			★			★	fee; cave formations
E/M	4.2			★			★	beautiful forests around Wilderness Lake
E	3.6				near		★	unusual pine forest
E	2.9	★			near	★	★	flat, easy walking
D	9.2	★		★	★			fee***; Pisgah Bay and swimming beaches
M	4.5	★			near		★	views of Honker and Barkley Lakes

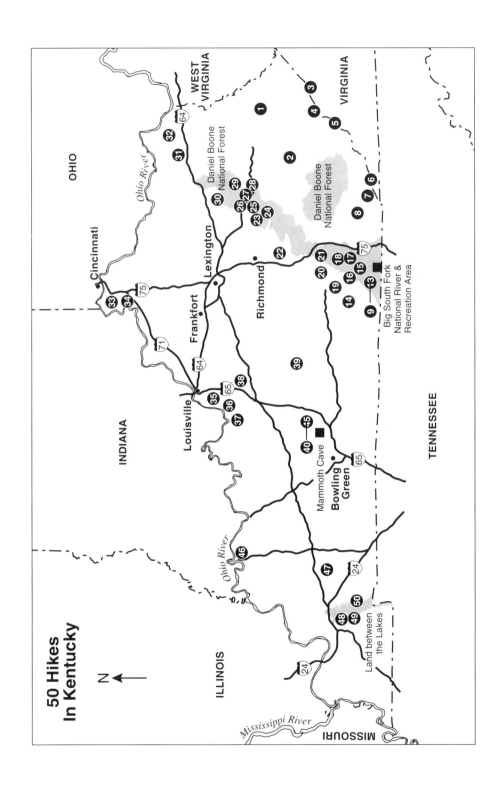

CONTENTS

Acknowledgments

This book could not have been written without assistance from many helpful people. I am grateful to the following people for helping with questions about parks, trails, and the natural history of Kentucky:

Jonathan Barker, Big Bone Lick State Park
Dwight Blevins, Tygarts State Forest
Jim Carroll, Mammoth Cave National Park
David Goode, Green River Lakes State Park
Gary Hawkins, Land between the Lakes National Recreation Area
Henry Holman, Mammoth Cave National Park
Mike Ladd, Pennyrile State Forest
Fred Marriott, Morehead Ranger District
Steven Shaper, Berea College Forestry
Jay Snyder, London Ranger District
John Stallard, Clinch Ranger District, Jefferson National Forest
K. K. Stuart, Cumberland Gap National Historic Park
Ed Swan, Somerset Ranger District
Carey Tichenor, Kentucky State Parks

Ron Vanover, Jenny Wiley State Resort Park

This work has been greatly improved by a number of gracious folks who reviewed draft chapters for hike descriptions in their areas:

Shad Baker, Pine Mountain Trail Conference
Joyce Bender, Kentucky State Nature Preserves Commission
Vickie Carson, Mammoth Cave National Park
Ries Collier, Cumberland Gap National Historic Park
Wilson Francis, Natural Bridge State Resort Park
Kathryn Harper, Land between the Lakes National Recreation Area
Jorge Hersel, Stanton Ranger District
Brian Lewis, Otter Creek Park
Steven Seven, Big South National River and Recreation Area
Bret Smitley, Cumberland Falls State Resort Park
Matt Walker, Land between the Lakes National Recreation Area

Introduction

From the natural arches of eastern Kentucky, across the magnificent caves that underlie the heartland, to the shimmering lakes and rivers of western Kentucky, the Bluegrass State offers a rich and varied landscape for those willing to explore it on foot. Each region of the state has its own characteristic landscape, and each holds unique surprises just waiting to delight those who explore around the next bend.

In every season the trails of Kentucky beckon. In winter, when the leaves have fallen and the underbrush has subsided, evidence of earlier visitors often emerges from the forest. Low walls of stone mark the boundaries of fields, and clusters of rusted artifacts mark long-abandoned homesites. Spring signals the rebirth of the landscape. An explosion of wildflowers carpets the floor of forest and glade, while birds brighten the air with song. In summer, it's time to head for the cool, clear waters of streams and lakes, or climb to windswept mountaintops. Fall signals a break from summer's heat. Autumn's patchwork of colors demand appreciation from overlooks high in the mountains.

Eastern Kentucky is known for coal mines and rugged, hard-to-reach mountains. But here at the western edge of the Appalachians are the long, high ridges of Pine and Cumberland Mountains. Tucked along these scenic mountaintops are the Pine Mountain Trail, Cumberland Gap National Historic Park, Pine Mountain State Resort Park, Breaks Interstate Park, and Bad Branch State Nature Preserve.

The Daniel Boone National Forest (DBNF) protects a million-acre strip across the eastern part of the state, stretching from the Tennessee border nearly to the Ohio River. This is a land of delicate waterfalls, quiet forests, and massive sandstone arches. This rocky wonderland contains two designated wilderness areas, the Big South Fork National River and Recreation Area, and state parks at Cumberland Falls, Natural Bridge, Carter Caves, and Greenbo Lake. Here are trails suitable for anything from a short stroll to a week-long wilderness adventure.

Kentucky's fertile Bluegrass Heartland lacks huge expanses of public spaces. But a fine assortment of well-located state, county, city, and private parks contain trails ideal for an escape into the woods. Areas such as Fort Knox, Otter Creek, Jefferson County Memorial Forest, the Bernheim Forest and Arboretum, and the state parks at Big Bone Lick and Green River Lake have extensive trail systems. Here the urban landscape quickly fades away and quiet, peaceful nature reigns.

Mammoth Cave is the mecca of Kentucky's cave country. The tours of its seemingly endless underground passages are among the wonders of the national park system. But above the ground, and across the Green River, is a spacious backcountry area and natural sanctuary that is ignored by most park visitors.

In western Kentucky, access to lakes and rivers makes hiking special. There's perhaps nowhere better suited to exploring

One of Kentucky's many natural rock arches

this landscape than the Land between the Lakes (LBL), a long narrow peninsula between Kentucky Lake and Lake Barkley, which offers a variety of trails designed for anything from casual strolls to long-distance excitement.

THE HIKES

Choosing 50 hikes from all the trails across Kentucky is a daunting task. Rather than choose only my personal favorites, I tried to select a variety of trails spread throughout the state. There are trails from the Land between the Lakes, from along the Ohio River, and from along the borders of Tennessee and Virginia. There's a variety in hike difficulty, too: the shortest hike in the guide is less than a mile long, and the longest is nearly 15 miles.

All the hikes in this guide have a few things in common. I was looking for great trails and great destinations: trails that led to arches, waterfalls, or spectacular overlooks. I was biased toward trails that passed along mountain streams, climbed through awe-inspiring forests, or visited the home of beautiful wildflowers. Though a few crowded trails are included (the Original Trail at Natural Bridge State Resort Park and the front-country trails at Mammoth Cave National Park, for example), I wanted to expose hikers to some less-used routes where they have better opportunities for solitude. I also looked for variety in landscapes: this isn't a book about 50 hikes to arches.

Finally, I looked for hikes on trails built for hikers. There are no long stretches here of eroded horse trails or raceways for speeding mountain bikers. Some of the routes here are on multiple use trails, but I tried to select those which few hikers would object to. Several of the loops do use small parts of low-use public roads; I assume most hikers would rather do a bit of road walking than backtrack on a long hike. I've done my best to steer you clear of areas frequented by off-highway vehicles (OHVs), but these pesky machines occasionally intrude on trails where they are not allowed.

I've also selected with a bias toward loop hikes. I know I would rather see new terrain on every mile of a hike, and I suspect many others would also. Car shuttles for one-way hikes are another means to avoid retracing your route, but these require at least one other person and are often impractical. I also tend to favor hikes that use part of the Sheltowee Trace Trail (STT). Kentucky's only long trail is literally the backbone for all the hiking trails in the Daniel Boone National Forest. Eleven of the hikes in the guide use some part of the STT, including those in the DBNF, the Big South Fork National River and Recreation Area, Cumberland Falls, and Natural Bridge state resort parks.

Finally, I've included two unconventional routes, which are tours through Mammoth Cave. These "underground hikes" can't be matched by trails anywhere else on the face of the earth, or under it. Both the Grand Avenue and Historic tours will be easy walks for most hikers. For the most part, both require simply walking through broad passages and up and down stairs. Mammoth Cave varies its tour schedule by season. Summer visitors may find themselves limited to the high-capacity tours as park rangers are stretched to their limits coping with the summer crowds. Don't expect solitude, or even quiet, on these two trips. However, even in the peak of summer heat and humidity, the temperature inside the cave hovers near a refreshing 54 degrees.

Backpackers have fewer options in Kentucky than do day hikers. Much of the land in the Daniel Boone National Forest is too fragmented to make long-distance hikes practical. However, in addition to the Sheltowee Trace Trail, there are large trail systems at Cave Run Lake, Clifty Wilderness, the Red River Gorge Geological Area, and around the Rockcastle River and Cumberland Falls that are used by overnight hikers. The forest service also manages the Land between the Lakes National Recreation Area, where the 60-mile North-South Trail is that region's only long backpacking trail.

The three areas managed by the National Park Service at Mammoth Cave, Big South Fork, and Cumberland Gap all offer superb backcountry camping. Backcountry camping is prohibited at most Kentucky state parks. Carter Caves and Greenbo Lake are exceptions where backpacking is allowed.

USING THIS BOOK

The statistics at the head of each chapter provide important information concerning the hike. Under "Total Distance" I give the length, type of hike, and what other user groups are allowed on the trail. Many of the trails described here are multiple use, meaning that they are open to other users such as horses, mountain bikes, or even vehicles. On multiple use trails, all users must cooperate so as to avoid adversely impacting the experience of others. In this section you'll also learn if there is any road walking needed to complete the hike.

I pushed a measuring wheel along most of the hikes, particularly the longer ones. The wheel is a great conversation starter; almost every hiker I met wanted to know how far I'd gone. I also measured a few of the trails that were open to mountain bikes with my bike odometer. I used these measurements in my descriptions, except when they differed only slightly from the "official" miles.

Most of the hikes are loops. Some are round-trip hikes, where you hike to a point and return by the same route. One-way hikes do not return to the starting point, and thus require a car shuttle. Semi-loops occur where part of the hike is round-trip and the rest is a loop. Some hikers call these lollipop or lasso hikes.

"Hiking Time" is a rough estimate of how much walking time will be needed for the average group to complete the route. These times do not include any stops, and so are the minimum amount of time a group can expect to be out on the trail. In general, the average group will walk about 2 miles per hour. Obstacles such as hills, stream crossings, rough footing, or hard-to-find trails will add extra time. Anyone hiking with small children should ignore the time estimates, and just make sure the kids enjoy the hike.

"Location" provides a reference point for the hike that anyone can find on a state highway map. Here you'll also find the name of the park or organization that administers the trail. Contact information for these organizations is listed in the Appendix. I recommend stopping by the visitors center for any park you plan to hike in to check on the very latest trail conditions.

I have listed the USGS quadrangle map(s) for each hike, along with any other useful maps. Many of the hikes follow trails that are new, or are not shown on the original quadrangle. Therefore, the maps in this book use USGS quadrangles for base maps. When you're hiking in the state parks, keep in mind that many of the trail maps issued by the parks, particularly those for the longer trails, are schematic. The National Geographic/Trails Illustrated maps for the Big South Fork and Mammoth Cave are prepared in cooperation with the National Park Service and are updated frequently.

These waterproof maps are well worth their cost.

A one-paragraph overview of the trip's highlights is given next. This is also the place to check for hazards, such as rough stream crossings, or administrative hurdles such as permits or fees. Use this information, along with the table "50 Hikes at a Glance," to find which hike is right for you.

Unlike parks in many other states, Kentucky state parks do not yet charge entrance fees. The National Park Service units in the state also are among the few in the system that do not charge. However, the United States Forest Service is moving toward a system of user-based fees. Some areas in the Daniel Boone National Forest have begun charging entry or parking fees. These fees will support local programs and services and should help to improve recreation on the forest.

"Getting There" provides detailed directions for driving to the trailhead, often the trickiest part of any hike. I've tried to pick the most direct routes to trailheads while at the same time minimizing the amount of driving on dirt roads.

Some suggestions for other hikes are offered following the main trail narrative. While many experienced hikers like the challenge of a long walk, many others crave a shorter, high-payoff trip into the woods. I've listed a "short and sweet" version of every hike that shows the easiest way to get straight to the good stuff. There are more and more families on the trails these days; the short-and-sweet hikes should be suitable for trail-tested kids. The other hiking options are briefly described and are often shown on the same map as the main hike.

SAFETY ON THE TRAIL

This is not a "how to" guide for safe hiking. Nonetheless, there are several simple safety hints that all hikers should keep in mind. First of all, drive safely on the way to the trailhead. I know of more hiking trips ruined by car accidents on the way to the trail than of accidents encountered while walking. Also, be careful where you leave your car. The trailheads described here should be safe, but never assume that a trailhead will be patrolled. Don't tempt thieves by leaving valuables visible. If you are unsure about security, leave your vehicle somewhere else. Include a small first aid kit in your pack for unexpected emergencies.

Though it sounds obvious, the key to staying found lies in paying attention to your surroundings. The descriptions and maps in this book should guide you safely around the trails, but this only works if everyone is paying attention. Many lost hikers I've encountered had no idea of the name of the road they started from and only a vague idea of their destination.

Poison ivy can be a problem on many trails; you'll encounter it both growing on the ground or climbing trees as a vine. I've tried to note the worst patches of ivy along the trail, but no doubt there are many others. The best way to avoid poison ivy is to be able to recognize it (remember: leaves of three, let it be). If you expect to hike in an area where poison ivy is abundant, wear long pants. Commercial ivy-block products also work for some people. Poison ivy is also more reactive in the spring, when there is more of the plant's oil on the leaves. If you suspect that you have come into contact with the plant, a vigorous wash with water as hot as you can stand is the best remedy.

I scouted many of the trails for this guide in midsummer, when biting insects are at their most voracious. The best way to avoid ticks and chiggers is to wear long pants and use insect repellent. Flying insects such as gnats and mosquitoes can also be annoying. Commercial repellents using deet or citronella are effective. The best way to avoid mosquitoes is to avoid trails through low, swampy places in midsummer. People who are allergic to gnats or stinging insects might want to carry an antihistamine with them.

More people fear snakes than any other creature in the forest. However, encounters with snakes on Kentucky trails are uncommon, and encounters with poisonous snakes even rarer. The eastern diamondback rattlesnake lives in the state. You can recognize this snake by its arrowhead-shaped head and by the distinctive rattle. The copperhead is also found here, but neither species is very common.

Heat is another of the dangers that summer hikers face. To avoid it, stay in the forest to avoid the open sun, wear a brimmed hat, rest often, and carry more water than you think you will need. Winter hikers can face the opposite problem from hiking in colder temperatures. The key to staying warm in winter is staying dry. Wear clothing that wicks moisture away from the body, rather than cotton clothing, which stays cold and clammy when wet. Avoid overdressing to the point that you sweat. Wearing clothing in light layers rather than a single bulky garment allows you to adapt as your effort and conditions change throughout a hike. Finally, it helps to have plenty to eat and drink on those cold days.

Don't assume that you can drink any of the water you find along the trails. Even if the water looks clean, it may not be. If you are out for the day, plan to bring all the water you will need with you. If you are backpacking, you will need to purify your water by boiling, filtering, or with a chemical treatment such as iodine tablets.

Jean Gauger

Journey's end

Water crossings are another potential hazard faced by hikers. Most large streams crossed by the trails described here have bridges, but some do not. Rock Creek, on the Koger–Yamacraw hike, is an example of an unbridged crossing that may be difficult or dangerous in high water. I've tried to describe typical conditions for any un-bridged crossings in this book. A rock-hop means that if you have good balance, and are lucky, you can get across with dry feet. A ford means that you'll be walking through the water. Of course, conditions can be more severe on any creek after a hard rain. Hikers should use their own judgment to determine if any stream is safe for them to cross.

GIVING BACK

With the pleasure of walking Kentucky's trails also comes some responsibility. Each of us needs to leave a trail in as good, or better, shape as when we found it. Mostly this will be simple things, such as not littering, controlling campfires, and protecting water sources. But often we can greatly improve an area with a relatively modest amount of work. Many of the people who visit our trails haven't yet learned not to litter. You can help by packing out litter that less-thoughtful visitors have left behind. Since places that start clean tend to stay clean, and places that have litter can get worse fast, a little bit of litter cleanup can go a long way.

Park and forest managers across the country are increasingly strapped for funds to maintain trails, and increasingly rely on volunteer labor, especially for routine work. Many parks have "Friends of" groups that support parks both financially and through volunteer work. Other environmental and trail groups such as the Sierra Club sponsor trail-work trips. For those with more time to donate, the American Hiking Society organizes volunteer vacations to places such as Jenny Wiley State Park and the

Pine Mountain Trail, where volunteers work for a week on trail projects.

An active group of volunteer trail maintainers helps the forest service on trails in the Red River Gorge. If you are looking for more information about this group try its website at www.gorgecrew.com.

If you do find hazards or other problems on a trail please report them to the agency that administers the trail. Trail managers can be surprisingly responsive to trail problems, so you might just prevent the next hiker from encountering the same problem that you did. Of course, if you find something along the trail that you really appreciate, let the manager know that too. Everyone likes positive feedback.

Trails and trail conditions are always evolving. Should you find things different than described in this guide, please let me know by contacting the publisher so that new conditions can be described as the guide is updated.

Kentucky offers a multitude of riches to those who explore the Commonwealth on foot. I hope that this guide prompts you step out on to the trails more often, and to enjoy your trip just a little bit more.

I

Eastern Highlands

1

Lakeshore–Moss Ridge Loop

Total Distance: A 3.0-mile loop on hiking trails

Hiking Time: About 1.5 hours

Location: Jenny Wiley State Resort Park, 3 miles northeast of Prestonburg

Maps: USGS Lancer; Jenny Wiley State Resort Park Visitor's Guide

Jenny Wiley State Park is centered around the fishing and boating opportunities at 1,100-acre Dewey Lake. The park offers other amenities including a golf course, sky lift, and a surprisingly fine network of hiking trails. A loop combining three trails at the eastern end of the park is a good sampler of what Jenny Wiley trails have to offer: lakeside vistas, quiet woods, and abundant wildlife.

Getting There

From the junction of US 23 and KY 302 south of Prestonburg, drive 4.3 miles north on KY 302 into Jenny Wiley State Park. Turn right on the road that leads to May Lodge and park in the lodge parking area.

The Hike

You'll begin the loop with a pleasant walk along the shore of Dewey Lake. From the far left end of the parking loop at May Lodge, start by a sign indicating the boat dock is 0.1 mile and the Lakeshore Trail is 2.5 miles. At the base of the stairs near the boat dock turn right and follow an asphalt road past the marina. Below the lodge the trail turns to dirt. While it hugs the lakeshore the trail is wide, smooth, and easy.

After a short climb, a side trail leaves to the right, toward Cottage 123, offering an opportunity to cut the loop short. Stay left on the Lakeshore Trail to complete the full loop. Some of the trees along the lakeshore include white oak, red maple, American hornbeam, pignut hickory, persimmon, and

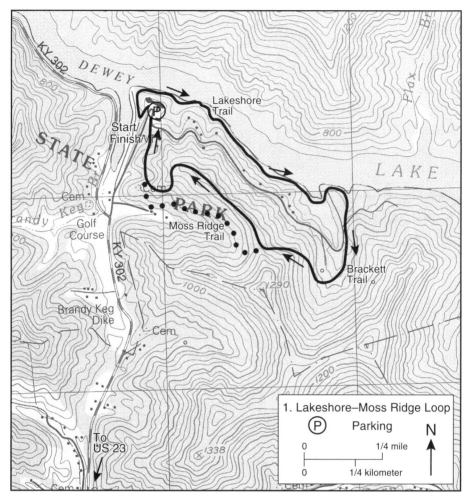

1. Lakeshore–Moss Ridge Loop

(P) Parking

N

0   1/4 mile

0   1/4 kilometer

sassafras. Keep your tree finder handy and see if you can identify more. Reach another small ridge and a sign indicating that there is no more hiking allowed along the lakeshore. Turn right and climb the ridge on a wide grass and moss-lined path. At 1.5 miles, reach a trailhead at the end of a paved road. This trailhead serves as both the end of the Lakeshore Trail and the start of the Steve Brackett Memorial Trail. Beyond the end of the pavement, a gravel road leads 3.5 miles to a Youth Camp. The paved road to the right offers another short-

cut opportunity; it's only a 1-mile walk back to May Lodge from here.

Brackett was the forester for 10 years at the park, and the eastern division forester for the Kentucky Division of Forestry. He built and marked most of the park's trails. To continue on the loop, follow the Steve Brackett Memorial Trail as it climbs farther up the ridge on trail marked with wooden posts. You'll cross a dry streambed on a wooden bridge, and a gas pipeline at the base of a set of stairs, before reaching a split with a faint roadway. The roadway is

The start of the Steve Brackett and Moss Ridge Trails

closed to hiking, so go left at this junction. After finally gaining the crest of the ridge, reach the junction with the Moss Ridge Trail at 2.5 miles.

Either leg of the Moss Ridge Trail will lead to May Lodge, but the right fork will keep you on the ridgetop the longest, and give you better views and cooler breezes. The ridge is a better place to spot the wild turkey that roam the woods and to enjoy the late-blooming fire pinks alongside the trail. Just remember that pink is the family name for this flower and that the flowers are actually a bright red. The flower contains five petals, each of which is "pinked," or notched, at the tip. Red blazes on the trees along the trail mark the boundary of U.S. Army Corps of Engineers property. After passing a radio tower, begin a steep descent. At 2.8 miles join the other fork of the Moss Ridge Loop. To the left it is 0.25 mile to the park amphitheatre. Your route goes right, and reaches the Moss Ridge Trailhead located on the cottage road at 3.0 miles. To reach May Lodge, continue down the cottage road to the lodge parking area.

The legend of Jenny Wiley is a sad one, but symptomatic of troubled times on the American frontier in the late 1700s. Wiley's troubles began in 1789 when a neighbor shot and killed two Cherokee Indians. When a war party returned for vengeance they found the Wiley homestead undefended. Wiley's brother and three children were killed, and the pregnant Wiley and an infant were captured. The infant, and later the newborn, died in captivity, but Wiley survived and one night was able to escape. Her flight from her captors was epic; she had no idea of either her location or the direction of home. However, she was able to reach the settlements, just ahead of the pursuit of her former captors. In the fall of 1790 she was reunited with her husband. They started another family, and Wiley lived to the age of 71 in the Big Sandy Valley of Kentucky, just north of the present-day park.

To honor the journey of Jenny Wiley, the state of Kentucky opened the Jenny Wiley Hiking Trail in 1980. However, much of the trail was on private land and management issues became rather complex. The foot trail was abandoned in 1998. In its place is now the Jenny Wiley Heritage Byway, a 155-mile road loop that traces the path taken by Wiley in her captivity and on her escape.

Other Hiking Options

1. Short and Sweet. An alternative to the several shortcuts on the route described here, the Sassafras Trail is a self-guided, 0.75-mile interpretive loop that occupies a small peninsula jutting into Dewey Lake. The trail was built in 1995 by volunteers from the American Hiking Society. Look for the trailhead, just 0.1 mile east of the campground entrance on KY 302.

2. The Jenny Wiley Trail extends 4.5 miles from Cottage 132, near the marina, west to the junction with KY 321. You can also access the trail at the campground check-in station, or at the base of the sky lift. The western 0.5 mile will be closed into 2002 due to construction of a $14 million emergency spillway for Dewey Lake. The project will require relocation of the west end of the trail and the western trailhead. Backpacking is not allowed on this trail.

3. Three miles of mountain bike trails near Arrowhead Point are also open to hikers. These trails follow the route formerly used by guided horseback trips in the park.

2

Boardinghouse Hollow Trail

Total Distance: A 1.8-mile semi-loop on a hiking trail

Hiking Time: About 1.5 hours

Location: Robinson Forest, 25 miles northeast of Hazard

Maps: USGS Noble; Boardinghouse Hollow Interpretive Trail

Robinson Forest is one of those out-of-the-way places that will have you wondering if it is worth all the miles of curvy roads that you must drive to reach it. But once you've reached the trail, and climbed to the top of the historic tower, you'll only wish that you hadn't waited so long to visit. Spring, with its prolific wildflower display and the early blooms of dogwood and redbud trees, would be the ideal time. Early spring flowers include bluets, fire pink, and bloodroot, and by late spring mayapples, foamflower, and violets are more common.

Getting There

From the junction of KY 80 and KY 15 in Hazard, drive 6.9 miles east on KY 80. Next drive 13.6 miles north on KY 476 to the hamlet of Rowdy, and the Perry-Breathitt County line. Southbound travelers will see a sign here for Robinson Forest. Cross Troublesome Creek on a suspicious-looking wooden bridge, and follow the paved road for 4.4 miles until reaching the forest boundary. Continue on the gravel road for another 0.8 mile to reach the forest camp. Pull off the gravel road and park just inside the camp fence. The trail starts north of the road at a large trail sign.

The Hike

From the trailhead sign, climb a set of stairs and then turn right onto the route built by Civilian Conservation Corps (CCC) crews in 1934 to put in place the material necessary to construct the fire tower. Boardinghouse Hollow is an interpretive trail, so you're lucky to have 14 displays along the

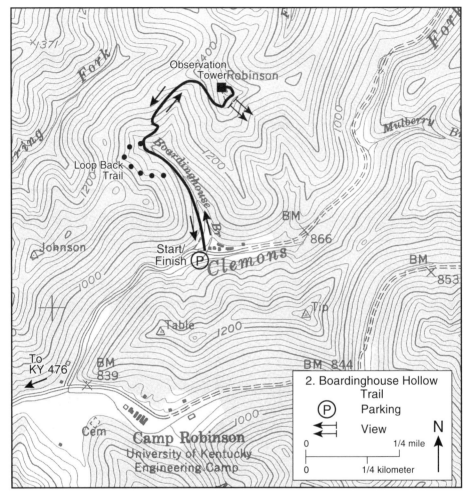

trail, as well as several dozen labeled trees and plants along the trail. The lower trail passes through a cool moist environment alongside Boardinghouse Gulch, which supports a cove hardwood forest of sugar maple, American beech, tulip poplar, red maple, and eastern hemlock. The short Cove Hardwood Trail that leaves the main trail at point 2, and returns at point 5, looked little-used on a spring visit and may be impassable in midsummer. The Loopback Trail, your return route, exits the main route to the left after station 5.

Beyond station 5, the trail climbs more steeply through oak-hickory and upland oak forests. The trailside signs identify white ash, paw paw, mockernut hickory, and redbud. Early May adds the deep orange buds of flame azalea to the mix. Near the top of the mountain, in drier and sunnier terrain in the oak-pine forest is composed of shortleaf pine, pitch pine, Virginia pine, and scarlet oak. Near the tower, cross under a power line before reaching the gravel road still used to service this active tower.

A natural arch in Robinson Forest

The tower is typical of those built by the CCC, with a tall, slender base of angle iron capped with a wooden observation room. The room is locked but the views from the top landing are just as fine. Here's a good chance to observe the damage done to Kentucky's pine forest by the southern pine beetle. The rust-red spots in the canopy indicate stands of pines that have been killed by the beetle. Since this is coal country you can also see a few cleared areas to the south in the Cyprus Amax Wildlife Management Area, but the view to the north appears to be unbroken forest.

You can return to the trailhead by using the Loopback Trail, if you are prepared to use a little rougher trail, and willing to brave the poison ivy found along it.

Robinson Forest was created from an original 15,000 acres purchased in 1908 for logging. Fifteen years later the cleared land was donated by the E. O. Robinson Mountain Fund to the University of Kentucky for an agriculture experiment station. Deer, wild turkey, and grouse have been successfully reintroduced to the area since the logging era. An attempt to reintroduce beavers into the forest failed. The forest is now used for a variety of teaching, research, and extension activities. In 1996, the fire tower was placed on the National Historic Lookout Register. It is one of the few functional towers left in Kentucky.

A survey of birds in large stands of older trees found 36 different species present, including a single common raven, which is listed as endangered in Kentucky. The most common birds found were red-eyed vireo and ovenbird. For many bird species loss of habitat due to fragmentation of forests by logging, mining, or road building is a major threat to their population. Some evidence exists that these large tracts of older forest are less likely to be used by cowbirds, another major threat to songbirds. Cowbirds lay their eggs in the nests of other birds, leaving them to raise the aggressive cowbird chicks at the expense of their own young.

Other Hiking Options

1. Short and Sweet. There are no other established hiking trails at Robinson Forest, but you can avoid the climb to the tower by only hiking the Cove Hardwood Loop.

2. The gravel access road at the fire tower leads into a wide web of other little-traveled roads that make for fine hiking. Robinson Forest is part of the Cyprus-Amax Wildlife Management Area. Hiking away from the Interpretive Trail requires a $10 user permit from the Kentucky Department of Fish and Wildlife Resources.

3

River–Geology–Overlook Loop

Total Distance: A 5.1-mile loop on hiking trails. Part of the loop follows a self-guided interpretive trail. Guides to the trail are available at the park visitors center.

Hiking Time: About 3 hours

Location: Breaks Interstate Park, 7 miles east of Elkhorn City

Maps: USGS Elkhorn City; Breaks Interstate Park Trail Map

Breaks Interstate Park is a unique, cooperative park managed jointly by both the states of Kentucky and Virginia. The park was established in 1954, and protects the "Breaks," where the Russell Fork River was able to cut through the mighty sandstones of Pine Mountain. The 4,500-acre park surrounds a 5-mile-long canyon that is up to 1,600 feet deep. This deep gorge carved by the river has been called the "Grand Canyon of the South" and is impressive by any standards. The park is graced by 9 miles of hiking trails, which make an almost infinite array of loop hikes possible. The route described here was chosen to give hikers the best balance between the beautiful overlooks high above the river and trails offering close-up views of Russell Fork River and Grassy Creek.

Getting There

From the junction of KY 80 and KY 197 in Elkhorn City, drive south on KY 80. In 3.7 miles, near the state line on a sharp bend where the road crosses Center Creek, pass an unmarked entry to a picnic area on the right side of the road. This is an alternate trailhead from the Kentucky side of the park. In another 3.2 miles, turn right onto VA 702, which is the park entry road. Go straight at the junction with VA 732, and past the visitors center, for 0.9 mile to the parking area for picnic shelter 2.

The Hike

Since there will be so many trail intersections on this hike, it would be a good idea to

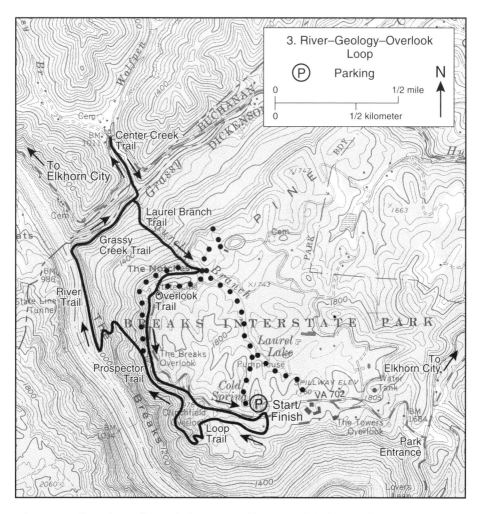

3. River–Geology–Overlook Loop

(P) Parking

N

0 — 1/2 mile

0 — 1/2 kilometer

orient yourself on the trail map before you get started. All you've got to do is take the Loop Trail to the Prospector Trail to the River Trail to the Grassy Creek Trail to the Laurel Branch Trail to the Geological Trail to the Overlook Trail and finally back to the trailhead. But it's not that hard; the trail blazes are color-coded, and since all of the trails have something to offer, it really doesn't matter exactly what route you take.

Start by hiking on the green-blazed Loop Trail through thickets of laurel and rhododendron that would yield spectacular blooms by July. In 0.4 mile reach a junction with the yellow-blazed Tower Tunnel Trail. The right branch leads back to the road, while the left branch (just a bit farther down the trail) leads to the first of the many "can't miss" overlooks above the Russell Fork. Across the river, and rising from the lush forests, are the bare stones of the Towers and Chimney Rock. This trail junction also marks the start of the orange-blazed Prospector Trail. Here a sign warns you that the Prospector Trail demands a 3-mile loop, while the River Trail requires 4 miles.

A view of the Russell Fork River from the River Trail

Turn onto the Prospector Trail, which then drops from the rim through a band of cliffs. You'll soon pass your first rockhouse. These shallow, overhanging cliffs may have sheltered pioneer or Native American families. They are still a welcome dry escape in rainy weather. You'll zigzag through more of these rock shelters, formed by rocks that have broken off the cliffs but still lean against them. Even in early May, rhododendron and azalea may bloom here. At 1.2 miles, reach the intersection with the blue-blazed River Trail.

As promised, the River Trail begins a rapid descent toward its namesake. The descent is steep, with many loose rocks, and is made more difficult by hikers who have cut the switchbacks that were carefully built into the trail. Switchbacks, though they make trails longer, make trails easier by making them less steep. Inexperienced hikers often cut switchbacks by taking a route directly downhill. This results in eroded hillsides that are ugly, unusable for wildlife, and dangerous. No matter what hurry you might be in, do your best to stay on the trail. Near the river, there is at least one "curiosity trail" that leads left off the main trail into oblivion. Eventually the River Trail reaches the base of a 100-foot-tall cliff band, and then later follows alongside the Russell Fork. At 2.2 miles, reach the mouth of Grassy Creek and the signed junction with the yellow-blazed Grassy Creek Trail.

There is a sandy beach at the confluence, and sites on both sides of Grassy Creek are ideal spots for a lunch break and even a summer swim. Next turn right on the Grassy Creek Trail, which leads past a 6-foot-high waterfall and numerous cascades. Closer to the confluence with Laurel Branch, the trail climbs away from the stream and becomes rough and rocky. At

2.7 miles, reach another important junction with the purple-blazed Center Creek Trail and the red-blazed Laurel Branch Trail at Laurel Branch.

To use the Center Creek Trail to reach the Center Creek Picnic Area and KY 80, turn left here, cross Laurel Branch, then make a tough rock-hop across Grassy Creek. On the far side of the creek, the trail appears to split. The left fork is an unofficial route that follows an old railroad grade downstream past the falls and some campsites. The right fork is the correct trail. It stays close to Center Creek, in places on narrow, precarious ledges of gently sloping sandstone. In 0.2 mile it reaches the picnic area, but there are no signs for the trail here.

To continue on our loop, turn right at the 2.7-mile junction and climb nearly straight up the Laurel Branch Trail. At 3.2 miles continue straight at a junction with the end of the Prospector Trail. At 3.3 miles, go right at a junction with the white-blazed Geological Trail. As expected, this trail traverses the base of a band of cliffs soaking in the sights of rock fins, chimneys, turrets, towers and deep cracks choked with chockstones. The Geological and Ridge Trails are a self-guided interpretive loop, so if you got the guidebook from the park visitors center you can follow along with the numbered posts.

The Geological Trail ends at 3.7 miles at the parking area for the State Line Overlook, which is a 150-foot side trip. From the overlook the roaring Russell Fork River is almost 1,000 feet below. You can also see the mouth of Grassy Creek, Stateline Tunnel along the railroad, and Potters Flat, a rare piece of level ground in this jumbled terrain. Next follow the green-blazed Overlook Trail. Be careful to stay on the canyon rim and not get seduced into following a steep "curiosity trail" through a crack in the cap rock. The walking is now both easier and highly rewarding. You'll pass side trails to both Pinnacle Rocks and Clinchfield Overlook, as well as enjoy views from many smaller, unprotected overlooks. At 4.8 miles, reach the end of the Overlook Trail. To return to Picnic Shelter 2, take the gravel footpath alongside the park road to 5.1 miles.

In addition to the prime hiking, Breaks offers other outdoor excitement. The Russell Fork River includes a 12-mile run with rapids rated up to class 4. The run depends on dam releases from the John Flanngan Dam, which normally occur only on weekends in October. Contact the park for a list of approved outfitters. There is also a 3-mile mountain-bike trail that circles a beaver pond and the cottage area. There is no backcountry camping allowed in the park.

Other Hiking Options

1. Short and Sweet. From State Line Overlook combine the Geological and Ridge Trails and follow the interpretive guide. Together these trails are called the Chestnut Ridge Nature Trail; the loop is 0.9 mile long.

2. Other loop hikes can be made using the Overlook Trail and either the Cold Spring or Laurel Branch Trails.

3. The eastern end of the 120-mile Pine Mountain Trail will be near Breaks Interstate Park at Potter's Flat, near Elkhorn City. The eastern end in 2001 was located near the police office in Elkhorn City. The Pine Mountain Trail is planned to follow the crest of Pine Mountain between Breaks and Pine Mountain State Park, and it will end near Cumberland Gap.

4

Pine Mountain Trail–
US 23 to Bryant Gap

Total Distance: A 7.6-mile round-trip hike that uses some paved and gravel roads

Hiking Time: About 4 hours

Location: About 3 miles south of Jenkins

Maps: USGS Jenkins East and Jenkins West

The Pine Mountain Trail east of Pound Gap represents the first step in an ambitious project by the Pine Mountain Trail Conference to build 120 miles of hiking trail along the crest of Pine Mountain from Breaks Interstate Park to Pine Mountain State Resort Park and then south to Cumberland Gap National Historic Park. Between US 23 and Bryant Gap lie spectacular crest-line views into Virginia and Kentucky, and the remarkable Skyview Caves.

Getting There

From the intersection of US 23 and US 119 west of Jenkins, drive south on US 23 over the Virginia Line at Pound Gap. Continue south for 0.4 mile to a gravel parking area at the intersection with VA 667 on the south side of the road. The trail starts back toward Pound Gap, where a remarkably steep paved road joins US 23 next to a BP travel station. There is no trailhead parking at this location.

The Hike

To start the hike from the trailhead, walk north on US 23 to the paved side road just beyond the BP station. This road may be signed Communications or Apostolic Drive. Look for the Pine Mountain Trail's trademark yellow blazes on the guardrail as you make the steep climb up the road. The views from the open roadway stretch far across Virginia's Jefferson National Forest. At 0.2 mile, leave the paved road at a turn near the ridgetop for a two-track gravel service road. Continue to climb along the crest of the

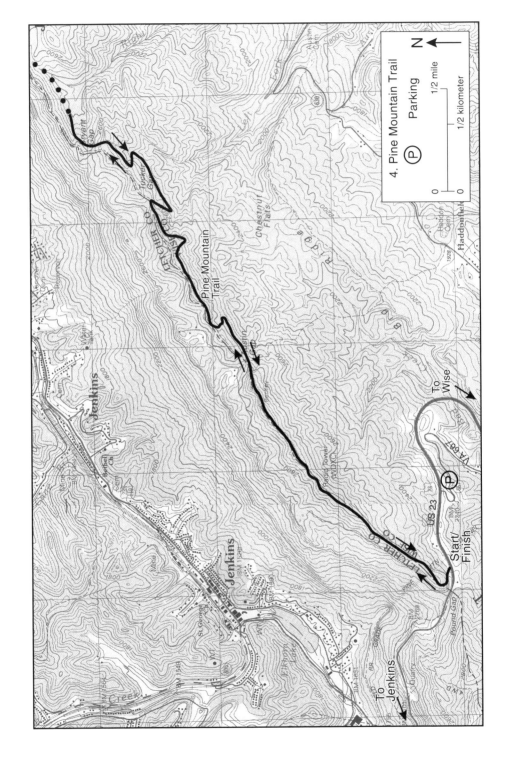

4. Pine Mountain Trail

Ⓟ Parking

N

mountain. You'll pass the broadcast tower for WIFX before reaching an impressive array of satellite dishes at the end of the gravel road at 1.0 mile.

Beyond the satellite dishes the trail becomes a narrow footpath. You'll continue along the crest of Pine Mountain, which here marks the boundary between Kentucky and Virginia and is also the north boundary of the Jefferson National Forest. Watch for the remains of a low stone wall. The wall is the remains of Civil War–era breastworks from a battle at Pound Gap. One of the officers commanding this struggle was James Garfield, later to become president of the United States. At 1.3 miles is a fine overlook on the Kentucky side, where Jenkins and the many coal mines that surround it are visible. The forest along the crest is mostly second growth. Pine and oak are perhaps the most common trees, but rhododendron, mountain laurel, holly, hemlock, and red maple are also found. Young sprouts of sassafras and American chestnut flourish in the newly dug dirt along the side of the trail. The trail follows so close to the crest of the mountain that often it must traverse across barren slopes of exposed rock.

At 1.6 miles, reach the Raven's Nest Overlook on the Kentucky side. After enjoying the sky-high vistas, begin a steady descent on switchbacks toward Austin Gap. In the middle of the steep hillside there is a side trail on the right to Staircase Caves. The side trail leads to the two main caves; there is another cave below the first two. At 1.7 miles, reach a sign at Austin Gap. At the gap rough, unmaintained side trails lead south into Virginia and north onto private property in Kentucky.

At 1.8 miles, reach a side trail on the Virginia side that leads steeply 500 feet down to Skyview Caves. As you walk down the steep rhododendron-covered slope it is hard to imagine a cave in this location that has a sweeping view of the horizon. Actually, the cave is a huge natural arch, more than 100 feet long and 100 feet across. The roof lies at the same steep angle as all the bedrock at Pine Mountain. The "sky view" is a small hole near the center of the roof that seems designed to be a smokestack for this idyllic campsite. Few, if any, arches on Pine Mountain reach the size of Skyview, and few arches anywhere have this private window into the heavens.

After Austin Gap, the Pine Mountain Trail leaves the crest to follow a gentle route on the Virginia side. At 2.6 miles, it turns sharply off the crest. The trail reaches signed Tucker Gap at 3.0 miles. Just west of Tucker Gap an unmarked trail leads north down onto private property in Kentucky. Just a few feet above the sign is a small overhang tucked into the rhododendron that would be a perfect rest stop, especially on a rainy day.

At Tucker Gap, the Pine Mountain Trail makes a sharp switchback and heads west into Virginia on trail built in 2001. At 3.1 miles, turn left onto a rare stretch of level trail. Follow along the slope until the trail makes another sharp switchback to the left at 3.5 miles. This switchback occurs just short of a small drainage that hides "moonshiner's mansion." The mansion is a shallow cave where relicts of this traditional industry can still be found. As the trail climbs toward the Bryant Gap it passes alongside other rocky overhangs. You'll see the remains of old washtubs and broken glass that may also date back to the time of the moonshiners. It is easy to imagine lookouts hiding in the thick growth at the edge of the rocky summits, anxious for any signs of the revenuers approaching.

The trail reaches the sign for Bryant Gap at 3.8 miles, where an old road crosses the crest. Beyond this point, the Pine Mountain

A double blaze like this means "watch for a turn."

Trail follows the old road to the left to reach another gap at 4.5 miles. The trail continues along the old road, high above a huge limestone quarry, to a point about 1 mile past Mullins Pond (11.7 miles), at which point it again follows a new footpath.

It doesn't take a trained geologist to recognize that Pine Mountain is a unique piece of Kentucky geology. Where most rocks in the state occur in relatively level layers, those at Pine Mountain are tilted high into the sky. Around 230 million years ago, during a massive mountain-building event, a large rectangular slice of the earth's crust broke loose and was pushed to the northwest. This block slid over rocks of the same age that remained in place. When this episode of mountain building was complete, and erosion began its turn at sculpting the landscape, the thick, erosion-resistant sandstones of the Lee Formation remained in place, forming the crest of Pine Mountain.

When complete, the Pine Mountain Trail will be one of the premier hiking trails in the region. It will link state parks at Breaks, Kingdom Come, and Pine Mountain with Cumberland Gap National Historic Park. The trail will also visit the Blanton Forest and Bad Branch State nature preserves and will include the awesome overlooks at High Rock in Bad Branch. The trail was originally envisioned to include the 38-mile Little Shepard Trail, a gravel road that serves as KY 1679 between US 119 near Whitesburg and US 421 near Harlan. Pending funding, the Pine Mountain Trail may be routed onto footpaths parallel to the Little Shepard Trail.

The Pine Mountain Trail is a key link in an even more ambitious effort to connect trails in the Cumberland Mountains with the world famous 2,000-mile-long Appalachian Trail. The north end of the Pine Mountain Trail lies close enough to the Appalachian Trail across the Jefferson National Forest that a connection is possible. At the south end, the trail will someday connect with the north end of Tennessee's planned Cumberland Trail State Park at the tristate marker in Cumberland Gap National Historic Park. Well over 100 miles of the 280-mile Cumberland Trail route from Chattanooga to Cumberland Gap have already been built.

The Pine Mountain Trail Conference is working hard to both extend the trail and to improve existing sections. In the fall of 2001 the group completed the first trailside shelter on private land near US 119. A group of volunteers from the American Hiking Society also rebuilt a section of trail on Carson Island Road at the mouth of Big Island Branch to complete the trail's connection to Elkhorn City. As you walk the Pine Mountain Trail remember that it is a work in progress, and realize that trail conditions may change faster than trail descriptions.

Other Hiking Options

1. Short and Sweet. If you are dropped off at the end of the paved road, a round-trip hike to Skyview Caves is 3.2 miles.

2. The Pine Mountain Trail continues 28.1 miles east to Elkhorn City. Mullins Pond near VA 631 is 11.7 miles from US 23.

3. The east end of the Pine Mountain Trail is at the police station on the east side of Elkhorn City on KY 80. The trail starts by following gravel Carson Island Road, but may not be blazed until it begins to climb Pine Mountain near Big Island Branch 1.2 miles from Elkhorn City.

4. For updates on the most recently completed trail sections, contact the Pine Mountain Trail Conference.

5

Bad Branch Trail

Total Distance: A 7.4-mile semi-loop open to foot travel only

Hiking Time: About 5 hours

Location: Bad Branch State Nature Preserve, 9 miles south of Whitesburg, and 18 miles east of Cumberland

Maps: USGS Whitesburg; Bad Branch State Nature Preserve Map

The 2,343-acre Bad Branch State Nature Preserve is the second largest of the state's preserves that are not associated with a state park. The preserve protects the watershed of Bad Branch, from the crest of Pine Mountain to its confluence with the Poor Fork of the Cumberland River. For hikers, Bad Branch is among the most accessible and rewarding of the preserves to visit. Both Bad Branch Falls, and the sweeping summit views from High Rocks, are enough to lure any hiker out on the trail.

Getting There

From the junction of KY 15 and US 119 in Whitesburg, drive south for 7.4 miles on US 119 over Pine Mountain. Turn left onto KY 932, and drive 1.7 miles to the signed trailhead parking for the Bad Branch State Nature Preserve.

The Hike

The trail begins in back of the signboard by the parking area and follows orange paint blazes. The first mile to the side trail to Bad Branch Falls is a gentle but steady climb. You'll cross Bad Branch twice on small wooden bridges. Here the trail's low elevation and proximity to the branch provide a lush environment quite different from the high, dry conditions found on top of Pine Mountain. The nature preserve contains one of the largest concentrations of rare and uncommon plant species found in the state, but you don't have to be an ace botanist to enjoy the show. Among the common flowers found here are chickweed and some other favorites include showy orchis.

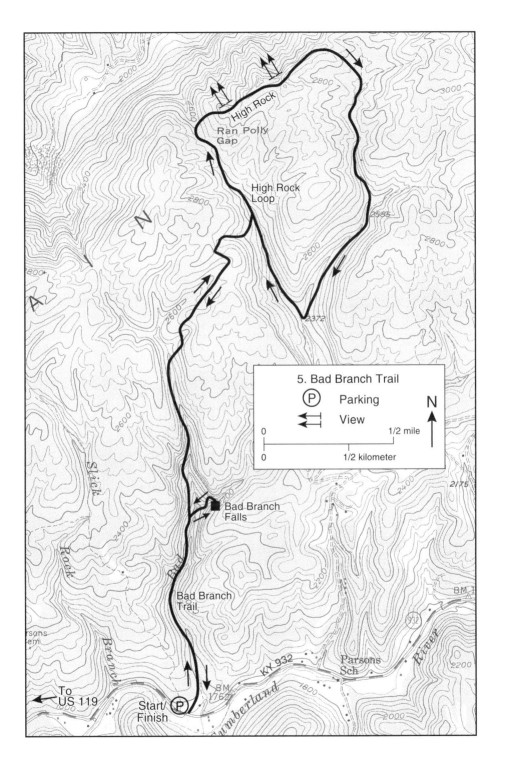

3000

2800

2000

2600

2400

2800

High Rock

Ran Polly
Gap

2585

2800

High Rock
Loop

N

A

2800

2600

2372

5. Bad Branch Trail

Ⓟ   Parking

⇆   View

N

0 _____ 1/2 mile

0 _____ 1/2 kilometer

2600

2400

2175

Slick

Rock

2400

Bad Branch
Falls

2200

Bad

Bad Branch
Trail

BM

932

River

sons
em

Branch

KY 932

Parsons
Sch

1800

2200

To
US 119

BM
1762

2000

Start/
Finish

Ⓟ

Cumberland

2000

At 1.0 mile is the signed junction for the side trail leading right to Bad Branch Falls. The side trail drops to a normally easy crossing of Bad Branch, then climbs above the falls before emerging into an overlook at the fall's base in 0.3 mile. Here is a 60-foot drop down a massive cliff fed into a plunge pool choked with immense boulders. The water's spray is cool and refreshing in summer, and forms spectacular ice displays in the depths of winter. The small viewing area lends an air of privacy appropriate for this secluded waterfall.

To continue to High Rock from the 1-mile junction, continue climbing alongside a side stream. The cool mountain stream and steep, shaded gorge combine to provide an environment similar to more northerly or higher elevation regions. Hemlock, tulip poplar, birch, basswood, buckeye, and beech are the most common varieties of trees. In spring you also might recognize flowering dogwood or umbrella magnolia by their distinctive blossoms. Cross the stream, then pass through a thick grove of rhododendron that shelters some rare painted trilliums.

Flowers of the trillium family are easy to recognize from their three petals, three leaves, and three sepals (the outer leaflike part of the flower). Painted trilliums take this symmetry one step further by adding a maroon triangle of "paint" to the base of the three petals. This flower is normally found farther north, but its love of cool, moist habitats also brings it to some spruce or fir forests in the southern mountains.

Next, the trail reaches a small divide that marks the start of The Nature Conservancy's portion of the preserve. Drop down the divide and reenter the Bad Branch drainage. Just beyond the crest is a huge overhanging boulder that the trail loops around.

At 2.4 miles, reach a signed junction with the High Rock loop portion of the trail. Turn left on the trail, which here follows a dirt road, perhaps abandoned during 1940s era logging, and begin climbing again. Soon the road becomes fainter, the forest more open, and slabs of sandstone are visible below the pines. The upper portion of the trail climbs on top of a single inclined layer of pebbly sandstone. Geologists use the term "dip slope" for areas like this, where the lay of the land follows a single angled rock layer. At 3.1 miles, reach the crest of Pine Mountain and the spectacular views of High Rock. Below is Whitesburg, the North Fork of the Kentucky River, and rich coal country. Many stands of pine in the viewshed have been destroyed by the southern pine beetle. Long high ridges such as Pine Mountain are also perfect habitat for raptors, and Bad Branch is home to Kentucky's only known nesting pair of common ravens.

Once you've finished lunch, and completed your bird count, continue along the mountaintop still soaking in the views. Closer at hand you might spot a pink lady's slipper, or even an early-blooming flame azalea. Drop south off the crest onto another faint old road, which follows along another side branch. You'll soon reach the confluence with Bad Branch at a wooden post at 4.5 miles. Turn right to cross the stream, then climb up the old road to close the loop at 5.0 miles. From this point retrace your steps up and over the divide, past the side trail to the falls, and back to the parking area at 7.4 miles.

If you loved the trail atop High Rock, and who wouldn't, then there soon will be a longer trail in the region that will interest you. The proposed Pine Mountain Trail is planned to cover 120 miles of the mountaintop from Breaks Interstate Park to Pine Mountain State Park and should connect with the preserve and lead to High Rock. In addition to state nature preserves such as Bad Branch and Blanton

Bad Branch Falls

Forest, the trail will also pass through Kingdom Come State Park and parts of the Jefferson National Forest. As of summer 2001, nearly 28 miles on the eastern end near Breaks were complete. Though parts of the trail may be open to horses, or even off-highway vehicles (OHVs), most of the new trails that will be built will be for foot travel only.

Other Hiking Options

1. Short and Sweet. The hike just to the falls and back is 2.6 miles round-trip. There are no other trails at the preserve.

2. Kingdom Come State Park near Cumberland, Kentucky, contains 14 miles of hiking trails near the crest of Pine Mountain.

3. The Kentucky State Nature Preserves Commission opened the Blunton Forest State Nature Preserve to the public in October 2001. This 2,500-acre tract contains the largest stand of old-growth forest remaining in the Commonwealth. A 2-mile hiking trail leads up the face of Pine Mountain to Knobby Rock. A 0.5-mile trail takes hikers along Watts Creek.

6

Sand Cave and White Rocks

Total Distance: An 8.7-mile semi-loop on a trail shared with horses

Hiking Time: About 5 hours

Location: Cumberland Gap National Historic Park, 13 miles east of Cumberland Gap, Tennessee

Maps: USGS Ewing; Cumberland Gap National Historic Park Trail System

The joys of hiking are many and varied. They can include both the big payoffs you get at the end of a hike from sweeping mountaintop vistas, and the smaller rewards from things you see along the trail. The hike to Sand Cave and White Rocks offers hikers both a high-impact payoff from the White Rocks overlook, and a more intimate, closeup visit to unique Sand Cave.

Getting There

From the Cumberland Gap National Historic Park visitors center just south of Middlesboro, drive 2.1 miles south on US 25 East through the new tunnel under Cumberland Mountain. Take the first exit south of the tunnel and turn left onto US 58. Drive 12.1 miles east to the small town of Ewing, Virginia, and turn left onto narrow VA 724. Drive 0.9 mile north, (with excellent views ahead of the cliffs at White Rocks) and go left at a fork. The right fork road leads to the horse trailhead, which you may use for your descent route. The hiking trailhead is located in another 0.1 mile at the Thomas Walker Civic Park in Ewing. The NPS hopes to begin leasing Civic Park for a trailhead. If this happens the trailhead will likely be renamed.

The Hike

From the park gate, walk up the park road past the covered picnic shelter to another cable gate and trail sign that marks the boundary with Cumberland Gap National Historic Park. The footpath is wide and easy to follow; just be careful not to step in the

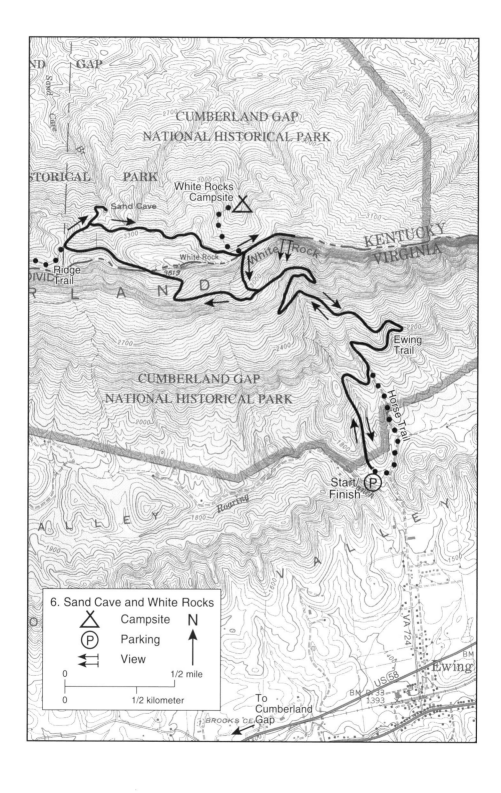

6. Sand Cave and White Rocks

△ Campsite
Ⓟ Parking
⇄ View

N

0 ———————— 1/2 mile
0 ———————— 1/2 kilometer

abundant poison ivy. You'll cross one small stream and pass a faint side trail leading left, before reaching a T-junction with a horse trail at 0.6 mile.

The combined horse and hiking trail turns left at the junction and soon begins climbing more steadily on a series of wide switchbacks. At around 2 miles a major turn to the right leaves you staring at the sheer cliffs below the White Rocks overlooks. At 2.5 miles, reach a junction where a foot-only trail leads directly to White Rocks on the right. You'll come down this trail, so continue left toward Sand Cave.

At 3.0 miles, a signed junction indicates that Sand Cave is to the left and Ewing is to the right. This junction can be confusing, since the trail to the right is unofficial and not shown on the park maps. It is still worth exploring, as it leads to the site of the now-removed White Rocks fire tower. A 5-minute walk will take you to a small clearing that marks the site. Only the concrete footings for the tower and two USGS benchmarks now remain. While the tower views are a thing of the past, the views that lie ahead from White Rocks overlook are just as rewarding.

Return to the signed junction and continue down the left fork toward Sand Cave on a sunny slope where chickweed continues to bloom even into the late spring. At 3.5 miles, reach a T-junction with the Ridge Trail, which leads 4.5 miles west to Hensley Settlement. Go right on the Ridge Trail to 3.7 miles, where a hitching rack for horses marks the start of the side trail to the Sand Cave.

The 0.2-mile side trail splits just before reaching Sand Cave. The easier lower fork leads to a small waterfall, and the upper fork takes a rougher route to the top of the great sand dune that fills the cave. Sand Cave is remarkable for both its size and beauty.

Though a hundred people could easily lounge inside, only on the most popular weekends are other visitors likely. If you're lucky, the noisy pigeons that nest in the roof of the cave will be your only companions. Lounge in the cool sand if you've arrived on a hot summer day, or enjoy the chain of icicles that line the roof of the cave, if you've arrived after a long winter cold spell.

The beauty of Sand Cave comes from the large beach-like dune that fills the cave. Unlike the jumble of fallen roof boulders and shade-loving plants on the floors of most Cumberland caves, here you're treated to cool, clean sand speckled with bright white quartz pebbles. Most caves are formed from hard rock layers that form the cave roof and from softer layers that erode away to create the cave opening. Typically, in the Cumberlands the hard layers are massive sandstones, while the softer layers are usually more easily eroded shales or very thin-bedded sandstones. What makes Sand Cave unique is that its soft layer is a thick, massive sandstone dotted with small pebbles of white quartz. The sandstone is poorly cemented, which means that its sand grains do not stick together well. This causes the rock to erode grain by grain, forming the dune on the cave floor, rather than to fall apart in huge boulders.

Return to the hitching rack at 4.1 miles, and turn left on a wide contour trail toward White Rocks. Along this stretch watch above for a huge outcrop of pebbly sandstone, and watch below for a wildflower display that includes numerous purple-spurred violets. After passing a faint trail to the right, which is the remains of the unmarked trail to the fire tower site, reach a poorly marked four-way junction at 5.0 miles.

To the left at this junction, an unmarked side trail leads 0.3 mile to the White Rocks backcountry campsite, located above the confluence of two small draws. The camp-site has three sites, each large enough for two small tents. In spring, water can be found below the confluence, about a 5-minute walk below the lowest campsite. Later in the year, water will be more difficult to find. You might plan on getting water at the small waterfall at Sand Cave if you plan to spend the night.

From the 5.0-mile junction, continue straight through the four-way junction along the ridgetop trail to White Rocks. You'll pass another hitching rack before starting the steep climb to the overlook at 5.3 miles. Be careful around the exposed cliffs, as you enjoy the views south into Virginia across the Tennessee Valley, and along the crest of Cumberland Mountain. When your eyes have had their fill, and your feet have had their rest, return to the four-way junction. At the junction turn left (if you're coming from White Rocks) and take the signed foot trail down toward Ewing.

Reach the main Ewing Trail at 6.1 miles. If you want, you can retrace your route back to the trailhead, or, for variety, at 8.0 miles continue straight ahead on the horse trail. After splitting from the foot trail, the horse trail leads south to a gate with a trail sign and a side road leading east. Go right at the next junction onto a gravel road. Continue downhill on the gravel road until reaching the paved road to the trailhead and Civic Park. Turn right briefly on the paved road to close your loop at 8.7 miles.

To use the White Rocks backcountry campsite you must obtain a free backcoun-try camping permit from the Cumberland Gap visitor center before starting an over-night trip.

Other Hiking Options

1. Short and Sweet. The 2.0-mile Fitness Trail loop seems to be the park's most popular trail. It begins at the far end of the visitor center parking area as a wide bark-chip path with many species of trees identified. After about a mile it reaches a lovely stream across from one of the park shop and the Bartlett Park Picnic Area. Trail's end is on the Pinnacle Road side of the parking area.

2. If you'd like to see more of the history at Cumberland Gap, try the 7.0-mile Tri-State Peak hike described in Doris Gove's *50 Hikes in the Tennessee Mountains* (Backcountry Guides).

3. Since the completion of the long-awaited tunnel through Cumberland Moun-tain in 1996, the route of old US 25 East over Cumberland Gap has been closed to traffic. The NPS hopes to be able to restore the road to its pre-industrial condition so that park visi-tors can see Cumberland Gap in much the same state as early pioneers or Native Americans did. Restoration of Cumberland Gap began in August 2001 with the removal of old US 25 East. The replica of the 2.5-mile section of the Wilderness Road should be completed some time in 2002.

7

Hensley Settlement

Total Distance: 10.6 miles round-trip on a route open to horses and official vehicles

Hiking Time: About 5.5 hours

Location: Cumberland Gap National Historic Park, 10 miles east of Middlesboro

Maps: USGS Varilla; Cumberland Gap National Historic Park Trail System

Of all the destinations in Cumberland Gap National Historic Park, the Hensley Settlement is perhaps the most remote. Yet on farms perched on the upper slopes of isolated Brush Mountain, hard-working mountain families tended crops and raised animals for several generations. The park has preserved the remains of some of these pioneer homesteads as a memorial to their proud community and as a window into their rugged way of life.

Getting There

From the Cumberland Gap National Historic Park visitor center just south of Middlesboro, leave US 25 East on the road to Pinnacle Overlook. Drive 1.7 miles, then turn onto KY 988. Drive 3.0 miles, then turn right onto KY 217. Drive 5.2 miles to the trailhead, which is 0.5 mile past Road 1344. There is no designated parking here, but hikers can use a small turnout on the north side of the road. There is no sign for the trail here, but the trail follows a gravel road beyond a locked gate, which is in the Shillalah Creek Wildlife Management Area. Park service vehicles use this road, so do not block the gate.

The Hike

The Hensley Settlement is nearly as hard to reach today as it was in the early part of the twentieth century. Several options are available. The shortest trail climbs 2.7 very steep miles up Chadwell Gap from the Virginia side. The Chadwell Gap trailhead is on private land and may be closed starting in

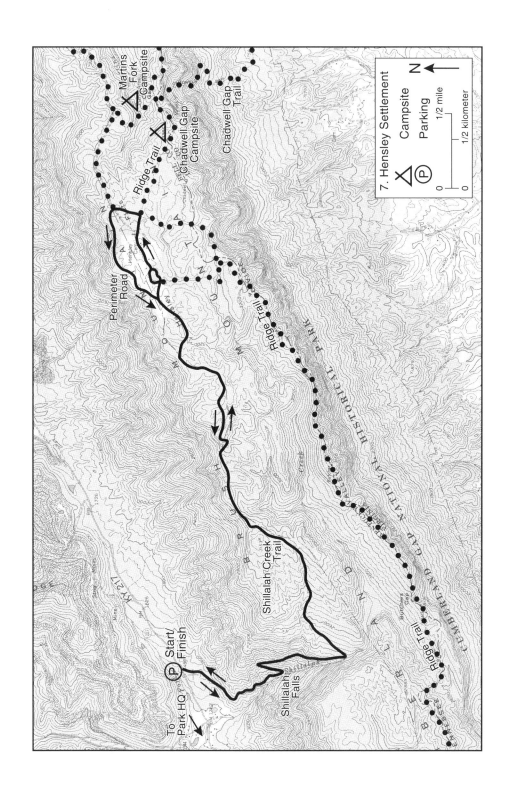

7. Hensley Settlement

△ Campsite
Ⓟ Parking

Martins Fork Campsite

Chadwell Gap Trail

Ridge Trail

Chadwell Gap Campsite

Perimeter Road

Ridge Trail

CUMBERLAND GAP NATIONAL HISTORICAL PARK

Shillalah Creek Trail

Shillalah Falls

Ridge Trail

To Park HQ

Start/Finish

KY 217

TENNESSEE

N

0   1/2 mile
0   1/2 kilometer

2002. Hensley Settlement is also a long, but relatively flat, 11.2 miles from Pinnacle via the Ridge Trail. A good compromise between length and steepness is the 4.6-mile route up Shillalah Creek Trail.

From bottom to top the Shillalah Creek Trail is a well maintained, but little traveled, gravel road. Since vehicles on the road will not be expecting hikers, stay alert and move aside if you hear a vehicle approach. With no challenges in route finding or boulder hopping the steady climb goes quickly.

From the gate opposite the trailhead the trail wraps westward behind the cottages at Shillalah Village. At 0.7 mile you reach a sign for the Shillalah Wildlife Management Area at the first switchback. To the right is Shillalah Falls, a seasonal 15-foot drop in a steep and boulder-chocked section of the creek. This lovely waterfall is an ideal photo stop or rest break. In late spring, look here for blooms of laurel and blackberry.

At the third switchback, your trail leaves Shillalah Creek, but an unofficial trail continues straight along the creek to visit other cascades. The wild turkeys that frequent the Wildlife Management Area are easy to spot in the surrounding woods, as are crested dwarf iris. You can identify the iris from the yellow crest on each of its three purple sepals (which in turn look similar to the flower's three petals). At 2.2 miles, enter an area posted NO TRESPASSING on both sides of the road. Just beyond, in lush growth of cinnamon ferns, a faint dirt road leaves right off the main road. At 2.5 miles, pass the gated entrance to a private inholding.

By now you've reached the crest of Brush Mountain, and the walking is less vertical as the road weaves in and out of the boundary between the park and Wildlife Management Area. Watch for squawroot, the yellowish brown stems of parasitic plants that grow in clumps from the roots of oak trees. At 4.6 miles, reach a chain gate at the edge of the Hensley Settlement. Beyond the gate the trail through the settlement branches right, while the "perimeter road" used by horses branches left. To connect these two branches in a complete loop around the settlement covers 1.4 more miles.

Leave plenty of time and energy to explore the settlement. The farms of Willie and Leige Gibbons are preserved along with many of their outbuildings, a schoolhouse, and community cemetery. It is now hard to imagine that this beautiful and peaceful place was once a thriving community that contained 80 people and 100 buildings. But this peace and isolation came at a price to the mountain families. As you explore, think of the effort and isolation of farming and raising a family so far from other communities. It was indeed the isolation and difficulty of farming here that led to the abandonment of the community. While some left to join large communities in nearby towns, others left for "better and easier" work in the nearby coal mines, a true indication of the difficulty of life on the mountain. Sherman Hensley, who arrived on the mountain in 1903 with his wife Nicey Ann, was the last to leave the community in 1951. The Willie Gibbons farmhouse burned to the ground in November 2000 in an incident of undetermined cause.

At the southeast corner of the settlement by a signboard, the Chadwell Gap Trail intersects the settlement loop. At the northeast corner, a rough trail enters from Brownies Creek. But you should return to Shillalah Creek by retracing your route.

The Shillalah Creek Trail is open to horses and mountain bikes. It is closed to hunters even in the Wildlife Management Area. However, the NPS uses the road for van tours daily in the summer season, and on weekends throughout the year. The tours leave daily, require reservations, and require a fee.

There is a backcountry campsite near the Hensley Settlement. Drinking water is available seasonally. You must obtain a free backcountry camping permit from the visitor center before starting an overnight trip.

Other Hiking Options

1. Short and Sweet. The hike to Shillalah Falls and back is a 1.4-mile round trip. Hikers unable to reach the settlement on foot should consider the NPS van tour.

2. The Sugar Run Trail climbs from two points along KY 988 to end at the Ridge Trail. From the trailhead the hike is a 4.2-mile round trip. From the picnic area the hike is a 4.4-mile round trip.

3. Cumberland Gap will someday be a pivotal point in the region's long-distance trail system. It is the proposed northern end of the Cumberland Trail State Park, a trail that will extend along the Cumberland Mountains across the entire length of Tennessee, and is the southern end of the proposed Pine Mountain Trail that will lead across the crest of Pine Mountain to Breaks Interstate Park.

8

Chained Rock Trail

Total Distance: A 3.4-mile one-way hike on the Laurel Cove, Chained Rock, and Rock Hotel Trails. This hike requires a 3-mile car shuttle or road walk, or can easily be reversed by strong hikers.

Hiking Time: About 2 hours

Location: Pine Mountain State Resort Park, 3 miles south of Pineville

Maps: USGS Pineville and Middlesboro North; Pine Mountain Visitors Guide

The hiking trails in Pine Mountain State Resort Park form two systems that are centered around either Herndon Evans Lodge or Laurel Amphitheater. But only the Laurel Amphitheater trails give hikers a taste of what the park is really about. Here you can climb Pine Mountain from nearly bottom to top, and reward yourself with two of the finest views in all of southeast Kentucky. And nowhere else can you see a rock that had to be chained in place to protect a town.

Getting There

From the junction of US 25 East and KY 119 about 1 mile south of Pineville, drive south on US 25 East for 0.3 mile to a paved road on the north side of the park golf course. Coming north from Middlesboro, this same junction is 0.5 mile north of the intersection of US 25 East and KY 190, which is the main entrance to the park. Drive west on this road, past the golf course, for 1.1 miles to reach the sometimes gated entrance to Laurel Cove Amphitheater.

The Hike

This hike starts off with a tour through Laurel Cove Amphitheater, home of the annual Mountain Laurel Festival. This rustic setting features seating on benches and on wooden planks with rock bases. Walk through the amphitheater, then descend to a picnic shelter. Across tiny Laurel Creek from the shelter is a trailhead sign indicating that the Laurel Cove Trail, your first leg, is about 1.75 miles one way.

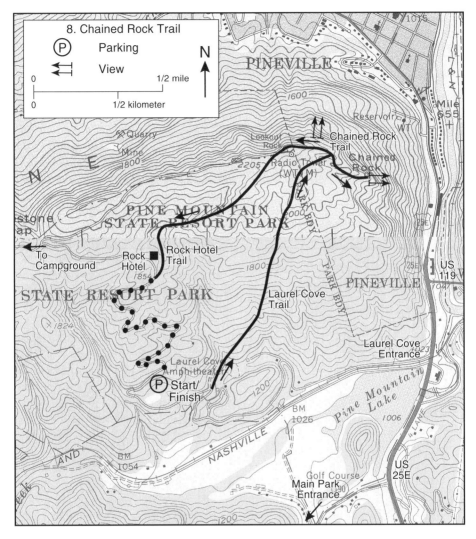

Most of the climb to the crest of Pine Mountain will be through a dry pine-oak forest. For better or worse, it's a good place to examine the workings of the southern pine beetle. The bark of several pines along the trail has been stripped off, giving an up-close view of the tunnels carved by the beetle in the soft living tissue of the tree. One of the other common trees along the trail is sassafras, best recognized by its mitten-shaped leaves, which can have one, two, or three lobes. About halfway up the mountain, the trail passes under a small arch. Arches are rare in the steeply tilted rocks of Pine Mountain and are more common in the flat-lying sandstone layers of rocks in areas like the Big South Fork or Red River Gorge. This rare treasure is only about 20 feet long, 8 feet wide, and 8 feet high.

Next, a short side trail leads left to a bare slab of sandstone and "through the trees" views. Beyond, the trail hugs a small stream and ascends on an intricate series of rock steps up a steep gully made to seem even narrower by a dense growth of rhododendron. At 1.7 miles, reach the well-worn junction with the Chained Rock Trail beside a small rockhouse. Through the years myriad unofficial routes to Chained Rock have developed, so the real trail can be hard to find. From the intersection it descends steeply, then goes down a set of stone steps with railings to a spot where the chain is visible at 1.9 miles.

Once at the chain you'll be torn between examining it, and enjoying the views from the rocks around it. The chain itself is 101 feet long, weighs 3,000 pounds, and spans 75 feet. Each link is 4 inches wide, 6 inches long, and weighs about 4.5 pounds. If you look carefully you can see pieces of a comparatively dinky older chain still in place. The town of Pineville lies below, obviously in the path of any wayward boulders that might escape from the mountain. Below also is the mighty Cumberland River, making the only cut through Pine Mountain for more than 100 miles. In late spring and early summer, the thick rhododendron blooms around the overlook add to the spectacle.

The story of the chained rock is a unique combination of civic pride and civic sense of humor. A menacing-looking boulder had always loomed above the city of Pineville, but residents had joked that they were safe from it because the rock was chained in place. Then in the early 1930s some tourists asked why the chain could not be seen from town. This gave some enterprising citizens the idea to install a real chain to replace a smaller one that had once been in place, but since had fallen into disrepair. The Pineville Kiwanis Club obtained a huge chain formerly used on a steam shovel at a rock quarry in Hagen, Virginia. The chain was shipped to town, hauled up the mountain by mules, and secured in place with considerable effort. With the chain in place, and visible from the town below, Pineville had what it needed: protection from the falling rock, and the tourist attraction that it wanted. Supposedly, the story of the chained rock was reported in more than 6,000 newspapers cross the country.

All went well on top of the mountain until recent years, when the chain, and the rock that it holds, became the subject of threats from "geology rights" advocates who want to "Free the Pine Mountain Rock." These groups believe that it is wrong to enslave the rock, and that chaining it to the mountain violates the rock's right to erode as nature intended. Whether they will be successful in removing the chain and freeing the rock remains to be seen.

Return to the Laurel Cove–Chained Rock junction at 2.1 miles, and continue straight ahead on the Chained Rock Trail. The trail here is wide and eroded. Ignore an unmarked path to the right before reaching another signed trail junction at 2.4 miles. The sign indicates that the Rock Hotel Trail is 2 miles one way, and the Laurel Cove Trail is 1 mile one way, but apparently the distances for the two trails on the sign have been reversed. To the right a trail climbs a short way to the parking area at Lookout Point, a worthy side trip for another view of the valley to the north of Pine Mountain.

Take the Rock Hotel Trail, which is marked by flat red stripe centered in round white blazes. You can ignore a side trail to the right to a overgrown overlook marred by dead pines. Be careful to watch for blazes on rocks in an open area filled with blueberry and laurel. At 3.0 miles, reach a junction with the side trail right to the Rock Hotel. Take this side trail down along a small stream lined with hemlock and rhododendron, and reach the Rock Hotel after a small climb at 3.2 miles. This deep rockhouse stretches for 100 feet along the bluff line and is up to 30 feet high, obviously large enough to hold a hotel full of people.

Continue on the side trail until you rejoin the Rock Hotel Trail only 100 yards from where you left it. Continue on the trail until you reach the main park road at 3.4 miles. If you weren't able to shuttle a car to this point, you have two options for your return. Obviously, you can retrace your route back to Laurel Amphitheater. If you ignore the side trips to Chained Rock and Rock Hotel, this will be a 2.8-mile journey. If you turn left, and walk down the road, you will have 2.6 miles of little-traveled pavement ahead of you.

While no backcountry camping is allowed in the park, there is a 36-site campground on the mountaintop that is open April through October. The campground lacks electric hookups but does have showers, so it is perfect for those looking to tent camp.

Two areas within the park are preserved as part of the Kentucky State Nature Preserves system. The small Hemlock Garden area behind Herndon Evans Lodge protects a small, old-growth forest of huge hemlock, beech, and tulip poplar. The larger area on the south slopes of Pine Mountain protects the habitats of two plants rare in the Commonwealth, and includes the trails from below the Chained Rock to above Laurel Cove.

Other Hiking Options

1. Short and Sweet. If you start from Lookout Point, Chained Rock is a 1-mile round-trip hike.

2. The other trails at Pine Mountain State Resort Park all start from Herndon Evans Lodge, located off KY 190, 4 miles from US 25 East. Hemlock Garden is a 1.1-mile semi-loop trail that passes by an CCC-era picnic shelter, and goes through some old-growth forest. Honeymoon Falls is a 1.5-mile semi-loop to a wet-weather falls. The Living Stairway and Fern Garden Trails are nested loops 0.5 and 1.4 miles long.

II

Daniel Boone Country—South

Blue Heron Loop

Total Distance: The loop is 6.4 miles around. A small part of the trail is used by horses.

Hiking Time: About 3.5 hours

Location: Big South Fork National River and Recreation Area, about 10 miles south of Whitley City

Maps: USGS Barthell; National Geographic/Trails Illustrated Big South Fork National River and Recreation Area

Blue Heron contains all that is great about hiking in the Big South Fork country. You'll see spectacular geology up close in the narrow passage through Crack-in-rock, enjoy spacious views over the Big South Fork from overlooks both next to the river and from high above it, and relive history in an restored coal mining camp.

Getting There

From the junction of US 27 and KY 92, drive west on KY 92 through Stearns for 1.1 miles. Turn south on KY 1651 for 1.1 miles to Revlo, then turn right onto KY 742. Drive west on KY 742 (Blue Heron or Mine 18 Road) to the end of the road at the Blue Heron visitor center and park. A fun alternate way to reach Blue Heron is to ride the Big South Fork Scenic Railroad that operates seasonally from Stearns.

The Hike

Even in a land where coal is king, many visitors are surprised to learn that the Blue Heron area isn't named for a bird. Blue Heron was the miners' name for a special type of coal mined at one of the many mining communities that dotted the Big South Fork in pre-park times. The community prospered when the mines were new and the digging relatively easy. But the good times didn't last. Usually the coal companies were diligent about drilling out their coal so they'd know how thick their seams were, and how far they stretched. But at Blue Heron, not enough holes were drilled to make an accurate estimate. The mines proved a disappointment to both the company and its workers.

Daniel Boone Country—South

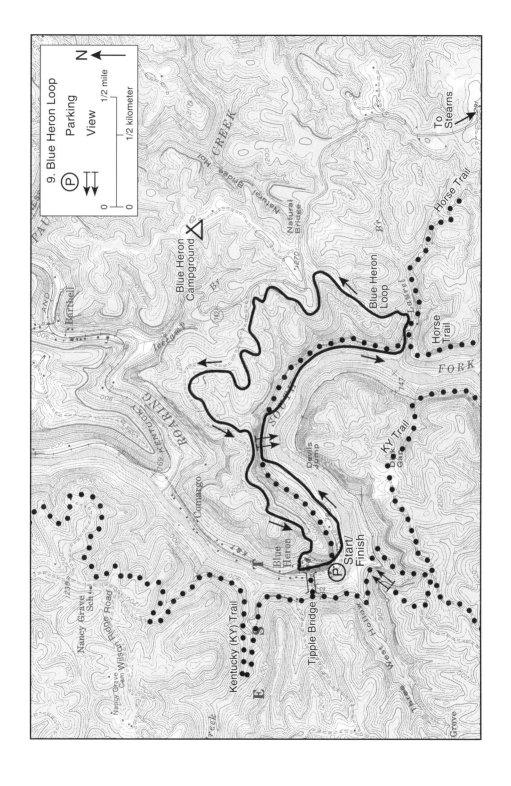

9. Blue Heron Loop

Ⓟ Parking

View

N

0   1/2 mile
0   1/2 kilometer

PAUL
BARTHELL

AND

Barthell

KENTUCKY

ROARING

Comargo

Bear Creek

Nancy Grave Sch.
Nancy Grave
Gem Wilson Ridge Road

K&T

Kentucky (KY) Trail

Tipple Bridge

Blue Heron

Start/
Finish
Ⓟ

West Three Creek

West Hollow

Devils Jump

KY Trail
Devils Gap

SOUTH

FORK

Blue Heron Loop

Horse Trail

Laurel Br

Horse Trail

To Stearns

Blue Heron
Campground

Natural Bridge Trail

Natural
Bridge

CREEK

Descending Crack-in-rock

You'll see plenty of remains of the mining era as you walk the loop, but be sure to leave plenty of time also to wander the interpretive displays and explore the Blue Heron tipple at the visitor center by the trailhead.

From the far end of the visitor center, follow the trail leading upstream along the river to walk the loop in a counter-clockwise direction. In 200 feet a horse trail will split left. At 0.4 mile, reach a side trail leading right to an overlook above Devil's Jump Rapid, one of the most feared rapids on this stretch of the river. There is a small campsite opposite the side trail. Soon after passing the rapid the loop enters a grassy area that is actually a reclaimed waste pile from the coal mines. After climbing two switchbacks, look for a set of stairs leading up the steep hillside to a right turn onto the horse trail leading to Bear Creek.

The horse trail follows mining tram route; so enjoy a mile of level walking with views of the river. Look closely here and you'll see some thin, exposed coal seams and small pieces of the soft black rock scattered across the trail. Make a right turn off the horse trail, and pass a large campsite above the river in a grove of pines. There's another campsite near the mouth of Laurel Creek at 1.9 miles, where there is also a major trail junction with the horse trail. The horse trail leads left to Blue Heron and right to the Bear Creek Horse Camp.

At the mouth of the creek, the Blue Heron loop turns left, crosses the horse trail, and begins a long climb up switchbacks and stairs toward the rim of the canyon. At the base of the rim is a long, narrow rockhouse. Reach the rim at 2.8 miles, where side paths lead right to KY 742 and the Blue Heron Campground.

Follow the trail alongside KY 742 and then along the road to Devils Jump Overlook, at one point climbing a set of stairs to walk alongside the road. At 3.5 miles, begin

Daniel Boone Country–South

a steady descent to reach another trailhead at 4.4 miles. Pass one more trailhead at 4.8 miles, before reaching a side trail left at 5.1 miles to an overlook above Devils Jump Rapid. The rapid and the narrows above it are even more intimidating from this aerial view than from your earlier, close-up encounters. At 5.6 miles, there's an overlook with benches and a wood canopy looking down onto the Blue Heron Tipple.

This overlook marks the start of the trail's descent to the river. At 5.8 miles, reach an elaborate set of stairs and walkways through the giant boulders of Crack-in-rock. The narrow, shadowed passage lends the trail here an air of mystery and suspense, as hikers try to guess just where the path will lead. Crack-in-rock is a set of huge boulders that have split from the main rim of the Big South Fork gorge. The rock split along vertical fractures and many of the blocks have come to rest leaning back against other blocks to form small arches.

The trail continues to descend, and reaches the Blue Heron visitor center at 6.4 miles. The visitor center contains an elaborate set of displays depicting the history of the coal and timber operations in the area, and the lives of the people who lived there. Here you can listen to the personal stories of life in the mining communities told in the original voices of the miners and their families.

The highlight of anyone's visit to Blue Heron will be a walk across the Tipple Bridge. The tipple is an elaborate operation that sorted the raw coal transported from the mines by size and quality for shipment to customers. Coal was brought in by rail on the tracks over the river, dumped into the top of the tipple, sorted, and cleaned, then loaded into railcars at the bottom of the tipple. The Park Service restored the tipple and bridge after taking over management of

the area. A walk across the bridge gives an unprecedented view of the Big South Fork and is a useful connector to the Kentucky Trail on the west bank of the river.

As you enjoy the Big South Fork, be thankful that the area ever became a park. After the ravages of coal mining and clear-cutting of timber, the land around the river was unable to support even the few people who chose to remain after the mines closed and the timber camps shut down.

The U.S. Army Corps of Engineers began looking at dam sites along the river to control flooding and to produce hydroelectric power for the region. A dam was first proposed at Devil's Jump as early as 1933. During the 1950s and 1960s, the dam was authorized by the U.S. Senate, but not by the U.S. House of Representatives. However, by this time others began to realize the unique recreation value of the river and the steep gorge surrounding it. With the region's only national park in the Great Smoky Mountains badly congested, and receiving more visits than any other national park, it was easy to see the benefits of converting the Big South Fork to a park instead of a reservoir.

By the early 1970s the battle between developers and conservationists was settled by a bill establishing the Big South Fork National River and Recreation Area. The 125,000-acre area was managed by the Army Corps of Engineers until 1991, at which time it was turned over to the National Park Service. Only 114,000 acres of the park have been purchased. Several land parcels along the edge of the park still remain private land.

Other Hiking Options

1. Short and Sweet. Walking around the displays at Blue Heron and over the tipple bridge is less than 1 mile.

2. Another pair of short hikes nearby are the trails to Split Bow Arch (0.6 mile, semi-loop) and to Bear Creek Overlook (0.5 mile, out and back). Both trails leave from the same trailhead 25 miles south of KY 742.

3. Across the Tipple Bridge is the Kentucky Trail, which leads south 1.6 miles to Dick Gap and 3.4 miles to Big Spring Falls. To the north, the Kentucky Trail leads 2.6 miles to Nancy Graves School site and connects with the Koger–Yamacraw Loop.

10

Yahoo Falls and Yahoo Arch

Total Distance: The entire 9.4-mile loop combines the Big South Fork Yahoo Falls trails plus the Daniel Boone National Forest Yahoo Arch, Negro Creek, and Sheltowee Trace Trails. The shortest route to Yahoo Falls, Kentucky's highest waterfall, is 0.5 mile round-trip. Progressively longer hikes lead to Yahoo Arch, Markers Arch, and to a loop using part of the STT.

Hiking Time: About 5 hours for the full loop

Location: Big South Fork National River and Recreation Area and Stearns Ranger District, 5 miles northwest of Whitley City

Maps: USGS Barthell and Nevelsville; National Geographic/Trails Illustrated Big South Fork National River and Recreation Area

If you like to have a lot of options when you hike, the Yahoo Falls area will be perfect for you. Depending on your energy level and the time available, you can walk anywhere between 0.5 and 10 miles here. Each extra mile adds another treat, so there's little incentive to stop and turn back before the loop is complete. The full loop has two road crossings, so if you can arrange a shuttle or car drop-off, almost any length of hike is possible.

Getting There

Two miles north of Whitley City, leave US 27 and turn west onto KY 700. In 2.8 miles, cross an alternate trailhead for Yahoo Arch Trail (DBNF #602). At 4.0 miles, turn right onto gravel with a sign reading 1.5 MILES TO YAHOO FALLS PICNIC AREA. Reach the picnic area shortly after entering the Big South Fork National River and Recreation Area (BSFNRRA). The trailhead is at the far end of the picnic area near a signboard and restrooms.

The Hike

Before you start the hike, take a good look at the Yahoo Falls trail map on the signboard at the trailhead. It looks complicated, doesn't it? Well don't worry. Even though the real trail system is every bit as confusing as the map, finding your way to the falls and back really isn't that hard. The main thing to remember is that the BSFNRRA divides the trails into three loops, the Topside (yellow blazes), Cliffside (green blazes), and

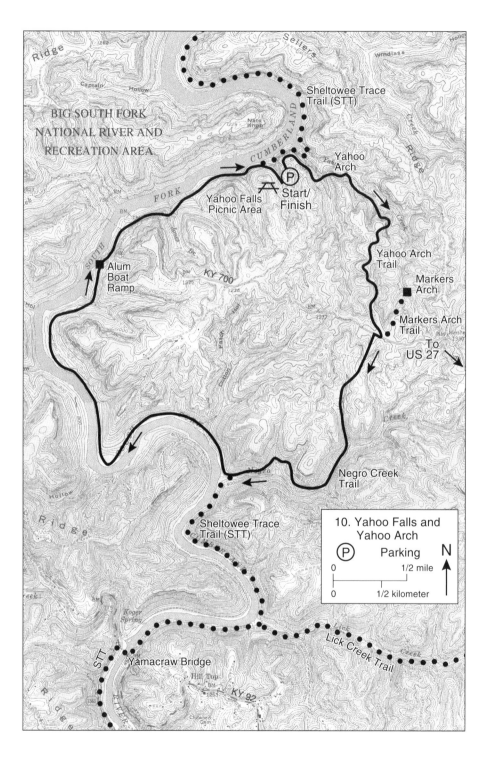

Ridge

Sellers

Windlass

Holly

Creek Ridge

BIG SOUTH FORK
NATIONAL RIVER AND
RECREATION AREA

Captain

Hollow

Nate
Knob

CUMBERLAND

Sheltowee Trace
Trail (STT)

Yahoo
Arch

FORK

Yahoo Falls
Picnic Area

P
Start/
Finish

Yahoo Arch
Trail

Markers
Arch

SOUTH

Alum
Boat
Ramp

KY 700

Markers Arch
Trail

To
US 27

Negro Creek
Trail

Sheltowee Trace
Trail (STT)

Ridge

Hollow

10. Yahoo Falls and
Yahoo Arch

P   Parking   N

0   1/2 mile
0   1/2 kilometer

Koger
Spring

STT

Yamacraw Bridge

Hill Top

KY 92

Lick
Creek

Lick Creek Trail

RIVER

Cascade (blue blazes). These loops overlap in several places; for example the section of trail that leaves from the trailhead is part of all three loops. Lying below all three loops, and closest to the Cumberland River, is the Sheltowee Trace Trail.

This loop will describe the shortest route to Yahoo Falls and Yahoo Arch. Hikers who have only time to explore the Yahoo Falls area should at least continue around the Blue Loop to Roaring Rocks Cataract.

From the trailhead, pass a short side trail on the left leading to an overlook. Take the next left turn, which leads downhill on a green-blazed trail. Pass by the next junction where a trail at your left leads to the STT. Beyond this junction, enter the huge natural amphitheater that holds Yahoo Falls. The falls pour over the lip of a mammoth rockhouse in a narrow ribbon of glistening water. Here, water freefalls 113 feet from the lip to crash into a tiny plunge pool. The creek that feeds the falls is a small one. It's the setting of the falls, not the power of its water, that make this a special place. The opening of this magnificent rockhouse stretches for several hundred feet in a broad semicircle.

On the far side of the Yahoo Falls, pass two branches of the blue-blazed Cascade Trail. Follow the yellow blazes uphill to a signed junction with the Yahoo Arch Spur trail at 0.3 mile.

Turn left onto the spur trail to Yahoo Arch (DBNF 602). As you approach the arch, watch the bluffs for a good lesson on how arches are formed. The first stage is the sheer solid cliffs formed from massive sandstone. As weaker layers below the sandstone are eroded, part of the base of the cliffs gives way, and shallow overhangs are formed. As overhangs become deeper, those with thin roofs may collapse forming an arch. At the back of the Yahoo Arch you can see the fallen blocks of sandstone that once formed the roof of the rockhouse at Yahoo Arch. Yahoo Arch is larger than most in the region, with a 70-foot by 50-foot span and a height of nearly 20 feet. If you look closely at the far side, notice that it is really a double arch, if you count a small opening on the left.

Leave Yahoo Arch at 1.1 miles, and climb stone steps to gain the top of a broad ridge. In late spring and summer, bluets, fire pinks, and robins plantain, along with scattered white blazes, decorate the old roadway that the trail follows. At 2.1 miles, just before the crossing of KY 700, reach a signed junction with the Markers Arch Trail (DBNF 603). Arch lovers should take the 0.5-mile side trip down to this small arch. Like Yahoo Arch, Markers Arch also resembles the remains of a collapsed rockhouse. The thin span is roughly 12 feet tall and 25 feet long.

Back at KY 700, walk 200 feet right up the road to gated DBNF Road 6003. This is the starting point for the Negro Creek Trail (DBNF 612). Follow the road for 0.2 mile past a recently burned area to the right of the trail. At a power line, look for an arrow on a pole that points toward stairs carved into a short rock face. The footpath, now marked with white diamonds, winds around the head of Negro Creek, then follows it on the slope above. As the trail approaches the Sheltowee Trace Trail, make three crossings of a two-track dirt road in quick succession.

Intersect the STT at 4.3 miles. Here a sign indicates that it is 3 miles right to Alum Ford, 3 miles left to Yamacraw Bridge and 4 miles back to Yahoo Falls. A large, overused campsite next to the river has a sandy beach ideal for a lunch break. On the rest of this hike, you'll never stray far from the river. Although powerboats use this section of the river, which is now part of Lake Cumberland, the walk is usually quiet and peaceful. There's a signed bridge over Cotton

Patch Creek, where the trail looks down into a giant's jigsaw puzzle of house-sized boulders wedged into the narrow creek bed. In spring the forest floor is covered by the bright yellow buds and variegated leaves of the yellow trillium, mayapple, and purple violets. At 5.8 miles, a faint side trail leads left to the Cotton Patch Shelter. No water, except for that from the river, is available here. Just beyond the shelter, a huge chimney marks an old homestead.

Walk through the Alum Ford Primitive Campground before reaching another crossing of KY 700 at 7.4 miles. Follow KY 700 to the right for 200 feet before turning left at a sign indicating that Yahoo Falls is 2 miles, US 27 is 8 miles, and Cumberland Falls is 24 miles. You'll pass two "pour over" waterfalls along small creeks, and pass the collapsed entrances of old coal mines, before reaching a junction with the green-blazed Cliffside Trail at Yahoo Falls at 8.7 miles. Unless you yearn for another view of the falls, turn right and begin a steady climb. The bluffs here are so steep that the park has installed metal ladders to get up the roughest sections. The trail rejoins the picnic area at 9.4 miles.

Other Hiking Options

1. Short and Sweet. The dense network of trails surrounding Yahoo Falls is confusing to many hikers, but provides numerous vantage points for viewing the falls and Roaring Rock Cataract. The round trip to the Yahoo Falls only is 0.5 mile.

2. Round trip to Yahoo Arch is 3.0 miles. Adding Markers Arch ups the total to 5.2 miles.

3. Yahoo Falls is also a convenient starting point for longer trips on the Sheltowee Trace Trail. South of the loop, the STT leads 3.0 miles to Yamacraw Bridge on KY 92. North of the loop, the STT leads out of the BSFNRRA 6.8 miles to cross US 27 north of Stearns.

11

Kentucky Trail–Ledbetter Trailhead to Troublesome Creek

Total Distance: A 9.4 mile out-and-back hike. A shortcut via Hill Cemetery Road makes an 8.8-mile semi-loop. Horses share some of these trails.

Hiking Time: About 5 hours

Location: Big South Fork National River and Recreation Area, about 16 miles southwest of Stearns

Maps: USGS Barthell and Oneida North; National Geographic/Trails Illustrated Big South Fork National River and Recreation Area

The Kentucky Trail is a 27-mile alternate route to the Sheltowee Trace Trail between the Peters Mountain Trailhead and Yamacraw Bridge. The section between Ledbetter Trailhead and Troublesome Creek travels some of the park's most remote backcountry and makes a fine day hike or overnight trip. Here the trail traverses the banks of both the Big South Fork and Troublesome Creek in an area where the inner gorge of the river is especially narrow.

Getting There

From the junction of KY 1363 and KY 92 at the west end of the Yamacraw Bridge, turn south onto KY 1363. Drive 2.3 miles and turn left onto Beach Grove (also called Devils Branch) Road. In 1.3 miles, go straight on the paved road at a four-way intersection where the Sheltowee Trace Trail crosses the road. Keep on the main road, which becomes gravel, for 2.7 miles to a junction just beyond Beach Grove Church. Go right at this junction for 0.9 mile, and then turn left onto gravel Ledbetter Road. The trailhead is 1.6 miles down this road on the left side of the road.

The Hike

From the Ledbetter Trailhead, follow the Kentucky Trail south along the dirt road. At 0.2 mile the road forks. The lesser-used road that splits right to Hill Cemetery can be used as an alternate return route from Oil Well Branch. At 0.6 mile, the trail leaves the road on a foot trail branching to the right. A sign indicates that the trail ahead is closed

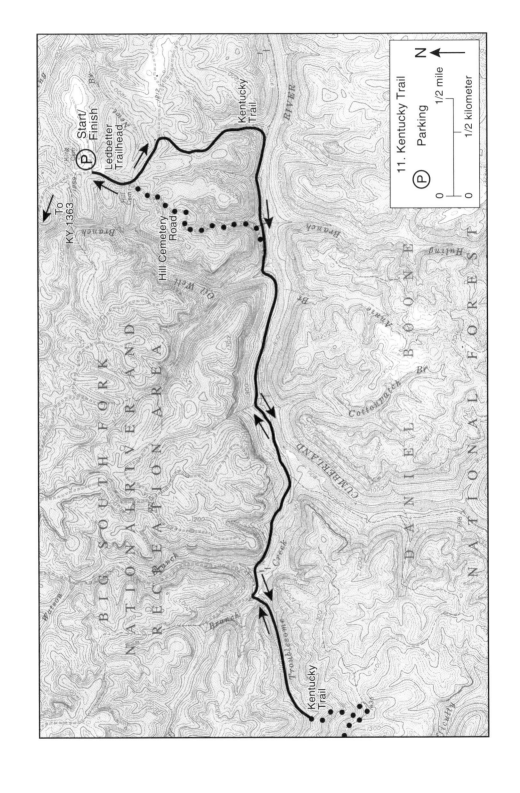

11. Kentucky Trail

(P) Parking

N

0   1/2 mile

0   1/2 kilometer

Start/ Finish

(P) Ledbetter Trailhead

To KY 1363

Kentucky Trail

Hill Cemetery Road

Oil Well

Kentucky Trail

Troublesome Creek

Branch

Branch

Cottonpatch

BIG SOUTH FORK NATIONAL RIVER AND RECREATION AREA

CUMBERLAND

DANIEL BOONE NATIONAL FOREST

RIVER

to vehicles and horses. Descend from the plateau through craggy cliff bands covered by thick, dark hemlock forest.

You will reach the Big South Fork River at a junction in 1.5 miles, just after crossing two short footbridges. To the left is a route sometimes illegally used by OHVs, which are banned from the inner gorge. Turn right and follow the powerful river, which is compressed into several small rapids by huge boulders that clog the riverbed. A small, sandy beach offers an invitation to swim. At 2.1 miles, a steep muddy road joins the route on the right. This is the bottom end of Hill Cemetery Road that split from the Kentucky Trail at 0.2 mile. Next to this junction is a large campsite on the riverbank.

Just beyond the junction, at Oil Well Branch, is the first of two new bridges built in 2001 by volunteers from the Student Conservation Association. Look for a sign on the left noting a short path leading to the Beatty Oil Well, which was drilled in 1818. From the sign, walk 50 feet toward the river, and past an older sign on a forked post. The well is marked by one foot of 6-inch diameter metal casing poking up from the ground on the riverbank. Watch out for poison ivy if you decide to search for the well.

According to B. G. Dreaver et al. in *Hiking the Big South Fork,* the Beatty Well was the first commercial oil well drilled in the country. The discovery was an accident, however; the hole was drilled in the hope of finding brine to make salt. The flowing well along the riverbank became the site of the first commercial oil spill in the country. It wasn't long before residents downstream began to complain about the crude oil in the river.

The next 2 miles of trail continue to follow the narrow gorge alongside the Big South Fork. Huge boulders, which have broken loose from the cliffs above, line the route and large cone-shaped piles of smaller debris, called talus, cover the base of some cliffs. Much of the area north of the river was burned in the 1999 Watson Fire. In some areas the fire burned extremely hot, destroying all life in its path, while in other areas the fire was cooler, and most trees survived with only a blackening of their base to mark the fire's passage.

At 2.9 miles is the second of the 2001 SCA bridges. Just beyond the bridge is a large campsite between the trail and the river. At 3.5 miles, leave the main path to the right to briefly follow a foot trail before rejoining the main road and proceeding up Troublesome Creek. If you stay on the main road here, ignore a less-used branch that fords Troublesome Creek, and continue south along the trail along the bank of the Big South Fork.

After crossing of Watson Fork, reach a signed junction at 4.1 miles. Here the old road branches right to lead to Divide Road in 2.7 miles. The Kentucky Trail takes the left fork and immediately reaches another fork. This right fork is signed as part of the Sheltowee Trace. Don't panic: the Sheltowee Trace at one time was planned to use this route, but problems crossing private land forced the trail onto Laurel Ridge Road to the north, so that this section never became part of the STT. Perhaps one day this confusing sign will be removed.

The Kentucky Trail takes the left fork where a sign indicates that Difficulty Creek is 3 miles. Continue along the north bank of Troublesome Creek enjoying views of the small creek and dense groves of rhododendron. Reach the small footbridge over Troublesome Creek at 4.7 miles, which marks the end of this hike. Beyond Troublesome, the Kentucky Trail climbs up and over the divide to Difficulty Creek. The west end of the Kentucky Trail is 7.7 miles away via

Cat Ridge Road, the Laurel Hill Trail, and Laurel Ridge Road.

You could return to the Ledbetter Trailhead by retracing your steps or by taking the shorter, and less scenic, Hill Cemetery Road. Hill Cemetery Road is 1.1 miles long. This shortcut saves 0.6 mile on the return. This road climbs very steeply from the bottom of the gorge through an area heavily damaged by the Watson Fire. Once on the rim of the gorge the road is usable by four-wheel-drive vehicles. It passes a low rockhouse with a classically arched roof. Just before joining Ledbetter Road pass Hill Cemetery, which was used by both the Hill and Watson families.

The wild heart of the Big South Fork is drained by three creeks named No Business, Difficulty, and Troublesome. Christened back in pre–chamber of commerce days, these creeks tell the story of the hard times and bleak prospects faced by the first pioneers who moved to the area. Poor soils and steep slopes made farming marginal, while working in the coal mines or on the timber crews offered hard work, low wages, and little job security. It is no wonder that people have abandoned what few settlements there were.

Back before pioneer times the Big South Fork was rich in game. Elk, deer, and black bear roamed the woods. But the early settlers killed off much of the game, and loss of habitat spelled the end for some species. Black bears have been absent from the region since at least the early 1900s. But by the 1980s, bears were moving back into the Daniel Boone National Forest north of the park, and park managers expected that soon some bears would enter the park itself.

A study commissioned by the BSF and carried out by the University of Tennessee determined that the Big South Fork contained excellent bear habitat and was large enough to support a viable population of bears. After a round of sometimes contentious public hearings, an experimental release of bears relocated from Great Smoky Mountain National Park was begun in 1996. Twelve adult females were transplanted to the Big South Fork in two stages. Some summer-released bears immediately fled the area, traveling as far as Knoxville and Chattanooga. Researchers had better luck with their second crop, pregnant females moved while hibernating in their winter dens.

The release has been a success so far. During the springs of 1999 and 2001 females with cubs were observed in the park. The park estimates that more than 30 black bears now call the Big South Fork home. Additional releases will be necessary to support a viable permanent population and to broaden the genetic diversity of the black bears. The park is currently expanding public education about the project with studies and surveys.

Other Hiking Options

1. Short and Sweet. The hike from the trailhead to the river and back via Hill Cemetery Road is 3.4 miles.

2. The Kentucky Trail leads 7.7 miles west from Troublesome Creek to Peters Mountain Trailhead, and 14.8 miles north from Ledbetter Trailhead past Blue Heron and Wilson Ridge to Yamacraw Bridge. The Sheltowee Trace–Kentucky Trail Loop between Peters Mountain Trailhead and Yamacraw Bridge is 42.6 miles.

12

Koger–Yamacraw Loop

Total Distance: This 11.1-mile semi-loop includes a short side trip to Koger Arch. Two short sections of this trail follow gravel roads.

Hiking Time: About 6 hours

Location: Big South Fork National River and Recreation Area and Stearns Ranger District, 5 miles west of Stearns

Maps: USGS Barthell; National Geographic/Trails Illustrated Big South Fork National River and Recreation Area

The Koger–Yamacraw loop combines the north end of the Kentucky Trail with the Sheltowee Trace Trail. These scenic trails are little used, but offer a visit to Koger Arch and streamside hiking along both Rock Creek and the Big South Fork. The loop does require two fords of Rock Creek, which can be dangerous in high water, and two short sections of little-traveled gravel road on Wilson Ridge.

Getting There

To reach the Yamacraw Bridge Trailhead from Stearns, drive 5.4 miles west on KY 92 and park in the gravel lot at the northeast corner of the bridge.

The Hike

From the trailhead, walk across Yamacraw Bridge to KY 1363. Almost immediately turn left off KY 1363 onto a dirt river-access road. Where the road makes a turn to the left, the Sheltowee Trace continues straight ahead into the woods. The Sheltowee Trace portion of this loop is infrequently blazed, but you will find a few of the STT white turtle blazes to guide you. Here the trail is wedged into a thin strip of land between the river and KY 1363. Pass a small beach at 0.7 mile, and then follow an overgrown two-track dirt road. Watch carefully for poison ivy here.

At 0.9 mile, the trail passes under the mammoth railroad bridge across the Big South Fork. The coal trains long ago quit rumbling toward Stearns, so the bridge is inactive. At 1.2 miles, the trail reaches a power

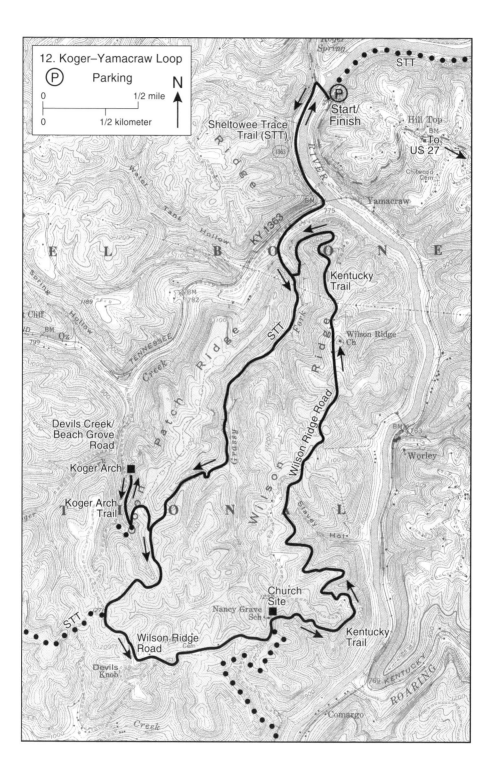

12. Koger–Yamacraw Loop

Ⓟ Parking

N

0 — 1/2 mile
0 — 1/2 kilometer

Sheltowee Trace Trail (STT)

STT

Roger Spring

Start/Finish

Hill Top

To US 27

Chitwood Cem

Yamacraw

KY 1363

Water Tank Hollow

Spring Hollow

Cliff

Tennessee Creek

Patch Ridge

Kentucky Trail

Wilson Ridge Ch

Wilson Ridge Road

STT

Grassy

Devils Creek/ Beach Grove Road

Koger Arch

Koger Arch Trail

Worley

Slavey Hol

Church Site

Nancy Grave Sch

Kentucky Trail

STT

Wilson Ridge Road

Devils Knob

Comargo

Creek

ROARING

KENTUCKY

line cut that may be choked with vegetation and nearly impassable in summer. Just beyond is a signed junction with the bypass route of the Sheltowee Trace around the Rock Creek Ford. The bypass route climbs the bank to KY 1363, and then follows Devils Creek (or Beach Grove) Road up to Wilson Ridge where it rejoins the STT. To continue on the main route, turn left at the junction and reach the ford across Rock Creek at 1.4 miles. Normally this wide stream is less than knee-deep and the rocky bottom is easy walking, but remember that the ford can be dangerous in high water.

Go straight across Rock Creek and climb the bank of the creek. Next, cross the main channel of a smaller side creek and look for a blaze on the far bank. From this point, the trail begins a long trip up the valley of Grassy Fork, one of the highlights of the loop. At 1.6 miles, the Kentucky Trail, your return route, enters on the left. The STT heads steadily up the valley on the bed of an old coal road. Farther up the valley, the trail begins multiple crossings of Grassy Fork and its tributaries. You'll pass a 6-foot-high cascade, some pretty sandstone cliffs, and a lush fern garden in the upper valley. At 2.5 miles, the portal of an abandoned coal mine has been broken open. This old mine, as are most others, is partly flooded and is likely to be very unstable. It's hard to overemphasize the danger that wandering into old mines presents. Opposite the old mine is a potential campsite.

The trail leaves the valley floor by following a small branch to the right and reaches a power line cut at 2.9 miles. This cut is also overgrown and difficult to penetrate in summer. Switchback underneath the road before crossing it on what is now an overgrown roadway. At 3.3 miles, turn right off the roadway onto an overgrown, unmarked foot trail where the roadway is blocked by a large

brush pile. Though it is tempting to assume that you are lost at this point, stay on the trail and reach an old road and signed trail junction on a ridgetop at 3.5 miles.

From this junction, the Koger Arch Trail (DBNF 633) leads right to Koger Arch in 0.2 mile. Just cross the road and descend a series of switchbacks to reach the arch at 3.7 miles. The DBNF lists this arch as 18 feet high and 91 feet long. This massive span is an oasis of cold air on hot summer days, and a welcome resting place after the difficult climb just completed. Native flowers appreciate the cold air also and you might spot red columbine blooming underneath the arch.

Return to the signed junction at 3.9 miles, and continue to follow the old dirt road. If you have battled the thick growth of summer in the power-line cuts, now is the time to reap your rewards. Much of this old road is lined with a feast of blackberries for hikers whose timing is right. There is also a dry campsite on the ridgetop. Follow the road until it comes to a four-way junction at 4.7 miles.

At this junction, paved Devils Creek–Beach Grove Road goes right down to Rock Creek and straight ahead toward Ledbetter Trailhead. The Sheltowee Trace Trail to the south follows the paved road straight for 0.1 mile before branching off to the right onto another dirt road. Our route leaves the STT and turns sharp left to follow gravel Wilson Ridge Road. This stretch of road is little traveled, and is necessary in order to connect the STT and Kentucky Trails. At 5.4 miles, pass the modern Nancy Graves Cemetery. Leave the road at 6.0 miles, opposite a wide muddy parking area on the left. This is the site of Nancy Graves School, which burned "long ago" according to a local resident. From the school site, bushwhack straight into the woods for 50

Yamacraw Bridge

feet until you intersect the Kentucky Trail, which will be marked by the white-on-red arrowheads of the BSF. If you come out in exactly the right place, you should see a trail sign indicating that Blue Heron is 3.6 miles to your right and the STT is 2.8 miles left.

Turn left onto the Kentucky Trail, which follows the rim of Wilson Ridge. Enjoy a small rockhouse and a vista across the gorge. This is also a good spot to look for yellow trillium during the spring wildflower bloom. The trail comes to a wooden bridge that has been obliterated by a fallen tree at 6.9 miles. You'll have to use the fallen tree to cross here, at least until the BSF can repair the bridge. Pass a few more small rockhouses before rejoining Wilson Ridge Road soon after reaching a power line at 7.5 miles.

Turn right onto the gravel road then keep left at the junction with Wilson Ridge Cemetery Road. At 8.5 miles, beside a solitary home, Wilson Ridge Road turns from gravel to dirt. Continue straight, and cross under the junction of a major power line with a smaller one. At 8.9 miles, turn left off the crest of the ridge at an unsigned split in the road. The trail soon switchbacks off the old road onto an intricately constructed section of trail featuring delicate rock steps. You'll cross one normally dry creek before rejoining the Sheltowee Trace at 9.6 miles. Turn right onto the Sheltowee Trace and retrace your route across the Rock Creek ford, and back to the trailhead at 11.1 miles.

This unofficial loop uses trails managed by both the BSF and Stearns Ranger District of the DBNF. From Yamacraw Bridge to Rock Creek the route is part of the Big South Fork. The remainder of the STT is in the national forest. The Kentucky Trail is also in the BSF until it reaches Wilson Creek Road, which is the boundary of the area.

Other Hiking Options

1. Short and Sweet. Koger Arch can be reached in 1.0 mile from the junction of the Sheltowee Trace and Devils Creek–Beach Grove Road. There is an alternate trailhead on Devils Creek–Beach Grove Road 0.8 mile from KY 1363, but there is no parking along the road. The 0.25-mile trail is marked with white diamond blazes.

2. To the north from Yamacraw Bridge the Sheltowee Trace Trail leads 1.4 miles to an intersection with the Lick Creek Trail (DBNF 631), and 2.9 miles to the Negro Creek Trail (DBNF 612). Princess Falls is located 0.2 mile along the Lick Creek Trail, and at 1.2 miles is the beginning of the 0.6-mile side trail to Lick Creek Falls (DBNF 631A).

13

Gobblers Arch and Mark Branch Falls

Total Distance: A 6.1-mile loop for hikers that uses a short section of forest service road. The loop combines the Sheltowee Trace Trail with the Gobblers Arch Trail (DBNF 636), and with small portions of DBNF Road 6105 and DBNF Road 569, Divide Road.

Hiking Time: About 3 hours

Location: Stearns Ranger District, about 20 miles west of Stearns

Maps: USGS Bell Farm and Barthell SW

The area around the Big South Fork is nowhere near crowded, by the standards of areas such as Red River Gorge or Great Smoky Mountains National Park. But still it is nice to know of a few backcountry hideaways, where any hiker can reach a beautiful spot with solitude almost assured. Gobblers Arch and Mark Branch Falls have the scenery that would draw a crowd in almost any park. But being a long way from anywhere protects them from being overrun. If you are willing to drive long miles on lonely gravel roads, this loop is for you.

Getting There

From the junction of KY 92 and KY 1363 on the west side of the Yamacraw Bridge over the Big South Fork, drive west on KY 1363 for 11.2 miles. Here the road splits between Bell Farm Horse Camp and Hemlock Grove Picnic Area. Follow the gravel road (DBNF Road 139) on the left, past the horse camp, for 4.5 miles to a T-junction. Straight ahead at the junction is the Peters Mountain Trailhead. The gravel road leading right is Divide Road (DBNF Road 569), which will take you to Pickett State Park in Tennessee; the gravel road leading left is Laurel Ridge Road (DBNF Road 575), which is also the Sheltowee Trace Trail. The Sheltowee Trace starts from the corner between Divide Road and DBNF Road 139 on the northwest corner of the intersection.

An alternate way to reach the loop during low water would be to drive to the Hemlock Grove Picnic Area, and ford Rock Creek to join the loop near the junction of the Sheltowee Trace and Gobblers Arch Trails.

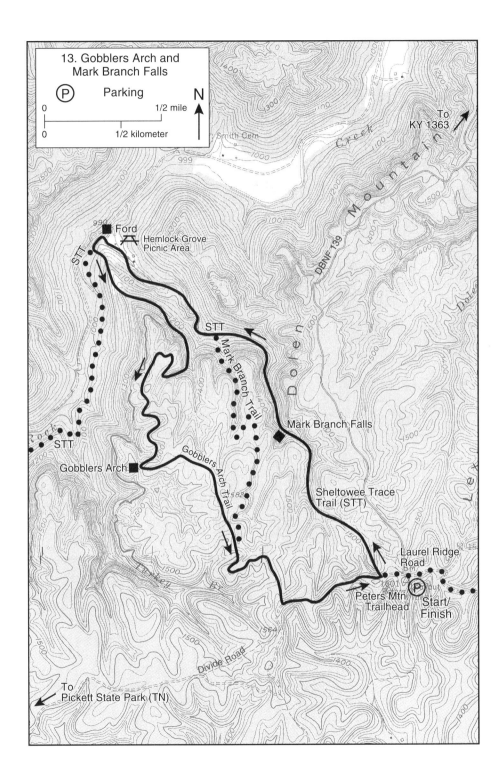

13. Gobblers Arch and
Mark Branch Falls

Ⓟ   Parking

N

0   1/2 mile
0   1/2 kilometer

To
KY 1363

Smith Cem

Creek

Dolen Mountain

999

990 Ford

Hemlock Grove
Picnic Area

STT

DBNF 139

STT

Mark Branch Trail

STT

Mark Branch Falls

Gobblers Arch Trail

Gobblers Arch

Sheltowee Trace
Trail (STT)

1582

Laurel Ridge
Road

Peters Mtn.
Trailhead

Start/
Finish

Finley Br

Divide Road

564

To
Pickett State Park (TN)

Gobblers Arch

The Hike

This hike is unusual in that it starts at the high end, rather than from the bottom. So make sure to take your time, and reserve plenty of energy for the climb back to the plateau from Rock Creek. From the Peters Mountain Trailhead, begin hiking north toward Pickett State Park on the Sheltowee Trace Trail, which is blazed with the trail's familiar white turtle emblem. The forest here is typical of the dry plateau supporting a variety of pines, hemlock, red maple, and sassafras. The trail soon dips beneath the first set of cliff bands. Traveling alongside a series of shallow overhangs in the sandstone cliffs, watch for fascinating iron concretions threaded through the rock.

The trail next drops into the very narrow valley of Mark Branch. Soon you can see where forest service trail crews have cut an almost unbelievable amount of downed timber from the trail. It appears as if Mother Nature had changed her mind about having

a valley here, and decided to fill it in with fallen trees. The forest service has done a commendable job keeping this route clear.

As you descend farther down the valley, hemlock and rhododendron become the dominant trees. At 0.6 mile is a small campsite opposite a rockhouse that might be useful as a shelter for long-distance hikers on the Sheltowee Trace Trail. Just beyond, watch for a large cave in the cliffs on the opposite side of the creek. At 0.9 mile, reach the base of a 30-foot waterfall, where Mark Branch pours over the rim of a resistant bed of sandstone into a tiny plunge pool. Through most of the year this is a modest column of water, but after heavy storms water gushes over the lip and over the pool.

Beyond the falls, the trail is less used and can be wet or muddy. There often is simply not enough room in the narrow valley floor to get the trail away from the creek, so this section can be wet in high water. But consider these obstacles a chance for close-up views

Daniel Boone Country–South

of the mammoth boulders and blowdowns that choke the valley floor. Eventually the valley opens up somewhat, and the trail becomes fern-lined and friendlier.

At 1.6 miles is the unsigned junction with the Mark Branch Trail (DBNF Trail 635). This trail is a useful bypass route for northbound hikers who might find the previous section of the Sheltowee Trace Trail closed due to heavy rain or storm damage. Mark Branch can be used to reach the Gobblers Arch Trail in 1.3 miles, and the Peters Mountain Trailhead in 2.3 miles, but these shortcuts do not go by Gobblers Arch.

Near the confluence of Mark Branch and Rock Creek at 2.2 miles, look for a signed junction with the Sheltowee Trace Trail in a small meadow by a large cedar and a tumbled rock cairn. In summer, look for the prominent orange heads of butterfly milkweed amid the meadow's vibrant growth. An unmarked route leads straight from the junction to a ford over Rock Creek. This unsigned route leads to Hemlock Grove Picnic Area, an alternate starting point for this hike. Riders sometimes use this ford as the start of trips on horseback to Gobblers Arch. To continue on the loop, follow the Sheltowee Trace Trail, which turns left up the bank of Rock Creek to reach the junction with the Gobblers Arch Trail (DBNF 636) at 2.3 miles.

Turn left onto the Gobblers Arch Trail and begin a steep climb. Watch out for poison ivy on the lower section of this trail. After the trail moves away from the nose of the ridge, pass to the left of an imposing chimney rock. Next is a shaded rockhouse where fire pinks flourish well into the summer. Continue along the bluff line until reaching a small draw, where the trail exits on a switchback to the right. Rejoin the ridge crest, where there is a small overlook above Rock Creek with "winter views." At 3.7 miles is a signed side trail to a better overlook above the creek. Beyond the overlook, the trail follows the base of a 20-foot high band of cliffs.

At 4.3 miles, reach Gobblers Arch. The arch is about 10 feet high, 50 feet wide, and 15 feet across. It appears more like a wide tunnel through a narrow ridge of sandstone than a classic arch. Though others have camped here before you, the Daniel Boone National Forest prohibits camping in arches and rockhouses. Walk through the arch, and climb switchbacks to reach the top of it.

At 4.5 miles, join DBNF Road 6105 at the road's end. Turn right on the road, and follow it past an old turnaround, beyond which the road is somewhat more used. At 5.1 miles is a signed junction with the Mark Branch Trail leading back down to join the STT near Mark Branch. At 5.6 miles reach Divide Road (DBNF Road 569), and follow it to the left to return to the Peters Mountain Trailhead at 6.1 miles.

Other Hiking Options

1. Short and Sweet. Via DBNF Road 6105 it is a 2.6-mile round trip to Gobblers Arch.

2. From the Gobblers Arch Trail, the Sheltowee Trace Trail leads 14.9 miles south to Pickett State Park. The Rock Creek Loop in the Tennessee portion of the BSF and the Hidden Passage Loop in Tennessee's Pickett State Park are two excellent loops that use parts of the STT.

3. To the east from the Peters Mountain Trailhead, the Sheltowee Trace Trail follows Laurel Ridge Road for 5.5 miles.

4. The 0.4-mile Buffalo Arch (DBNF 634A) and 2.4-mile Parker Mountain (DBNF 634) Trails are both in the Stearns Ranger District.

14

Natural Arch Scenic Area

Total Distance: A 6.1 mile semi-loop trails on the Natural Arch and Buffalo Canyon Trails that uses a short stretch of a gravel road. No horses or mountain bikes are allowed.

Hiking Time: About 3 hours

Location: Somerset Ranger District, 7 miles northwest of Whitley City

Maps: USGS Nevelsville; DBNF Natural Arch Scenic Area

The Natural Arch Scenic Area protects 945 acres of the Somerset Ranger District centered around spectacular Natural Arch. This mammoth structure rivals Natural Bridge in the state park near Red River Gorge for the most impressive sandstone span in the Cumberland region. While most visitors stay on the 1-mile Natural Arch Trail, a longer and more rewarding hike on the Buffalo Canyon Trail circles the Scenic Area. This 5-mile loop passes through a superb wildflower area, lingers along Cooper Creek, and returns past lesser-known Chimney Arch.

Getting There

From the junction of US 27 and KY 927, 7 miles north of Whitley City, drive west for 1.8 miles on KY 927. Parking for the scenic area is on the right side of the road and includes a picnic area and restrooms. Natural Arch is a self-service fee area. In 2001, the fee was $3.

The Hike

The toughest part of the hike around Natural Arch can be tearing yourself away from the parking area. At the far end of the parking area is the classic postcard view of the arch. This view of Natural Arch is alone worth the drive, even if you don't do any hiking at all. But of course you'll want to visit the arch up close, so head east around the picnic area along the paved path, which is the start of the Natural Arch Trail (DBNF 510). You'll pass several other overlooks above the arch before starting to descend a

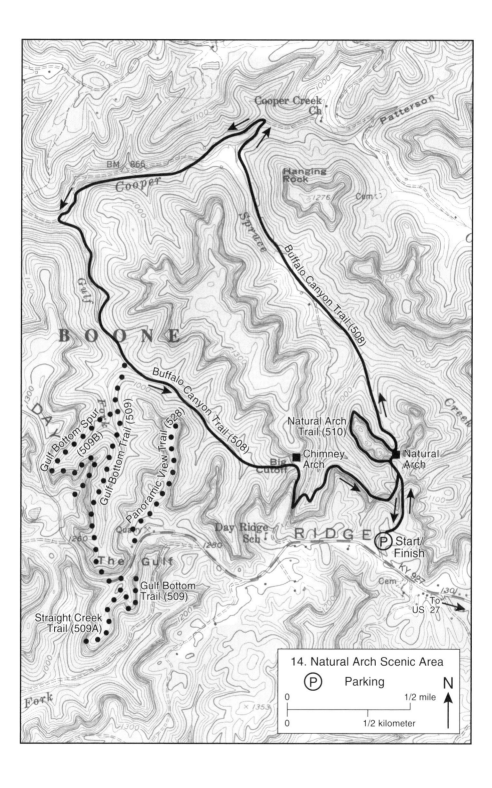

Cooper Creek
Ch

Patterson

Hanging
Rock

BM 866

Cooper

Cem

1276

Spruce

Gulf

Buffalo Canyon Trail (508)

B O O N E

Creek

Buffalo Canyon Trail (508)

Gulf Bottom Spur
(509B)

Gulf Bottom Trail (509)

Panoramic View Trail (528)

D A Y

Natural Arch
Trail (510)

Natural
Arch

Chimney
Arch

Big
Cutoff

Quarry

Day Ridge
Sch

R I D G E

Start/
Finish

The Gulf

Gulf Bottom
Trail (509)

Straight Creek
Trail (509A)

KY 927

Cem

To
US 27

×1353

Fork

14. Natural Arch Scenic Area

P   Parking

N

0   1/2 mile

0   1/2 kilometer

Inside Natural Arch

series of stone steps. Keep an eye out for nature's smaller wonders as well; false Solomon's seal, yellow krigia, aster, bird's foot violet, and robins plantain bloom alongside the trail. At 0.5 mile, you will come to a trail junction where you should go right. The left fork is the Buffalo Canyon Trail, which is your return route.

Just beyond the 0.5-mile junction, you reach the start of the Shawnee Nature Trail. Here the Natural Arch Trail splits just before reaching the arch. Go right at this junction, and climb up to the underside of Natural Arch. The arch was formed by what is called headward erosion of a long narrow ridge. This simply means that the hard massive and resistant sandstone that forms the span of the arch began as a long, narrow ridge. The ridge was attacked by erosion from two opposing sides. Rain and wind were able to erode the softer underlying rocks more easily than those that form the span of the arch.

Eventually some of the softer rocks below the top of the ridge are worn through, creating a small opening in the ridge. As the opening enlarged, some of the unsupported rock of the span fell away, creating the typical curved shape of the arch.

Natural Arch is 60 feet high and 100 feet across. It is the largest in Kentucky, south of the Red River Gorge. Note that the arch is formed from a thick sandstone bed (you can see the individual sand grains in the rock), with many white quartz pebbles embedded in it. This rock is part of the Lee Formation from the Pennsylvanian period and is over 300 million years old, older even than the time of the dinosaurs. Rock this old deserves special respect, so make sure not to leave any evidence of your passage. Better yet, pick up any trash that less careful visitors might have left behind.

You can circle the arch on the Shawnee Nature Trail (part of the Natural Arch Trail),

Daniel Boone Country—South

or simply enjoy an up-close view of this breathtaking feature. To continue from the arch on the Buffalo Canyon Trail (DBNF 508), go to the left side of the arch and follow the trail in the shadow of a large overhang. You'll follow the white diamond-shaped blazes past a sign indicating that Great Gulf is 3 miles and Chimney Arch is 4 miles. The trail next heads down a sunny slope, which can be a wildflower bonanza in the spring. Keep your flower book handy and see if you can spot common varieties such as chickweed, rue anemone, hepatica, foamflower, violets, bellwort, or maybe even a pink lady's slipper.

Though you're hiking mostly under hemlock trees, you next make two crossings of the upper reaches of Spruce Creek. The wildflower show isn't quite over though. Spring hikers still have the chance to add yellow trillium, phlox, spring beauty, fire pink, and betony to your list for the day. At 1.5 miles, the trail turns left onto little-traveled gravel DBNF Road 5266. A few minutes after passing the Young family farm the road makes a ford of normally shallow Cooper Creek. Just beyond the ford, at 2.2 miles, turn left off the main road onto a two-track road that follows along Cooper Creek.

You'll see the Young farm again through the trees as you walk along Cooper Creek. Make another usually easy crossing before reaching an overused campsite next to an inviting swimming hole at 3.1 miles. This is the midpoint of the hike, and a great spot to stop for lunch.

Beyond the campsite, the Buffalo Canyon Trail continues to follow the white diamonds along the Gulf Fork of Cooper Creek. At 3.7 miles, reach the junction with white-blazed Gulf Bottom Spur Trail (DBNF 509B), which enters from the right. You'll

next have three normally dry crossings of Cutoff Branch before reaching Chimney Arch at 4.6 miles. Chimney Arch lacks the classic symmetry of most natural arches. Instead of gently sloping to the ground, the left side of the arch is nearly vertical, controlled by a pre-existing crack in the rock.

Beyond Chimney Arch, cross the upper reaches of a branch of Spruce Creek, then pass a low rockhouse on your right. Higher up in the same cliff band you can later spot a tree that seemingly grows straight out of the cliffs. Close the loop at the junction with the Natural Arch Trail at 5.6 miles, and retrace your route to the parking area at 6.1 miles.

Like many parts of the Daniel Boone National Forest, the Natural Arch Scenic Area contains many pine trees that have been killed by the southern pine beetle. The forest held a small salvage sale in August 2001 to remove some of the damaged trees. Hikers should be aware that dead trees and branches could remain a hazard, particularly in high winds.

Other Hiking Options

1. Short and Sweet. The hike just to Natural Arch and back is a 1-mile round trip.

2. Farther west on KY 927 are three trails that lead either to overlooks above Natural Arch or can be used to intersect the Buffalo Canyon Loop. The Panoramic View Trail (DBNF 528) leads 0.6 mile to an overlook above Natural Arch. The Straight Creek Trail (DBNF 509A) leads 0.2 mile to an unprotected overlook. The Gulf Bottom Trail (DBNF 509) is a 1.7-mile loop along the top of the bluff line, then down metal stairs into the Great Gulf. The Gulf Bottom Spur (DBNF 509B) connects the Gulf Bottom and Buffalo Canyon Trails.

15

Blue Bend Trail

Total Distance: The loop is 4.7 miles long.

Hiking Time: About 2.5 hours

Location: Cumberland Falls State Resort Park, 16 miles southwest of Corbin

Maps: USGS Cumberland Falls; Cumberland Falls State Park Visitor's Guide

The Blue Bend loop was established in 1996 and is the newest trail at Cumberland Falls State Resort Park. It traverses the Cumberland Falls State Nature Preserve before descending to the Cumberland River and joining the Sheltowee Trace Trail. The nature preserve section is a paradise for birders and wildflower lovers, while the STT offers prime river views and leads past scenic rockhouses.

Getting There

From I-75 get on US 25 West near either Corbin or Williamsburg. Drive west to intersect KY 90. The Cumberland Falls State Park Office is 7.5 miles west on KY 90. Continue another 0.8 mile, across the Cumberland River, to reach the trailhead for Blue Bend and Eagle Falls. You can stop at the park visitors center near the falls for a trail map and information.

The Hike

This hike begins directly across KY 90 from the popular Eagle Falls Trail. A hike around Blue Bend is the opposite of Eagle Falls in more ways than one. The other cars parked at the trailhead likely belong to hikers out on the Eagle Falls Trail. Expect to have Blue Bend to yourself. Instead of hearing the roar of falling water, on this trail your background music will be made by singing birds. And lastly, you'll stroll along a quiet stretch of the Cumberland River, instead of beside the noisy falls and shoals of the lower river.

The Blue Bend Trail begins by following a long-abandoned dirt road, where you'll

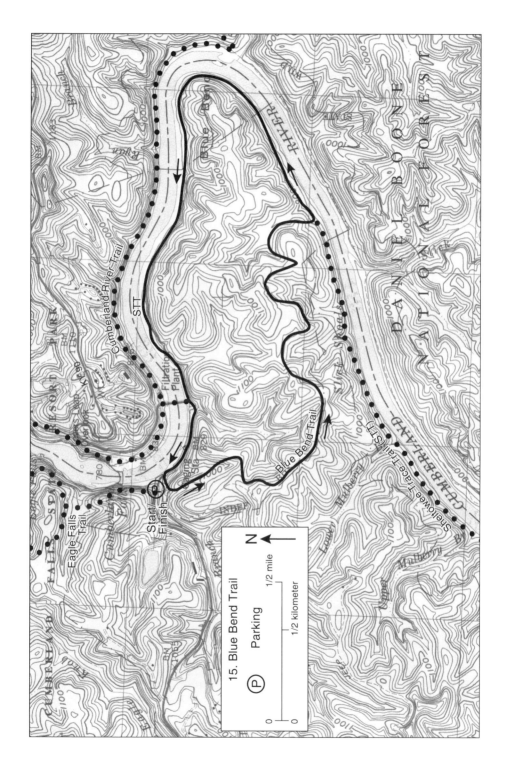

15. Blue Bend Trail

Ⓟ Parking

N

0   1/2 kilometer
0   1/2 mile

Downstream from the falls

cross a low gate. Follow the blue blazes and climb steadily past slopes where bluets and white violet flourish in spring. Clusters of tiny bluets are one of spring's special delights. The four small petals of this delicate plant are arranged like compass points around a yellow eye. At 0.5 mile, reach a T-junction with another old road on the ridgetop. Turn left onto this road and follow it through an open forest of Virginia pines, holly, sweetgum, and a few dogwoods. Some of the common songbirds that you may see, or hear, along the trail include Carolina chickadee, tufted titmouse, juncos, sparrows, and goldfinches. Both the red-bellied and downy woodpeckers are also found in the park. At 1.0 mile is a second gate. This one marks the boundary of the Cumberland Falls State Park Nature Preserve. The preserve protects 1,300 acres of the park west of the Cumberland River that is home to several species of rare plants and animals.

The trail continues along the ridgetop and keeps right at the next fork in the road. By fall, flowers are less common, but you might spot the bright red blooms of cardinal flower here. At 1.5 miles is a sign that tells you the Sheltowee Trace is only 0.6 mile away. Just 100 feet past where another faint old roadway enters on the left is another sign stating the Trace is only 0.4 mile farther. Here the trail leaves the ridgetop to descend steadily on a worn two-track road. You'll know the Cumberland River, and Sheltowee Trace, are just ahead when you pass a low, sandy-floored rockhouse on the right.

The junction of the Blue Bend and Sheltowee Trace Trails at 2.1 miles is marked by a sign indicating that KY 90 and Gatliff Bridge are 2.2 miles to your left. To the right, red blazes mark the boundary between the state park and the Daniel Boone National Forest. Though unsigned, the Sheltowee Trace goes right along the

Cumberland River toward Sycamore Shoals. There is a campsite under a pair of huge beech trees only 300 feet to the right. The portion of the Cumberland River that flows through the park has been designated a Kentucky Wild River.

The Blue Bend Trail goes left at the junction and follows the STT back to KY 90. This quiet river walk is paradise for wildflower lovers in spring. The diverse forest of the plateau has been replaced by the dark evergreens—hemlock and rhododendron. The prolific blooms of the mayapple love the same moist, shady habitat as does the hiker's bane—poison ivy. Mayapple is one of the few flowers more easily recognized by the leaves than by the flowers. This low plant looks like a small green umbrella open on the forest floor. Plants with two leaves support a single white flower on a short stalk growing below the leaves. Ripe fruit of the mayapple can be made into jelly. Though modern biotech researchers have found some compounds from the plant useful in the treatment of cancer, the plant can be poisonous. Robins plantain, purple violets, and crested dwarf iris are some of the other flowers blooming later in the spring.

At the tip of Blue Bend the trail narrows and passes a large rockhouse opposite a sandy beach along the river. The route then pulls away from the river to explore the base of a band of cliffs. You'll round Blue Bend below the base of a high cliff. At 3.2 miles a dilapidated roadway enters on the left. The trail continues along the hillside in a dark forest dominated by hemlock and rhododendron. At 4.2 miles the trail crosses a small creek, then climbs steeply up the far bank. Just beyond is a sign indicating that Cumberland Falls is 0.5 mile ahead and KY 700 is 5 miles behind you. Reach Gatliff Bridge at 4.5 miles, and turn left and walk 0.2 mile along the road back to the trailhead.

The Cumberland River below the falls is a popular whitewater run during high river flows. Contact the park for a list of outfitters currently offering river trips.

The rocks that form the Cumberland Falls are the oldest rocks of the Pennsylvanian period, famous in Kentucky for the thick coal beds that were deposited during that time. Geologists call the sandstone and pebble conglomerates that form the falls, and the gorge around it, the Lee Formation. The layers below the Lee Formation are the easily eroded Pennington Shale and more resistant Chester Limestone, both of which were deposited in the earlier Mississippian period.

Other Hiking Options

1. Short and Sweet. If your time is limited, try an out-and-back hike on the STT along the river.

2. From Blue Bend, the Sheltowee Trace continues south toward the Big South Fork and Pickett State Park. It is 3.6 miles south to the next road intersection at KY 700, but this hike requires either a long return hike or a shuttle between the trailheads.

16

Eagle Falls Trail

*Total Distance: The entire loop is a
1.5-mile semi-loop, including a side trip
to Eagle Falls.*

Hiking Time: About 1 hour

*Location: Cumberland Falls State Resort
Park, 16 miles southwest of Corbin*

*Maps: USGS Cumberland Falls;
Cumberland Falls State Park
Visitor's Guide*

If you have time for only one hike at
Cumberland Falls, this is the trail to take. A
short, easy walk will lead to dramatic views
of Cumberland Falls. The trail then enters a
loop, from which a side trail leads to the
slender water column of Eagle Falls. Few
trails anywhere are as well designed for
viewing two completely different waterfalls.
The waterfalls and wildflowers make this
trail a perfect place to introduce youngsters
to the outdoors.

Getting There

From I-75 get on US 25 West near either
Corbin or Williamsburg. Drive west to inter-
sect KY 90. The Cumberland Falls State
Park Office is 7.5 miles west on KY 90.
Continue another 0.8 mile, across the
Cumberland River, to reach the trailhead for
Blue Bend and Eagle Falls. You can stop at
the park visitors center near the falls for a
trail map and information.

The Hike

The Eagle Falls Trail begins at a gravel trailhead on KY 90, just across the Gatliff Bridge,
and opposite the trailhead for the Blue Bend
Trail. The first 0.5 mile of the trail is relatively
easy and is the most scenic. It is also a favorite with wildflower watchers, who come to
see robins plantain and bluets, along with
purple and white violets. If you have children
with you, do your best to keep them on the
trail and away from the poison ivy that also
flourishes here. The trail follows a line of
bluffs close to the edge of the Cumberland
River. You'll pass one rockhouse and then
climb a set of stone steps before reaching

the trail's highlight, a spectacular overlook almost directly above the falls. Your view of the falls from the overlook will be relatively private. The powerful river separates you from the hordes across the river at the park visitors center. The shallow bluffs and rocky overhangs along the trail add to the sense of intimacy. Just watch your step; it is a short drop from the cliffs to the river, and it's a swift current surging toward the falls.

The trail beyond the first overlook has some steep sections of stairs, but is well worth the effort. In spring, the variety of flowers includes pussy toes, fire pink, little brown jugs, halberd-leaved violet, Solomon's seal, and yellow violet. You will also pass a side trail leading left uphill to an overlook and a CCC-era picnic shelter. At about 0.5 mile, there is a split where an old sign indicates Trail 10 turns left and Trail 9 continues right. This junction can be a bit confusing since the official park map now shows both sides of the split to be part of Trail 9. Until 1999, the Gorge Overlook Trail connected this junction and the overlook. However, that trail was abandoned, and the number 10 reassigned to the Blue Bend Loop.

Beyond this junction are deep rock overhangs and wide-open fenced overlooks perched high above roaring Cumberland Falls. Here is another great photo spot, with the falls and lower river gorge displayed. Below the falls you may see rafts, kayaks, or canoes that begin a scenic float trip downriver from this point.

Shortly, a steep side trail leads right down to the river, and to the base of Eagle Falls. You'll descend wooden stairs, then rock steps until finally a steel cable may be your only good hold. The falls lies at the head of an intimate alcove of steep sandstone perfect for a picnic. In contrast to the Niagara-like power of Cumberland Falls, here a small stream pours over a thick rock

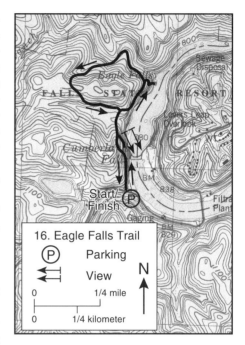

16. Eagle Falls Trail

Ⓟ   Parking

⇄   View

N

0 ——————— 1/4 mile

0 ——————— 1/4 kilometer

shelf in a narrow column of water. It's a great spot to stop for lunch and enjoy both the river and falls.

When you are ready to complete the loop, hike back to the junction with the main trail. The rest of the loop begins with a climb alongside Eagle Creek and leads past a small rockhouse. The loop is a bit tougher than the hike to the falls. The path is marked by yellow plastic diamonds and is easy to follow. Here, however, are even more wildflowers, including some common ones such as wild geranium, spurred violet, chickweed, foamflower, buttercup, cinquefoil, squawroot, and crested dwarf iris, and some rarer ones like jack-in-the-pulpit and yellow lady's slipper. The unusual jack-in-the-pulpit is best recognized by its distinctive mottled foliage. A green hooded pulpit covers the "jack," which stands within it. The pulpit is often vertically striped, but can also be mottled. The actual flowers are tiny, and cluster at the foot of the jack.

Eagle Falls

Pass the abandoned end of old Trail 10 near the end of the loop. Once you've closed the loop, retrace your steps back to the trailhead. On your return you might also take the side trail leading to the overlook and shelter constructed by the Civilian Conservation Corps in the 1930s.

Cumberland Falls is a State Resort Park and so has a full array of amenities. The park has a campground (open seasonally), woodland rooms, cabins, and a full-service lodge with a restaurant offering one of the best breakfast spreads in the region. Inside the lodge building is the Bob Blair Museum, containing displays on the cultural and natural history of the area. Fishing in the river is popular, as are guided horseback rides. An Olympic-sized pool is open in summer. Contact the park for a list of outfitters that guide river trips.

Cumberland Falls State Resort Park was created in 1931 with a grant from Senator T. C. DuPont, who grew up in Kentucky. The

1,776-acre park was one of the four original Kentucky state parks. The original park lodge was built in 1933 by the CCC and named for the senator. The first lodge burned in 1940, was rebuilt in 1941, and then expanded in 1951.

Other Hiking Options

1. Short and Sweet. You can hike out to the best of the overlooks and back in less than 1 mile round-trip.

2. In addition to the hikes described in other chapters, Cumberland Falls has a number of short hiking trails perfect for exploring. From DuPont Lodge, Trails 3 and 6 lead down to the Cumberland River by the falls. Trail 4 is a self-guided interpretive trail that explores the contributions made by members of the Civilian Conservation Corps to the park in the 1930s. Trail 5 connects the camping and cabin areas to Trail 4. Trails 7 and 12 form a confusing network between KY 90 and the Sheltowee Trace Trail.

17

Cumberland River Trail

*Total Distance: The loop is 7 miles around
on the Cumberland River (Trail 2) and
Sheltowee Trace Trails at Cumberland
Falls State Resort Park, and in the
Daniel Boone National Forest. Add
0.5 mile if you choose to visit the
Pinnacle Tower site.*

Hiking Time: About 4 hours

*Location: Cumberland Falls State Resort
Park, 16 miles southwest of Corbin*

*Maps: USGS Cumberland Falls;
Cumberland Falls State Park
Visitor's Guide*

The Cumberland Trail is the longest trail in
the Cumberland Falls State Park area.
Combined with the Sheltowee Trace Trail
on the Daniel Boone National Forest, it is
also the only trail with the opportunity for
backpacking, but you must camp on the forest, not in the park. But don't choose this
trail simply for its length; the Cumberland
Trail visits some of the park highlights, including Cumberland Falls, rockhouses,
overhangs, and a visit to an abandoned fire
tower.

Getting There

From I-75 get on US 25 West near either
Corbin or Williamsburg. Drive west to intersect KY 90. The Cumberland Falls State
Park Office is 7.5 miles west on KY 90.
Continue 0.5 mile down to the river and
park at the Cumberland Falls visitors parking area. You can stop at the park visitors
center near the falls for a trail map and
information.

The Hike

This is the longest loop trail in the
Cumberland Falls area, and it can be
walked either as a backpacking trip or as
a moderately long day hike. Overnighters
should remember that there is no backcountry camping allowed in Cumberland
Falls State Resort Park, so be sure to find
a spot in the Daniel Boone National Forest.

If you've parked at the visitors area next
to the falls, the best way to pick up the trail
is to head for the strip of trees between
the parking area and KY 90. Here you'll find

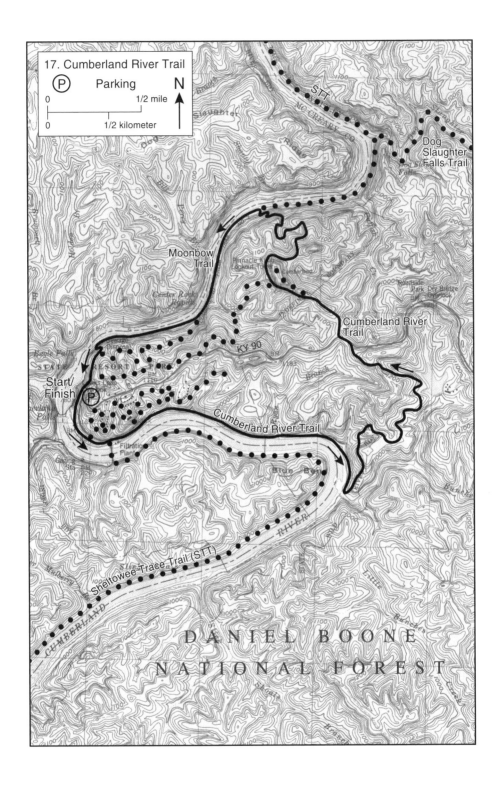

17. Cumberland River Trail

Ⓟ Parking N

0 ——————————————— 1/2 mile

0 ——————————————— 1/2 kilometer

Dog Slaughter Falls Trail

Moonbow Trail

Cumberland River Trail

Start/Finish

Ⓟ

Cumberland River Trail

Sheltowee Trace Trail (STT)

DANIEL BOONE

NATIONAL FOREST

the Sheltowee Trace Trail. Follow it upstream to the end of the parking area, then cross KY 90 and walk along the road leading to a picnic area. Just as you enter the parking area, a side trail leads left at a sign TO TRAIL 4. This short diversion leads to a huge rockhouse with a picnic table and a slender, wet-weather waterfall.

At the end of the picnic area at 0.5 mile, leave the road for a narrow trail that will continue to follow along the river. Spring hikers should have their wildflower guides open and ready; this is one of the park's best trails for flower lovers. Bluets, little brown jugs, and robins plantain are among the most prolific in spring. Foamflower, crested dwarf iris, cinquefoil, and several types of violets also grow here. Later in the year, laurel and galax will bloom.

Beyond the junction with Trail 5 which leads to the campground, Trail 2 receives much less use. After passing the concrete park boundary marker at 1.3 miles, you reach a flat area that could be used for camping. Continuing alongside the river, look for signs of hungry beaver who have attacked some impressively large trees. Keep the flower books out; you may be able to add trillium, trout lily, chickweed, rue anemone, mayapple, and wild geranium to your list.

At 2.1 miles, the trail intersects a dirt road and follows it to the left uphill and away from the river. In the cool, moist area beneath a rockhouse, check for the bright red flowers of columbine, a rare flower in this area. After gaining the ridge, the trail passes underneath a power line at 3.1 miles. Bear right at a signed junction with a dirt road. From the junction, descend through an area rich in both pine and myrtle to reach a gate at the junction of KY 90 at 3.7 miles. The trail resumes about 100 yards to your left across the highway at another gated dirt road. Small pull-off areas at both roads make this an alternate starting point for the loop.

Continue up the road and reach a second gate at 4.1 miles, which marks the state park boundary. Just beyond is a side trail leading right 0.25 mile to Pinnacle Tower, an abandoned fire lookout. A locked gate keep hikers off the tower, which in any case is no higher than the surrounding forest. Just beyond the tower site trail your route turns right off the old roadway. Next is the junction with Trail 11 at 4.3 miles. A left turn onto Trail 11 provides a slightly shorter, but more hilly, route back to the park. After circling in back of the bluffs below the tower, Trail 2 soon starts to switchback downhill past a rockhouse toward the Cumberland River. At 5.0 miles, reach the signed junction with the Sheltowee Trace Trail.

Turn left on the Sheltowee Trace Trail, also called Trail 1, or the Moonbow Trail, here. This section of river next to the trail is a favorite of white-water enthusiasts. The steep, boulder-strewn riverbed would seem at best a daunting obstacle for even skilled boaters. But this is a great stretch for hikers also. The trail winds up and down rock stairs, around rockhouses, and passes underneath an arch formed by a massive rockfall. Trillium, crested dwarf iris, and sundrops form a colorful floral carpet. At 5.9 miles is the first of two junctions with Trail 7. After the second junction, just as Eagle Falls comes into view across the river, take a sharp switchback left at 6.7 miles and walk uphill. If you miss this switchback, and many people do, you can follow casual trails along the riverbank to the end of the visitors center trails. Along the river's edge you may see an unusual deposit of black rock. This is a gravel bar formed from coal, unusual because coal is soft and easily broken up by the mixing action of a river. The presence of coal in the gravel bar indicates that there

Along the Cumberland River

must be a layer of coal at river level very close by.

Meanwhile, the Sheltowee Trace Trail reaches the first of two very closely spaced intersections with Trail 12 at 6.8 miles. Next, the trail merges with the paved walkways leading from the visitors center to overlooks below Cumberland Falls. Summer hikers can enjoy a reward of cold drinks or ice cream before returning to the parking area.

Cumberland Falls is the only place in the western hemisphere where "moonbows" are found. Moonbows are just like rainbows, except that they form from light from the moon rather than light from the sun. Moonbows are so rare because so many different things must happen together. Moonbows need strong light from a full moon, a clear sky, clear air, and the prodigious spray of water that only a powerful waterfall can make. Besides Cumberland Falls, only Africa's Victoria Falls on the Zambezi River produces similar moonbows.

Be aware that the park is always more crowded close to the full moon.

Even without the moonbow, every visitor finds Cumberland Falls a wonder. Most waterfalls on the Cumberland Plateau occur when small streams pour over the edge of a rockhouse. At Cumberland Falls, a full-fledged river crashes 68 feet into a foaming, churning pit of white water. Most likely you'll hear the falls well before you see it. Normally the falls are more than 100 feet wide, but the river has been recorded to flow as little as little as 4 cubic feet per second. Maximum recorded flow on the river was almost 15,000 times stronger.

Other Hiking Options

1. Short and Sweet. A web of trails downstream from Cumberland Falls start from the developed visitors area on the east side of the river. Exploring all the available overlooks and walking down to the sandy beach below the falls is less than 1 mile round-trip.

2. The 0.2-mile trail to Moonshiners Arch (DBNF 418) starts 3.1 miles east of the entrance to DuPont Lodge at an unsigned turnout. The trail to this small arch is not well maintained.

3. The 10.5-mile hike on the Sheltowee Trace between Cumberland Falls and Laurel Lake is a popular hike, especially for backpackers. From the falls it is 2 miles to Trail 2, 2.9 miles to the Dog Slaughter Falls Trail, 7.4 miles to Bark Camp Trail, and 10.7 miles to the Mouth of Laurel Boat Ramp. Backcountry shelters are found at Bark Camp and Star Creeks.

18

Bark Camp Trail

Total Distance: A hike to the Cumberland River and back is 5.6 miles round-trip.

Hiking Time: About 3 hours

Location: London Ranger District, 11 miles southwest of Corbin

Maps: USGS Sawyer

The Bark Camp Trail (DBNF 413) is pleasant hike along Bark Camp Creek. The stream passes numerous rockhouses and ends at an impressive series of cascades near the Cumberland River. There is a backcountry shelter on the Sheltowee Trace Trail near the trail's end. This is a great day hike or an easy overnight trip.

Getting There

From US 25 West 2.9 miles north of the junction with KY 90, take County Road 1193 west. In 4.5 miles continue straight onto County Road 1277 where 1193 turns right. Drive 1.2 miles, then turn left onto gravel DBNF Road193. Take the gravel road south for 1.9 miles and park at a small turnout where the road crosses Bark Camp Creek. The trailhead can also be reached from KY 90 near Cumberland Falls in 8.8 miles by following gravel DBNF roads 195, 88, and 193.

The Hike

Creekside walks are always a hiker favorite, no matter what the season. The rollicking splash of water rolling downstream provides a soothing serenade, even on a dreary winter day. In spring, the cool, wet areas along the bank are home to wildflowers rarely seen elsewhere in the forest. And when summer rears its steamy head, cool waters are ready to refresh. In fall, the stream is a magnet for fisherman seeking the rainbow trout stocked by the Daniel Boone National Forest.

Bark Camp Creek isn't the only attraction along this trail. The route follows the base of

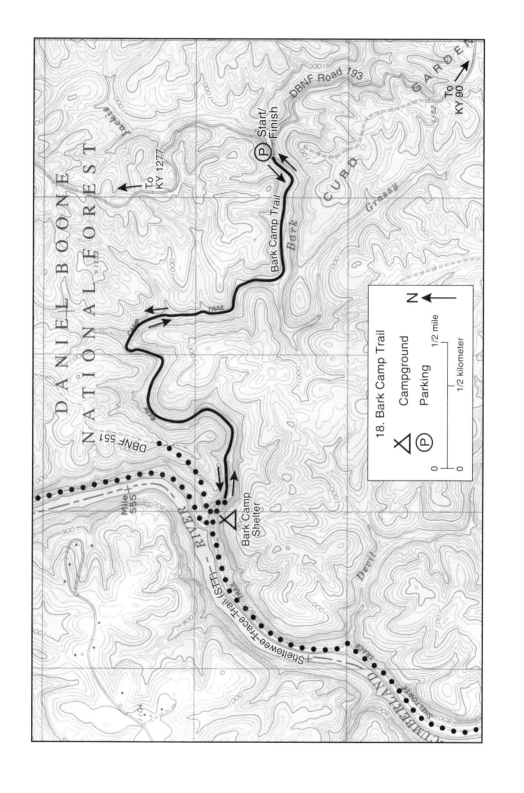

Bark Camp Creek

high sandstone cliffs for much of its length. The cliffs, overhangs, rockhouses, and two seasonal waterfalls along the way make this seem like a much shorter walk, and the attractions are plentiful enough to keep younger hikers entertained throughout.

Like the geologic formations, spring wildflowers are more plentiful toward the two ends of the trail. The more abundant flowers include bluets, little brown jugs, crested dwarf iris, and galax. Lucky hikers may also spot columbine, squawroot, pink lady's slipper, and the elusive jack-in-the-pulpit. The pink lady's slipper is a rare, slow-growing member of the orchid family. It grows only in a symbiotic relationship with a special type of fungus that helps the plant absorb nutrients from the soil. Once seeds of the pink lady's slipper germinate, the plant waits up to two years for the fungus to develop, then can wait several more years before flowering.

Several overused campsites are found in the first mile of the trail. Less considerate hikers may have left behind some trash, so it's not a bad idea to pack a plastic bag to "carry out" what others have "carried in." There's a less-used campsite just short of the junction with the Sheltowee Trace Trail; located on a small bluff above the creek, this site offers some privacy not found at the upper campsites or at the Bark Camp Shelter.

Rockhouses are important plant habitats in the forests of the Cumberland Plateau. Conditions here are cooler, wetter, and less sunny than elsewhere in the forest. At least four species of ferns and seven species of flowering plants, including members of the otherwise common buttercup family, are known to occur only in rockhouses in the eastern United States.

Before joining the Sheltowee Trace Trail, the Bark Camp Trail reaches a junction with

the flood bypass route for the Sheltowee Trace. The bypass leaves to the right, where the sign states FS 551 is about 0.25 mile and the Laurel Boat Ramp is 3 miles. However, the bypass climbs for at least 0.5 mile before reaching the end of a sandy, little-traveled road.

Just beyond the bypass junction is the junction with the main Sheltowee Trace Trail. To the left is the Bark Camp Shelter in 0.25 mile, Dog Slaughter Creek in 5 miles, and Cumberland Falls in 8 miles. To the right is the Mouth of Laurel Boat Ramp in 3.3 miles. It's worth making the extra trip to see the Bark Camp Shelter, an Adirondack-type structure similar in construction to those used on the Appalachian Trail. The shelter's location on a stretch of river accessible to power boats contributes to some excess wear and tear. But the trip to the shelter takes you across the multispan wooden bridge across Bark Camp Creek. The bridge takes perfect advantage of the views of the cascades that tumble over the huge boulders that clog the final few hundred yards of the stream.

Much of the use of this trail is by fisherman seeking the trout regularly stocked in the creek.

The Daniel Boone National Forest was originally named the Cumberland National Forest. The Cumberland region in turn, got its name from the explorations of Dr. Thomas Walker in the 1700s, who named the Cumberland River for England's Duke of Cumberland. This apparently was not quite the honor it might seem, as Walker felt that the winding river and the duke were equally crooked.

The name Cumberland has grown to include the entire Cumberland Plateau and the mountains that surround it. A confusing array of recreation areas have taken the name as well. In addition to Cumberland

Falls State Park and Cumberland Gap National Historic Park in Kentucky, there are Cumberland Mountain State Park and the South Cumberland Recreation Area in Tennessee, plus the Cumberland Trail State Park. And, of course, there's the Big South Fork (of the Cumberland) River and National Recreation Area. President Lyndon Johnson saved us all from further confusion by signing an order in 1966 changing the name of the national forest to Daniel Boone.

The forest consists of 692,000 acres that are federally owned and spread over a 2.1-million-acre area. Lacing the forest are 423 miles of hiking trails. There are two wilderness areas, three Kentucky Wild Rivers, and a National Wild and Scenic River. The DBNF manages three lakes, 22 campgrounds, and 23 picnic areas. Other special areas in the forest include the Red River Gorge Geological Area, Natural Arch Scenic Area, and the Pioneer Weapons Wildlife Management Area.

Other Hiking Options

1. Short and Sweet. Hikers pressed for time could turn around after visiting the rockhouses along the first 0.5 mile of the trail.

2. The Sheltowee Trace Trail leads 3.3 miles from Bark Camp Creek to the Mouth of Laurel Boat Ramp.

3. The Dog Slaughter Falls Trail (DBNF 414), located 6 miles to the south, follows a similar streamside route to the Cumberland River. Hikers could combine the Dog Slaughter and Bark Camp Trails into an 11.2-mile trip using a short car shuttle.

19

Beaver Creek Wilderness

Total Distance: A 1.9-mile semi-loop on the Three Forks Loop (DBNF 512) and Three Forks of Beaver (DBNF 512A) trails, with an optional 1.4-mile off-trail side trip to campsites at the three forks.

Hiking Time: 1 hour for the loop plus another hour for the side trip.

Location: Somerset Ranger District, about 16 miles northeast of Whitley City

Maps: USGS Hail. The 1990 DBNF Clifty Wilderness and Beaver Creek Wilderness Recreation Guide (R8-RG) contains a number of serious errors and should not be used.

Beaver Creek was the first wilderness area created in Kentucky. The area is rough, rugged, remote, and rarely visited by hikers; the hostile terrain can be intimidating. However, the short hike out to the Three Forks of Beaver Creek Overlook is easy, well marked, and ends at a remarkable view above the three forks. For backpackers, there is also an optional side trip down to campsites along the three forks.

Getting There

From the junction on US 27 and KY 90 north of Whitley City, drive north on US 27 for 4.2 miles to the junction with gravel DBNF Road 50. This road may be marked with a WATCHABLE WILDLIFE sign and signs for Hammonds Camp and Jasper Road. Follow Road 50 for 2.4 miles, then turn right onto DBNF Road 51. Drive 0.7 mile on Road 51 to the Three Forks Beaver Trailhead. The trail starts at the far end of the trailhead, next to Road 51C, which is the return route.

The Hike

Though much of the Beaver Creek Wilderness remains the roughest hiking in the state, the walk to the Three Forks of Beaver Creek Overlook is easy, pleasant, and rewarding. Be sure to take your camera along for the walk; this is a photo-worthy vista at any time of year.

From the trailhead, follow signed Trail 512, which is marked with white diamond blazes. The trail will wander through a forest dominated by pine and oak trees that is

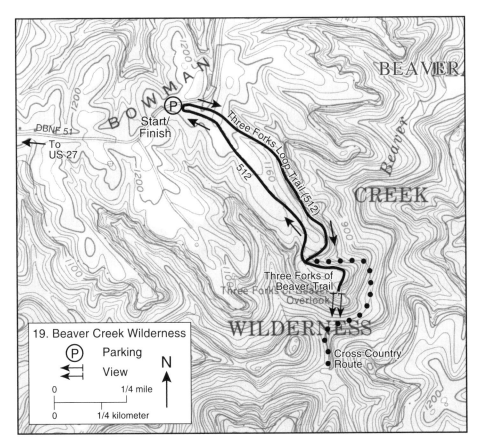

19. Beaver Creek Wilderness

typical of the dry ridgetops of this part of Kentucky. You'll also see red maple, sassafras, tulip poplar, Fraser magnolia, and hemlock trees. At 0.5 mile, a short side trail leads left to an overlook at the rim of Beaver Creek Canyon where a sign marks the boundary of the Beaver Creek Wilderness. This overlook, with its view into the narrow, jumbled canyon, is just a taste of things to come.

At another trail sign, the route turns away from the rim beside a pair of large and small beech trees. The scraggly branches of Virginia pine are common here, as are the prickly leaves of holly in the understory. At 0.8 mile, come to a T-junction with a grassy former road. The Three Forks Loop Trail (512) goes right and north along the road back to the trailhead. To follow the Three Forks of Beaver Trail (512A) to the overlook, turn left and south onto the road. The road splits in 50 feet. The right branch is the trail, and should be marked with a WATCHABLE WILDLIFE sign.

The right branch quickly narrows and begins to tunnel through the laurel and blueberry that flourish beneath a canopy of pines. This combination of spring flowers and fall berries make this a great hike in either season. At 1.0 mile, reach the fenced overlook above the three forks of Beaver Creek.

The Freeman, Middle, and Hurricane forks of Beaver Creek are all in view below.

The bridge over Beaver Creek

The streams have carved tall turrets into the narrow divides between them, and have sculpted shear cliffs to form the canyon walls.

From the overlook, retrace your route back to the T-junction. Because the boundary of the Beaver Creek Wilderness is drawn along the rim of the canyon, this hike has not yet entered the wilderness proper. If you would like to enter the wilderness, and feel that your route-finding skills are up to the task, an unblazed and unmaintained route to the three forks also begins near the T-junction. This 1.4-mile round-trip route begins on the south part of the grassy road. Instead of taking the right branch of the road toward the overlook, keep left and descend on a rough road. This route gets narrow and overgrown not far from the rim. A few old water bars remain, indicating that this may once have been a maintained trail. The wilderness boundary is well signed.

Once into the wilderness, the trail drops steeply through the cliffs that guard the inner canyon. In summer, this is the most overgrown part of the trail, but when the leaves are down it is the prettiest, with views of cliffs and rock overhangs on both sides. You'll pass a huge overhanging boulder (that could serve as an emergency shelter) just as you get your first view of Hurricane Fork. Reach the confluence of the Middle and Hurricane Forks near a possible campsite in a grove of hemlock trees. The route continues past a crossing of the Hurricane Fork, and follows the Middle Fork upstream a short distance to a larger campsite, and the confluence with the Freeman Fork, which is 0.7 mile from the T-junction. A few old i-shaped blazes lead across the Freeman Fork, but there is no trace of a route beyond them. There are several nice campsites located in the spacious creek bottoms at this confluence. From the confluence, retrace your route back to the T-junction.

To complete the Three Forks Loop from the T-junction, turn right on the old road. Stay on the ridgetop to reach a cleared wildlife opening, where a series of interpretive displays begins. The displays explain the value of using native plants in landscaping and of revegetating damaged lands. There are also two small ponds that provide homes for frogs, newts, and salamanders. Follow the trail straight across the opening, and continue on the road through the woods on the other side. Return to the trailhead at 1.9 miles.

The 4,791-acre Beaver Creek Wilderness was part of the Eastern Wilderness Act of 1975 that created 13 wilderness areas. The act protected some of best-loved hiking areas in the mountains from New Hampshire to Alabama. The lack of an extensive trail system, poor upkeep of what trails there are, and confusing maps of the area have kept Beaver Creek the least used of any of these areas. However, these same qualities can attract wilderness users who don't like trails, want the feeling of exploring the land that they pass through, and who value solitude in the woods.

Other Hiking Options

1. Short and Sweet. The 1.9-mile roundtrip hike to the overlook is the only easy way to see the wilderness.

2. A second trail system enters the wilderness from the Bowman Ridge Trailhead located 1.7 miles farther on DBNF Road 51. The Bowman Ridge (DBNF 514) and Beaver Creek (DBNF 532) Trails begin together at this trailhead. The trails split in 0.2 mile. The Bowman Ridge Trail descends to a bridge over Beaver Creek at 0.9 mile and climbs the opposite rim to reach the Swain Ridge Trailhead on DBNF Road 52 at 1.9 miles. The Bowman Ridge Trail follows a road that was closed with the creation of the wilderness, and it still remains easy to follow. The 1990 DBNF Beaver Creek Wilderness Map shows a confusing variety of trails here.

The Beaver Creek Trail follows an old logging road for the first 1.7 miles down to Beaver Creek at an overgrown clearing. There is no marked route, and virtually no footpath, for the next 1.3 miles until you reach a spacious campsite only 0.2 mile from the Beaver Creek Bridge and the Bowman Ridge Trail. Because of the difficulty in finding the start of the logging road out of the valley near the clearing, it is probably easier to descend Trail 532 and ascend 514 if you try to hike this loop.

3. Maps of the wilderness area show the Middle Ridge Trail (518) extending from DBNF Road 839 down the Middle Fork to Trail 514 at the bridge over Beaver Creek. However, there is not (and never has been) a hiking trail between these two points. There is, however, an old road that leads from the trailhead on Road 839 down to the Middle Fork, where it disappears in an overgrown area. Since the publication of the 1990 Clifty Wilderness and Beaver Creek Wilderness Map by the DBNF, countless hikers have been lured onto this route, only to endure frustration trying to follow this nonexistent trail. Forest service maps showed this connection simply to indicate that it was possible to walk along the valley of Beaver Creek. Unfortunately, many maps still show this as a trail, and the forest service continues to maintain the Road 839 Trailhead.

20

Bee Rock Loop

Total Distance: A 4.9-mile loop on the Bee Rock Loop (DBNF 529) and Rockcastle Narrows (DBNF 503) Trails, which can be combined with a short walk on the road through the Bee Rock Campground.

Hiking Time: About 2.5 hours

Location: Somerset Ranger District, about 20 miles southwest of London

Maps: USGS Ano

The Bee Rock hiking paths have the well-groomed feel of scenic front-country trails. This loop gives hikers the chance to sample the best of hiking near the Rockcastle River—with towering overlooks, close-ups of cliffs, and views of the Rockcastle Narrows.

Getting There

From Exit 38 off I-75 on the south side of London, follow KY 192 west for 18.9 miles to DBNF Road 623. This road begins immediately after crossing the Rockcastle River and serves the Bee Rock West Campground. Drive 0.5 mile on the road, past the west end of the Bee Rock Loop Trail, to park near the footbridge across the river.

The Hike

The Bee Rock Loop features the rock-and-roll scenery famous along the Cumberland Plateau. The loop first climbs past the sheer sandstone rock of the Rockcastle Gorge, then descends to follow the rolling waters of the Rockcastle River.

From the footbridge over the Rockcastle River, walk 0.2 mile back on the campground road to the start of the west leg of the Bee Rock Loop Trail. Follow the white diamond blazes up a small branch on an old road through a thick hemlock forest. Soon the trail approaches the rim of the Rockcastle Gorge, and begins to climb through the massive layers of sandstone that form the rim. You'll pass one low rockhouse then a second "split-level" house. The main room here has a long smile-shaped main opening and another lower level off to the right.

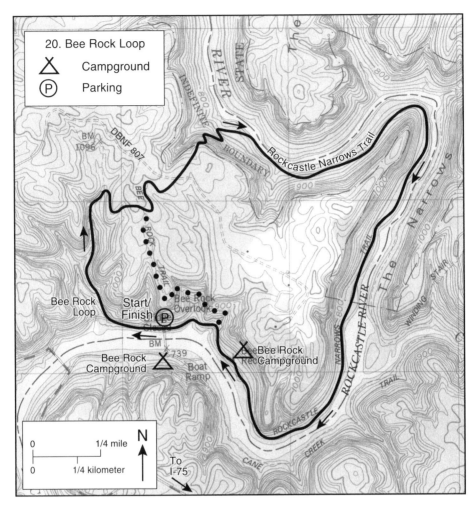

Across the trail from the split-level is a rare "mushroom rock," where a massive boulder sits on a much narrower rock base.

Next, you'll pass the first of the mile markers the DBNF has placed every 0.5 mile along the trail. This one indicates that you have walked 0.5 mile from the campground road. Just beyond, at 0.8 mile, turn right off the road onto a footbridge. The trail now rolls along the contour, keeping to the same elevation through a forest of pine, holly, Fraser magnolia, oak, and red maple. At 1.1 miles, reach a T-junction with abandoned DBNF Road 5063. Trail 529 turns right down this road and leads past the Rockcastle River overlook directly to the campground. Your route turns left off the road and within 50 feet reaches the start of Trail 503. Trail 503 meanders along the ridgetop until reaching DBNF Road 807 at 1.3 miles.

After crossing Road 807, descend steadily from the rim through a set of cliff bands, then wind alongside shallow rock overhangs covered with maidenhair ferns and rhododendron. The trail clings precariously to the steep hillside. Some recent trail relocations on the descent have made the grade less steep and the walking easier.

Once you reach the riverside, the walking is nearly level and much easier on a path that follows the trace of an old road. At 1.8 miles there is a sign pointing left to Beach Narrows, and another telling you that there is 2.5 miles of trail left to hike. Two faint roads will join the route before a larger road intersects the trail at 2.2 miles. Enjoy some views of the river along the trail even at the height of summer's luxurious growth.

At 3.1 miles, a marked side trail leads 300 feet down to the river at the Rockcastle Narrows. This all-day hangout spot gets up close to the class-3 white water of this Kentucky Wild River. The huge boulders shed from the plateau rim litter the narrow valley like pieces of a giant's puzzle set. If you look closely at some of the larger rocks in the river you can spot the high-water marks left over from many years of spring floods.

Return to the main trail, and continue toward the campground. Just beyond the 1-mile post the cliffs to the right of the trail reach nearly 100 feet above the river. You'll leave the old road to the right, then rejoin it near another side trail leading to the river, before reaching the end of the trail at 4.4 miles. Walk back on the campground road passing the east end of the Bee Rock Loop Trail at 4.7 miles. Close the loop at the footbridge at 4.9 miles.

The Rockcastle River has been designated a Kentucky Wild River. The 17-mile run from KY 80 to KY 192 at Bee Rock is rated class 3–4. Below Bee Rock, the Rockcastle flows into the backwaters of Lake Cumberland.

The Bee Rock West Campground is open from April until October. Just across the river is the Bee Rock East Campground, which has a boat ramp and is open year-round. Both campgrounds have some of the nicest sites in all of the national forest. The sites are spaced far apart, situated either next to the river or on private bluffs above it, and have broad smooth, level areas for tents. Several sites on the east bank are very private and can be accessed by short side trails.

Bee Rock is a fee area. In 2001, the day-use fee was $3, and overnight camping cost $5.

Other Hiking Options

1. Short and Sweet. The east leg of the Bee Rock Loop leads 0.5 mile to the side trail to an overlook above the Rockcastle River.

2. The Bee Rock Loop Trail is 2.2 miles around.

21

Rockcastle Narrows

Total Distance: A 9.4-mile semi-loop on the Rockcastle Connector (DBNF 401A), Rockcastle Narrows East (DBNF 401), and Sheltowee Trace (DBNF 100) Trails. The crossing of Cane Creek can be dangerous in high water.

Hiking Time: About 5 hours

Location: London Ranger District, about 20 miles southwest of London

Maps: USGS Ano

The Rockcastle Narrows hike begins across the river from the Bee Rock Loop. While the Bee Rock Loop has a friendly "front-country" feel, the Rockcastle Narrows hike has a rougher backcountry feel. But the attractions along the trail are still first-rate. You'll see both the Rockcastle Narrows and Cane Creek and can make a sort side trip to Vanhook Falls.

Getting There

From Exit 38 off I-75 on the south side of London follow KY 192 west for 18.8 miles to DBNF Road 624 on the east side of the Rockcastle River. Drive 0.4 mile through the Bee Rock East Campground, and park either at the boat ramp or at the end of the road near the gate marking the start of the trail.

The Hike

Begin by hiking along the Rockcastle Connector Trail (DBNF 401A), which starts out as an old road and is sporadically marked with white diamond blazes. Beyond a low hilltop capped with a concrete pad, the route turns into a footpath. The trail often ventures close enough to the river to offer some nice views of both its gentle and rollicking sections. You'll cross only one side stream, beside a house-sized boulder, before reaching the valley of Cane Creek at 1.6 miles in an area where there are some possible campsites.

Hike just far enough upstream to find Cane Creek choked with boulders shed from the plateau rim above. Close to the

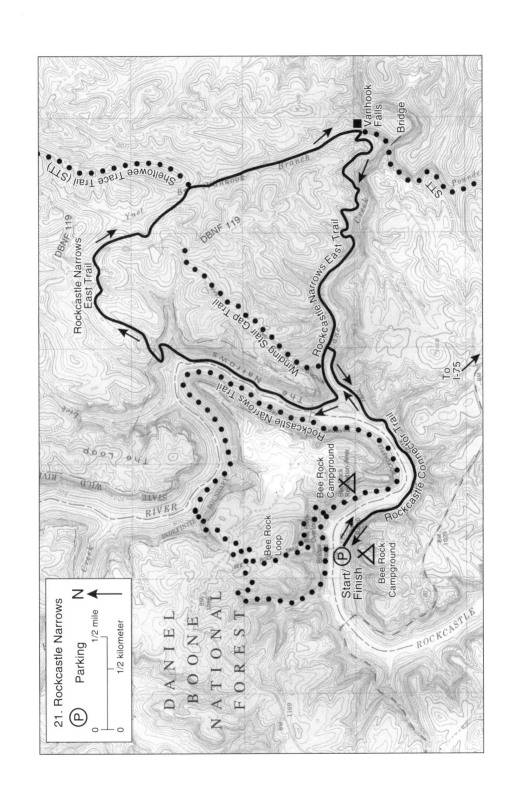

creek the trail disappears, so you will need to work your way down the bank and try to make a dry crossing on the larger rocks. In spring, or in any high water, this crossing could be dangerous, and should be avoided.

On the far bank of the creek, the trail is again difficult to find. Try climbing straight up the bank for about 200 feet. You should find a well-trodden trail here near an old fire ring. This is the start of the loop on the Rockcastle Narrows East Trail (DBNF 401). Take care to mark the place where you first intersect the trail. You will need to repeat this crossing on your return hike. To continue around the loop, go left. In another 200 feet or so you should find an unsigned trail entering on the right. This is the lower end of the Winding Stair Gap Trail (DBNF 402).

Past the junction with the Winding Stair Gap Trail, a short side trail leads left to a campsite near the confluence of Cane Creek and the Rockcastle River. You next return to the river's edge and follow a pretty route through rhododendron and hemlock trees. At 2.4 miles, a side trail leads left to an overlook above a rocky set of narrows. Just beyond is another fine campsite. At 2.9 miles, cross a substantial side stream just above a small cascade. Beyond this crossing, look for a sharp right turn that marks the start of the climb away from the river.

A few switchbacks along the climb lessen the grade somewhat, but the climb still remains steep. Near the plateau rim the trail joins an overgrown logging road at 3.5 miles. Follow the logging road until you reach a stop sign at the junction with gravel DBNF Road 119 at 3.8 miles. The stop sign doesn't protect you from much traffic; the road is gated closed about 2 miles north at its junction with DBNF Road 457. Turn left onto Road 119, and go about 250 feet, where a sign points to a right turn off the road and down toward the valley of Vanhook Branch.

The Rockcastle Narrows East Trail descends along the right bank of Vanhook Branch. The trail here is wide and the forest open. You'll cross Vanhook Branch just before reaching the intersection with the Sheltowee Trace Trail (DBNF 100), and the north end of the Rockcastle Narrows East Trail, at 4.8 miles. Turn right onto the STT, which continues a steady descent above the branch, but out of sight of it.

At 5.9 miles, the STT reaches the south end of DBNF Road 119 at a signed junction. The road is now a rough jeep trail that looks little like the wide gravel road you saw at the first crossing. From this junction, the start of the Rockcastle Narrows East Trail is 150 feet along a right turn up the road, though this is not apparent from the junction. If you go left at the junction, and stay on the STT, you will reach Vanhook Falls in 0.1 mile and the bridge over Cane Creek in 0.25 mile. The Falls is a small water column that pours over the lip of a deep rockhouse. Both the Falls and the bridge are scenic side trips.

The south end of the Rockcastle Narrows East Trail is signed 150 feet up DBNF Road 119. A sign indicates that Winding Stair Gap Trail is 1.75 miles and Cane Creek is 2 miles. An older sign also indicates that this was once called the Cane Creek Trail. The trail descends gradually alongside Cane Creek, midway between the creek and the cliffs above it. Few blazes mark this leg of the trail, so be careful not to miss a switchback to your left at 6.8 miles. Beyond the switchback, the trail crosses over the lip of a small waterfall. The trail moves closer to the creek as the valley narrows and high cliffs tower above.

At 7.8 miles you should close the loop near the place where you first crossed

Cane Creek. If you missed your crossing, you should intersect the unmarked, but blazed, lower end of the Winding Stair Gap Trail. Recross Cane Creek, and locate the Rockcastle Connector Trail on the other side. Retrace this trail to return to the trailhead at 9.4 miles.

The Rockcastle Narrows Loop traverses the heart of the 6,700-acre Cane Creek Wildlife Management Area. The DBNF first stocked Cane Creek with 20 whitetail deer in 1978, and the area is now an important habitat for these game animals.

Other Hiking Options

1. Short and Sweet. A hike out and back on just the Rockcastle Connector Trail is 2.8 miles.

2. If water is high, the Sheltowee Trace Trail can be used to access the loop from the open portion of DBNF Road 119. This approach to the loop is 0.5 mile shorter, but requires considerably more driving.

3. The Winding Stair Gap Trail leads from the crossing of Cane Creek 1.2 miles to a point midway along the closed portion of DBNF Road 119.

III

Daniel Boone Country—North

22

Indian Fort Mountain

Total Distance: A 3.0-mile semi-loop

Hiking Time: About 2 hours

Location: Berea College Forest,
3 miles east of Berea

Maps: USGS Berea and Big Hill;
Berea College Indian Fort Mountain Trails

The Berea College trail system is one of those pleasant surprises that hikers sometimes stumble across. Here is a place with beautiful trails leading to spectacular overlooks that is situated just off the interstate by one of the Commonwealth's prettiest towns. The trail network at Indian Fort Mountain is a complex web that leads to five different overlooks on the mountain. The semi-loop described here combines the Indian Fort Overlook with a side trail to West Pinnacle.

Getting There
From Exit 76 off I-75 drive east on KY 21. Keep right on KY 21 where the road splits at the Boone Tavern in the town of Berea. At 5.1 miles, reach the signed parking area on the left side of the road for the Indian Fort Amphitheater.

The Hike
From the parking area follow the paved path for 0.1 mile to Indian Fort Amphitheater. Here a trail sign indicates that the mountain was sacred to the prehistoric Hopewell Culture who lived in the area between 2,100 and 1,600 years ago. Beyond the trail is dirt, but wide and easy to follow. Pass an unmarked side trail leading right to East Pinnacle at 0.5 mile before reaching a major, signed junction at 0.6 mile. The trail to the right also leads to East Pinnacle. The trail left leads to West Pinnacle and is your return route. Your route continues straight ahead.

As you approach the crest of Indian Fort Mountain, several other trails will split off the

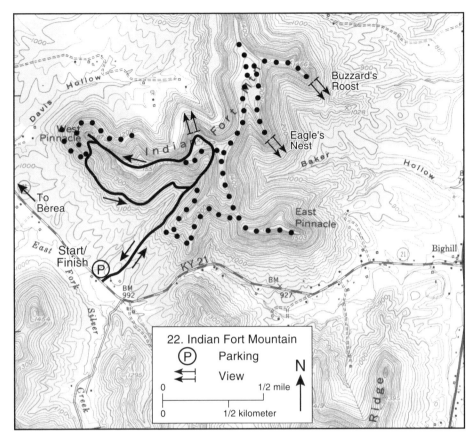

22. Indian Fort Mountain

P Parking

View

N

0   1/2 mile

0   1/2 kilometer

main path. Just continue straight to the crest, which you will intersect near the roof of a deep rockhouse known as Devils Kitchen at 0.8 mile. There's no trail down into this opening, so you must be content with your view from above. Next pass "Jail House Rock," a wide crack in the rock rim that has been covered with iron bars. Finally, the overlook at Indian Fort comes into view.

From this vantage point, you can see west toward the town of Berea and West Pinnacle and north to Robe Mountain. Indian Fort Mountain lies at the edge of the plateau country. To the west lies rolling farmland, while the land to the east is mostly rugged forests. In late spring, wild roses bloom at the overlook.

Though most hikers simply return to the trailhead from this point, adventurous hikers can reward themselves by visiting the other overlooks along the trail system. To reach the West Pinnacle, continue hiking along the rim to the west until you reach a trail junction marked by a lone post at 1.0 mile. Keep right at this junction, and descend a steep and worn route straight down the ridge crest. This unlikely looking route levels off after reaching the base of a cliff band, but remains little used and may be hard to follow. The trail leads through a forest of pines, oak, maple, and sassafras, where fire pinks can also be found. About 50 feet before reaching a cap rock, regain the ridge crest. Don't be tempted to stop here; the

Devil's Kitchen

real West Pinnacle is just a few minutes ahead. Stay on the trail and watch carefully for poison ivy growing alongside it. At 1.5 miles note a faint side trail leading left off the ridge; this will be part of your return route.

At 1.6 miles, reach West Pinnacle, which is actually a pair of high capstones. You can enjoy some views from the overlook without getting to the top of the capstones, which looks to require some rock-climbing skills. Otherwise the view is partially obscured by trees. The capstones are formed from a hard pebbly sandstone layer that overlies a more easily eroded sandstone with cross-beds.

From West Pinnacle, return by retracing your route to 1.7 miles, where a faint side trail leads south off the crest. If you missed the side trail on your outbound leg, look for it at a line of short stubby, toadstool-like sandstone formations. At 1.8 miles, reach a junction where the signed Walnut Trail leads to the right. Soon after, another old

road by a post with no sign also leads to the right. Keep left on the trail, which is now a wide old roadway. At 2.4 miles, intersect the main trail at a signed junction. To return to the trailhead, turn right and walk past the amphitheater to reach the parking area at 3.0 miles.

Berea College was founded in 1855 by opponents of slavery on the then-radical idea of equal education for men and women of all races. The college also set out to provide work in lieu of tuition for as many of its students as possible. The founders were driven from the area during the Civil War, but returned afterward and continued to teach. From 1904 to 1950 Kentucky law prohibited interracial education, but the school became mixed again as soon as state law permitted.

Berea's popularity grew so much that in 1911 the school was forced to focus its efforts on students from the "neglected" region of Appalachia. After 1968 the college confined its efforts to undergraduate education, often receiving the highest awards for its academic programs. Berea still provides work-based full-tuition scholarships to all students and retains its commitment to serving southern Appalachia.

The Berea College Forest protects 8,000 acres of woodlands east of the college and helps to protect the water source for the city of Berea. The forest was logged in the 1880s, but it is now covered in mature second-growth pine and oak on the drier ridgetops, and has grown up into a hardwood forest of basswood, oak, maple, walnut, ash, and hickory in the moister valleys. The forest is used for timber, recreation, education activities, and watershed management. It serves as a natural lab for studies of entomology, forestry, and water and timber management in the school's Forestry Department. In more than 100 years as a working forest it has produced 16 million board feet of saw timber alone.

The forest contains about 8 miles of hiking trails. Trails north of Eagle's Nest and Buzzard's Roost on Robe Mountain have been closed because of conflicts with private land. The forest also contains four water reservoirs and a treatment plant that provide the surrounding area with nearly 800 million gallons of water per year. The 1,300-acre Ownsley Fork watershed and 150-acre lake were purchased in 1970.

Much of the forest was logged in the late 1800s and early 1900s. Other parts of the forest had been cleared, then overfarmed or overgrazed, and were badly eroded. Early efforts at managing the forest were directed at controlling fires, stabilizing soils, thinning, and replanting trees. Many stands of Virginia and shortleaf pines have now reached old age and in normal forest succession would be replaced by hardwood stands. These stands are being hit hard by the southern pine beetle. To counteract the beetle, the forest is replanting shortleaf pines.

Other Hiking Options

1. Short and Sweet: The round-trip hike to Indian Fort Overlook is only 2.0 miles long.

2. Other fine overlooks at East Pinnacle (1.4 miles one-way), Eagle's Nest (1.6 miles one-way), and Buzzard's Roost (1.8 miles one-way) make fine day hikes.

23

The Original Trail

Total Distance: This 3.8-mile loop hike includes a side trip to Lookout Point. The route uses the Original, Laurel Ridge, Rock Garden, and Battleship Rock Trails.

Hiking Time: About 2.5 hours

Location: Natural Bridge State Resort Park, about 3 miles east of Slade

Maps: USGS Slade; Natural Bridge State Resort Park Trail Guide

The Original Trail was (as one might guess) the first trail built at Natural Bridge State Park. And due at least in part to park signs calling it "the easiest trail to Natural Bridge," it is by far the park's most popular trail and may even be the most heavily used trail in the state. The Original Trail deserves its fame; it is an historic, well-graded route to a spectacular arch and a wonderful overlook. From the parking area to the junction with the Balanced Rock Trail the route is part of the Sheltowee Trace Trail.

Getting There

From Exit 33 off the Mountain Parkway at Slade, drive south on KY 11 for 2.8 miles. Turn right into the main park parking area. The Original Trail starts at the far end of the parking area.

The Hike

Since there are a number of routes leading to Natural Bridge from the same place, hikers should pay attention to the trails at the start. Almost everyone first hikes up the Original Trail, but there are four other routes that can be used to return to the lodge area. All are exciting and scenic, but the Rock Garden Trail is the longest, and least used, so it may be the best complement to the Original Trail.

The Original Trail begins at the far end of the parking area, by a large sign. Since the route is so heavily used, much of it is up stone steps, is graveled, or is fenced to keep hikers on the route. Not far from the start, the trail splits, and a shortcut to the nature center goes left. The Original Trail goes right and climbs to a paved walkway by some benches.

The walkway leads left to the nature center, where there are displays on the mammals of the Red River Gorge Area. To the right the walkway leads to a parking area in back of Hemlock Lodge. Cross the walkway and go straight uphill to a junction with the Balanced Rock Trail (and Sheltowee Trace), which lead left. Go right and immediately come to another junction, this time with the Battleship Rock Trail (your return route), which joins from the right. Stay left, and continue to climb on the Original Trail.

The trail climbs past a trail shelter built in the 1930s by the Civilian Conservation Corps. Next is a small cave on the left side, which you can explore with the aid of a flashlight. Beyond the trail continues a steady climb. The climb is not long enough or steep enough to trouble most experienced hikers, but it can seem far too long to those unused to walking on trails. Just before reaching the Natural Bridge is a shortcut to the right to the Battleship Rock Trail and Devils Gulch.

At 0.7 mile, the Original Trail reaches the base of Natural Bridge. On the opposite side of the front of the bridge is the upper end of the Battleship Rock Trail. On the back side of the bridge are junctions with the Hood's Branch Trail on the left and the Rock Garden Trail on the right.

Your best close-up view of the bridge is from below. Here you can see the graceful curve of the top of the opening. To reach the flat top of the bridge you must follow the trail up the thin crack on the far left side of the bridge. This long "squeeze" leads to some steps. To the right at the top of the steps is the upper end of the Balanced Rock Trail

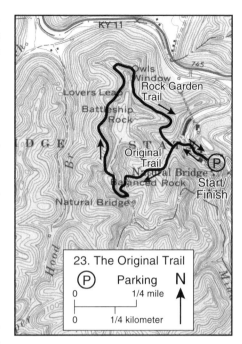

23. The Original Trail

Ⓟ   Parking   N

(which leads to the Sheltowee Trace Trail). Straight ahead is a large gazebo. To the left is the top of the bridge.

The top of Natural Bridge is not fenced but is wide enough to be safe for those who are paying attention to their surroundings. From the top of the bridge you can see across the park, over the valley of Whittleton Branch to Red River Gorge. You will probably also see a prominent overlook to your left with many people on it. This is aptly named Lookout Point, a worthy destination for a larger-scale view of Natural Bridge.

To reach Lookout Point, cross the arch and continue on the Laurel Ridge Trail to the top of the Sky Lift. The Sky Lift is a ski-type lift that climbs the back side of the park. In 2001, the fee was $5 for adults and $4 for children ages 3 to 12. Cross under the Sky Lift and continue along the level trail until you reach the open views of Lookout Point. From Lookout Point, return to the base of

Natural Bridge

the Bridge to continue your loop on the Rock Garden Trail.

The Rock Garden Trail follows the base of the cliff band from which Natural Bridge has formed. These cliffs offer one of the best displays of concretions visible to hikers in the park. The concretions form swirls or honeycomb patterns in the sandstone. They occur because the iron oxides that hold the individual sand grains of the rock together can be harder than the sand itself. As the sandstone is eroded, the concretions remain in relief as the sand is gradually worn away. These types of rocks also form rockhouses, the shallow overhangs that early peoples might have used as shelter, and you'll see some of these also.

The trail next follows the ridgetop through an area of laurel and rhododendron that must be beautiful in early summer. The trail finally begins to descend down three narrow stairways carved into bare sandstone. You'll pass a marker indicating that you've gone 1 mile down the trail—which means there is only 0.75 mile to go. Pass a house-sized boulder beside a wooden bridge before coming to an area where there are views of Hemlock Lodge below. As you leave Hemlock Lodge behind, the well-worn Battleship Rock Trail joins from the right. Just beyond, intersect the Original Trail, and turn left on it to return to the parking area.

Red River Gorge was still wild and unknown in the 1880s when the Kentucky Union Lumber Company first built railroad tracks up the river. The forests were soon cut, and the logs were hauled by oxen to the railroads and brought to the huge mill at Clay City. The loggers came first for the prime hardwoods—mostly white oak, chestnut, and yellow poplar. By the end of World War I, the logging boom was dead, the area almost completely cut over, and the rail lines and logging camps abandoned.

The park was established in 1895 by the railroad, which built a campground, picnic area, and the Original Trail. By 1926, the railroad was out of the park business, and it donated Natural Bridge to the state. It thereby became one of the four original holdings in the Kentucky state park system. The state built the original Hemlock Lodge in 1927, and by the late 1920s the park could be reached by a gravel road from Slade. The park built a new lodge in 1963. The original lodge burned in 1969.

Natural Bridge remains one of Kentucky's most popular, and most beautiful, state parks. In addition to the park trails, Sky Lift, and Hemlock Lodge, the park contains two campgrounds at Middle Fork and Whittleton Branch (the site of the 1930s Civilian Conservation Corps Camp), cottages, and an immensely popular public swimming pool. There are also two snack bars, gift shops, and an activities center with nature displays. There is an active schedule of interpretive programs with several events per day offered in the summer. Red River Gorge is also one of the region's prime rock-climbing areas. Though there is no climbing allowed on the state park lands, surrounding private and national forests lands contain several exciting areas.

Other Hiking Options

1. Short and Sweet. Natural Bridge and Lookout Point can be reached from the Sky Lift in a 0.5-mile walk.

2. The Lakeside Trail is a 0.6-mile round-trip hike along the lake that is also part of the Sheltowee Trace Trail.

3. The Battleship Rock and Balanced Rock Trails can be combined into a 2.0-mile loop that also leads to Natural Bridge.

24

Hood's Branch and Sand Gap Trails

Total Distance: A difficult 10.4-mile loop, which also includes part of the Sheltowee Trace Trail and a visit to Natural Bridge.

Hiking Time: About 5.5 hours

Location: Natural Bridge State Resort Park, about 3 miles southeast of Slade

Maps: USGS Slade; Natural Bridge State Resort Park Trail Guide

The hiking trails at Hood's Branch and Sand Gap are literally the opposite side of hiking at Natural Bridge State Park. The short trails on the Hemlock Lodge side of the park are heavily used and well worn. Few hikers explore the longer trails on the Sky Lift side of the park; a shame since these trails combine a backcountry sense of solitude with front-country highlights.

Getting There

From Exit 33 off the Mountain Parkway at Slade, drive 2.2 miles south on KY 11 to the entrance of Natural Bridge State Park. Cross the Middle Fork of the Red River and turn right. Drive 0.7 mile, past the Sky Lift, to a parking area by the snack bar and mini-golf area.

The Hike

The Hood's Branch and Sand Gap Trails form a 10-mile loop on the back side of Natural Bridge State Park between the Sky Lift and Natural Bridge. This long walk is an all-day affair. Once hikers reach the Sand Gap Trail there is no opportunity for an easy shortcut.

The Hood's Branch Trail starts behind the snack bar and mini-golf course just beyond the main parking area for the Sky Lift. Start the trail with a climb up some wooden steps, then take a sharp left above the maintenance area where a path joins from the right. Hood's Branch begins as if the trail means to climb all 500 feet to Natural Bridge in one breathless gulp. But after the junction with the end of the Sand Gap Trail at 0.1 mile, the grade eases.

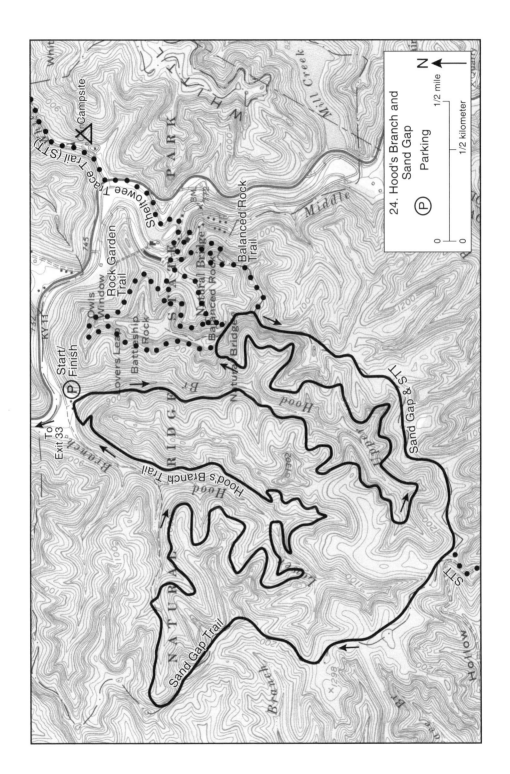

24. Hood's Branch and
Sand Gap

Ⓟ Parking

N

0   1/2 kilometer
0   1/2 mile

Mushroom

The trail follows above the west bank of Upper Hood's Branch through hardwood forest. At 0.6 mile there is a small wooden shelter to the right that was built in the 1930s by workers from the Civilian Conservation Corps, and restored in 1979. As you climb higher along the branch the trail makes several crossings on wooden bridges. The forest changes to a mix of boggy open areas and dark hemlock forests. Along some side branches are lush, bright green fern gardens. Even in midsummer you can spot flowers such as spiderwort in bloom.

At 1.6 miles, reach the junction with the upper loop of the Hood's Branch Trail. This trail does not rejoin the main Hood's Branch Trail, but is a side loop. Go left from the junction on a wooden bridge over Upper Hood's Branch. Make one more bridged crossing of a very small stream before reaching the 1-mile marker. This marker is for hikers coming down the trail from Natural Bridge; you've only got a mile to go to the bridge, and have walked 2.0 miles.

Just past the 1-mile marker is a deep rockhouse. You'll now walk along the base of the cliff band that forms Natural Bridge and the other rocky delights of the park. The cliffs are covered in thick rhododendron that hides some of the trailside rockhouses and overhangs.

After a short, steep climb reach the end of the Hood's Branch Trail at the base of Natural Bridge at 3.0 miles. Next, climb through the long, narrow crack at the base of the bridge and climb the stairs to the top of the arch. Carefully walk out onto the bridge for a view of the Hemlock Lodge side of the park and a look up Whittleton Branch in the Daniel Boone National Forest. If you haven't done the Original Trail hike, you should consider the side trip to Lookout Point for the classic view of Natural Bridge.

From the top of Natural Bridge, your route follows the Balanced Rock Trail to a junction at 3.1 miles. Here the Balanced Rock Trail (and the Sheltowee Trace to the north) goes left down to Hemlock Lodge, and the start of the Sand Gap Trail (and the Sheltowee Trace to the south) goes right. The Sand Gap Trail, also called Trail #5, is blazed here with a few white paint diamonds and the STT symbol. The next 2 miles are the easiest hiking on the loop. The trail follows a narrow ridgetop along the south boundary of the park. In a short distance, the park land is also part of the 994-acre Natural Bridge State Nature Preserve, which was dedicated in 1981. The preserve protects the habitat of the small yellow lady's slipper, a Kentucky endangered species, and the Virginia big-eared bat, which is a federally endangered species.

At 4.6 miles, the Sheltowee Trace splits to the left, just short of an old metal gate at the park boundary. A sign indicates the STT leads 7 miles south to Standing Rock and 16 miles south to the Kentucky River down a dirt road where some new development can be seen. From the gate, turn right and continue north along the ridgetop and the park boundary on the Sand Gap Trail. The forest here is typical of the dry ridgetop environment. Shortleaf pine, red maple, scarlet oak, and chestnut oak dominate the canopy, while sassafras is a common smaller tree. The trail veers off the left side of the ridgetop to visit a small overlook with views through the forest at 5.8 miles.

After crossing to the right side of the ridge in a small saddle, reach a small pocket-cave above the left side of the trail. Begin the descent from the ridge at 6.3 miles. Turn sharply to the right after crossing a small stream on a wooden bridge and begin a short steep climb. For the next few miles, the trail will climb in and out of the headwaters of Lower Hood's Branch. Notice how the vegetation changes as the trail alternates between the wet valleys and dry ridgetops. At 8.7 miles cross a small stream on a wooden bridge by a bench.

Make two more short climbs before reaching another, welcome bench at 9.3 miles. There's a high bridge over a side branch just before you regain sight of the main creek. After a double bridge, the trail begins to follow an old road. At 10.0 miles leave the nature preserve, and at 10.3 miles reach the intersection with the Hood's Branch Trail. Turn left onto the Hood's Branch Trail and reach the trailhead at 10.4 miles.

Other Hiking Options

1. Short and Sweet. Hikers can use the Sky Lift (for a fee) to ascend to Natural Bridge, then enjoy a 3.0-mile downhill walk on the Hood's Branch Trail.

2. The Sheltowee Trace Trail leads 3.7 miles south from Natural Bridge to KY 1036. Much of the rest of the STT immediately south of the park is on roads or is open to OHVs.

25

Whittleton Arch

Total Distance: A 4.4-mile round trip on the Whittleton Arch (DBNF 217) and Whittleton Branch (DBNF 216) Trails

Hiking Time: About 2.5 hours

Location: Red River Gorge Geological Area, Stanton Ranger District, about 3 miles east of Slade

Maps: USGS Slade; DBNF Red River Gorge Geological Area

Whittleton Arch is a good example of the high payoffs of hiking at Red River Gorge. Here is a scenic arch that is easy to reach from trailheads on both the Daniel Boone National Forest and Natural Bridge State Resort Park. In the early days of the timber boom at Red River Gorge loggers strung a railroad branch up the narrow valley of Whittleton Branch to extract the trees they had harvested from the forests atop the gorge. Nowadays all that remains from the railroad is a short section of corduroy along the trail and a healthy stand of second-growth forest. Don't merely consider the forest as background while you hike to the arch. Here is a chance to marvel at the power of nature to regenerate itself.

Getting There

From the Slade Exit off Mountain Parkway, drive 3.3 miles east on KY 15 to the junction with DBNF Road 39, which is Tunnel Ridge Road. On the right side of this junction is a small pullout and signs for the Whittleton Branch and Sheltowee Trace Trails. To reach the south trailhead at Whittleton Campground from the Slade Exit, drive 2.5 miles east on KY 11 to the campground entrance. You must park in the day-use area and not at site A37, where the trail begins.

The Hike

Whittleton Arch can be reached from either a trailhead on KY 15, or from the Whittleton Campground on KY 11 in Natural Bridge State Resort Park. Though most hikers will

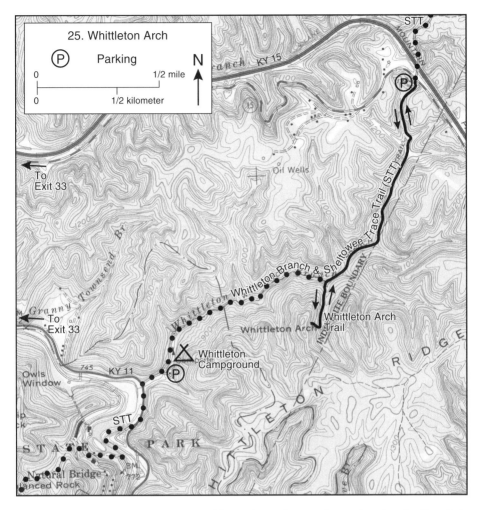

return to the trailhead from the arch, the hike is short enough that many will want to hike the whole trail. The Whittleton Branch Trail is also part of the Sheltowee Trace Trail.

From the small parking area on KY 15, follow the foot trail south down steps that have been carved into the sandstone bedrock. White blazes lead down three switchbacks into the bottom of the narrow valley. This dark and damp area is dominated by hemlock, pitch pine, and rhododendron, with Christmas fern in the understory. The pines of Red River Gorge have not suffered from the southern pine beetle like their neighbors to the south, perhaps because colder winters have kept the beetles' population in check.

Once in the valley, you cross a small side branch on a wooden bridge. The next branch has no bridge, and water may flood the trail immediately after a hard rain. The valley is so narrow in places that the trail and stream must share the same route. In others, the trail is lined with moss and ground cedar, giving the trail the appearance of a narrow green tunnel.

At 0.5 mile, Whittleton Branch cuts through an especially thick and hard layer of sandstone. Rockhouses line both sides of the trail, and Whittleton Branch drops over a 6-foot cascade. Farther down the trail, the cliffs loom to nearly 60 feet high, and you can study the unusual concretions revealed in the deeply pockmarked sandstone.

Just beyond a second wooden bridge, reach the signed junction with the Whittleton Arch Trail at 1.2 miles. Turn left onto this side trail and cross Whittleton Branch on a sturdy wooden bridge. Reach the arch at 1.4 miles. Whittleton Arch appears to have formed from the collapse of the rear of a large rockhouse. There is a small wet-weather waterfall that pours over the right-side of the opening of the arch. This impressive arch is about 55 feet long, 40 feet wide, and 30 feet high. The open and airy base of the arch is an ideal spot for a lunch break before starting your return hike.

To hike from the side trail junction to Whittleton Campground, continue south on the trail from the junction. Here the trail makes many crossings of the stream on wooden bridges, surely a major challenge for those who laid the first rail tracks through here. Notice how the water in the stream disappears and reappears. The branch flows over limestone in the lower reaches, and its water comes and goes from underground passageways. At 2.0 miles come to the Whittleton Campground Trailhead near site A37. To reach the parking area, you must walk through the campground to the day-use parking area at the campground entrance station.

The first rail line was pushed into Red River Gorge in the 1880s by the Kentucky Union Lumber Company. The track up Whittleton Branch was run by the Mountain Central Railway and operated until 1928, just two years after the establishment of Natural Bridge State Park.

The Red River Gorge Geological Area was designated in 1974 and protects 26,000 acres around the Red River. The Geological Area results from a bitter land use battle that was fought over the gorge in the 1960s and 1970s. On one side was the Army Corps of Engineers, who proposed a $34 million dam that would flood 5,000 acres on the North Fork of the Red River for flood control. On the other side were conservationists and fiscal conservatives, who felt that the dam would not be cost effective, would endanger or destroy critical habitats, and would benefit only a small number of downstream landowners. The dam project was killed in 1975 by a formal objection by Kentucky governor Julian Carroll.

Further protection of the area came in 1985 with the creation of the Clifty Wilderness, and in 1993 with the designation of the Red River as a National Wild and Scenic River. The river is home to sensitive fish species and 23 types of mussels. Along with the common white-tailed deer, bobcats, coyotes, and an occasional black bear have been spotted in the Red River Gorge Geological Area. The Geological Area contains over 100 arches. Of the approximately 5.5 million annual visitors to the DBNF, 500,000 per year visit the gorge.

Other Hiking Options

1. Short and Sweet. It is slightly shorter to reach the arch from Whittleton Campground.

2. From Whittleton Campground, the 0.3-mile Henson Arch Trail leads to an unusual arch in the Natural Bridge State Resort Park. Instead of being formed from sandstone, Henson Arch is formed from limestone. It looks more like part of a collapsed cave than an arch. Part of the roof remains over a cylinder-shaped hole. The smooth, fluted, and vertical walls remind one of the underground waterfall at Cascade Cave in Carter Caves State Park, or of a smaller version of

Mammoth Dome in Mammoth Cave National Park. The arch is named for Clarence Henson, a former park superintendent.

3. From the trailhead on KY 15, the Sheltowee Trace Trail leads north about 0.7 mile to the Grays Arch Trailhead.

26

Courthouse Rock and Double Arch

Total Distance: An 8.1-mile semi-loop to Courthouse Rock, with an out-and-back leg to Double Arch. The hike uses the Auxier Ridge, Courthouse Rock, Auxier Branch, and Double Arch Trails.

Hiking Time: About 4 hours

Location: Red River Gorge Geological Area, Stanton Ranger District, about 8 miles north of Slade

Maps: USGS Slade; DBNF Red River Gorge Geological Area

The trails on the west side of the Red River Gorge Geological Area pack some of the area's biggest punch. Sure they are packed with stone arches and rockhouses, but no other trails in the area, and perhaps the state, can match the wide-open views from Auxier Ridge. Here is a perfect escape from any claustrophobic feeling of being trapped in the woods.

Getting There

From the Slade Exit off the Mountain Parkway drive 3.3 miles east on KY 15 to Tunnel Ridge Road (DBNF Road 39). Turn left and drive 3.6 miles north on the gravel road to the Auxier Ridge Trailhead. Tunnel Ridge Road is now closed beyond the Auxier Ridge Trailhead. However, you are welcome to walk the road, which leads to the Double Arch Trailhead (an alternate starting point for this hike) in 1.4 miles. Courthouse Rock and Double Arch are really two separate destinations. But since the trails to both are short, and both start near same trailheads, they can easily be combined into a single moderate hike.

The Hike

From the parking area, walk north on the Auxier Ridge Trail (DBNF 204). The trail leads north across the forested ridgetop to an intersection with the Courthouse Rock Trail (DBNF 202) at 1.0 mile. If you chose to hike the loop, the trail to your left will be your return route. Stay right and continue on the ridgetop on the Auxier Ridge Trail.

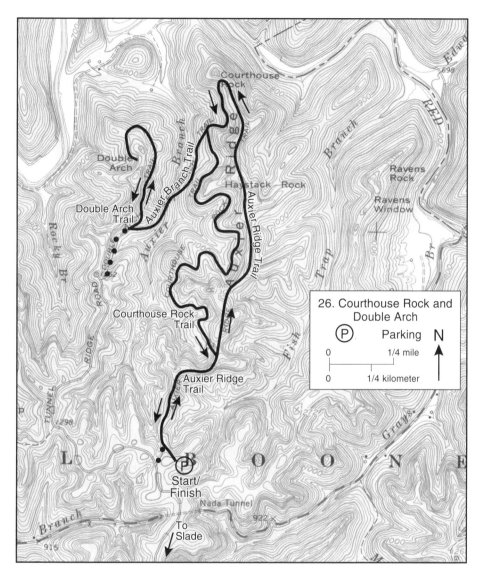

26. Courthouse Rock and Double Arch

Ⓟ   Parking   N

0 — 1/4 mile

0 — 1/4 kilometer

Approaching Courthouse Rock is 0.5 mile of unrestricted views from the narrow, cleared top of the ridge. You'll work your neck as much as your legs trying to keep up with this "out West" scale scenery. But be sure to keep at least one eye on the path; there are no fences at these overlooks to protect the oblivious hiker. There are many dry campsites scattered along the ridgetop, but remember that Red River Gorge regulations prohibit camping within 300 feet any roads or trails.

Courthouse Rock is one of those places you can spend all day exploring. Here long, narrow Auxier Ridge has broken up into a series of high turrets and graceful towers nearly 100 feet high. You'll need rock-climbing skills and equipment to climb to their tops, but many great overlooks are easily accessible. To the west is the ridge containing Double Arch; on the other side is the sheer dome of Raven Rock, capped with an unruly grove of trees, like a bad toupee. Vandals have destroyed the trail signs for the Auxier Ridge Trail at the popular overlooks at Courthouse Rock, but the stairs that mark the start of the descent down the trail are easy to find. If you'd like to walk the loop with the Courthouse Rock Trail, and visit Double Arch, descend off the ridge crest at 2.3 miles.

A short distance from the ridge crest there is a junction with the Courthouse Rock Trail leading left. To go to Double Arch, bear right onto the Auxier Branch Trail (DBNF 203). Just below the junction, a faint old road merges into the trail on the left. At the valley bottom, follow Auxier Branch a short distance before leaving it near a spot others have used for a campsite. Climb gradually to the intersection with the Double Arch Trail (DBNF 201) at 3.4 miles.

At this junction the Double Arch Trail leads left 0.3 mile to a trailhead on a now-closed portion of Tunnel Ridge Road. Go right toward Double Arch. The trail stays nearly level as it traverses north along the base of a massive cliff band. You can see other arches in the making in the graceful, arched roofs of large rockhouses within the cliffs. If you keep a sharp lookout, and are lucky, you'll spot Double Arch at the top of the cliff long before you reach it. The trail wraps around the nose of the ridge and traverses the west side for a short distance before reaching the arch at 4.8 miles.

Double Arch is one of the most unusual in the Red River Gorge Geological Area. It is not uncommon for arches to occur side by side at Red River Gorge, but Double Arch is unique in that two arches are stacked on top of each other. The arches are similar in style to the "classics," like Natural Bridge or Grays Arch, that have formed by the erosion of thin ridges of highly resistant sandstone. The upper arch is a narrow slot, perhaps formed by the collapse of a single sandstone bed. The main lower arch is about 20 feet long, 15 feet wide, and 12 feet high. Framed perfectly in the opening of the arch is a view of Courthouse and Haystack Rocks on adjacent Auxier Ridge. Step carefully, though, as you enjoy the view. A fall from the arch over the cliffs below would certainly be fatal.

Once you've enjoyed all Double Arch has to offer, retrace your route back to the junction of the Auxier Branch and Courthouse Rock Trails, just below the top of Auxier Ridge. At this point you have walked 5.6 miles. It seems that the Courthouse Rock Trail was designed to absolutely minimize any elevation gain along its route. The trail is so level that one expects that it began life as a railroad grade or logging road, perhaps left over from timber operations conducted in the early 1970s. Unfortunately, the trail sacrifices scenery for ease. You can see cliff bands through the trees above you, but there are no close-up glimpses of rockhouses or other features. But the trail does visit a variety of habitats, from thick groves of laurel and rhododendron to lush groves of ferns and hardwood forest. After a brief ascent on switchbacks reach a signed junction with the Auxier Ridge Trail at 7.1 miles. Turn right on the Auxier Ridge Trail and retrace your outbound route back to the trailhead at 8.1 miles.

Other Hiking Options

1. Short and Sweet. The trip to Courthouse Rock and back from the Auxier Ridge Trailhead is 4.0 miles round-trip. It is not necessary to hike the entire distance to enjoy the fine overlooks from the ridgetop.

Double Arch

2. Koomer Ridge Campground on the east side of the Red River Gorge Geological Area has a similar system of short, high-impact trails. The Silvermine Arch Trail (DBNF 225) is a 0.9-mile trail to Silvermine Arch. In 2001, the trail was rebuilt around a set of collapsed stairs. The 1.0-mile Hidden Arch Trail (DBNF 208) can be combined with the Koomer Ridge Trail past this small arch. The Cliff Trail (DBNF 206) is a 0.8-mile connector along the bluff line between the campground and the Silvermine Arch Trail.

27

Grays Arch–Rough Trail Loop

Total Distance: This 9.4-mile loop also includes the Buck Trail and parts of the Koomer Ridge and Pinch-Em-Tight Trails.

Hiking Time: About 5 hours

Location: Red River Gorge Geological Area, Stanton Ranger District, about 4 miles northeast of Slade

Maps: USGS Slade; DBNF Red River Gorge Geological Area

Of all the stonework on display at Red River Gorge, Grays Arch is perhaps the most impressive. This colossal arch has all the graceful curves and rugged beauty that hikers desire in a backcountry arch. The arch also anchors one end of the only hiking loop in the main gorge area long enough for overnight trips. You don't need to take a long hike to see Grays Arch, but likely you'll be inspired to stay in the woods as long as you can.

Getting There

From Exit 33 from the Mountain Parkway at Slade, drive 3.3 miles east on KY 15. Turn left on Tunnel Ridge Road (DBNF Road 39) and drive 0.9 mile to the Grays Arch Trailhead.

The Hike

From the trailhead at Grays Arch, start on the Grays Arch Trail (DBNF 205). At 0.3 mile, reach a junction with the Rough Trail (DBNF 221). The Rough Trail leads left 1.3 miles to KY 77, while the trail to the right continues to Grays Arch. This section is considered part of both the Rough and Grays Arch Trails. Beyond the junction the trail is wide and sandy, a result of the heavy use this route receives. In about 0.5 mile, pass through a cleared area kept open for wildlife habitat.

Don't expect to see Grays Arch until the trail has dropped off the ridgetop. You'll descend past a shallow rockhouse and down several flights of wooden stairs before reaching a trail junction at 1.1 miles. This

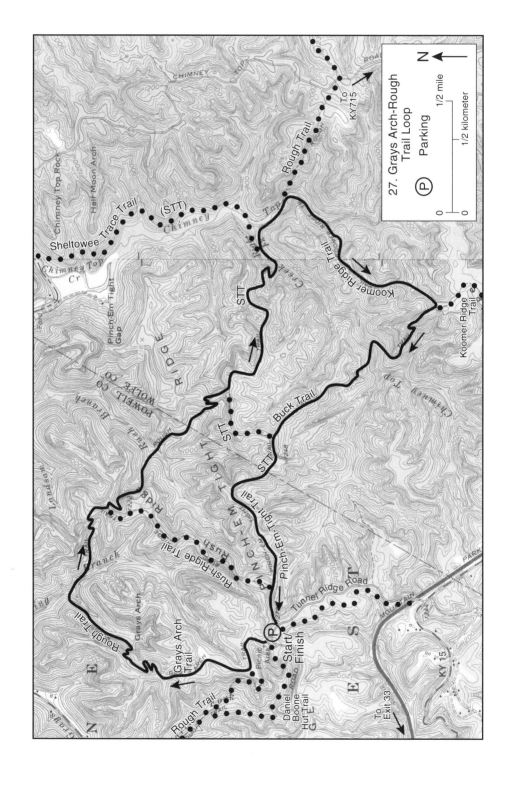

27. Grays Arch-Rough
Trail Loop

Ⓟ Parking

N

0   1/2 mile

0   1/2 kilometer

spot offers a great topside view of the arch. The spur trail to your right leads about 500 feet to the base of Grays Arch. The arch sits at the narrow end of a long sandstone ridge. The rock is a massive bed of sandstone, dotted with pebbles of clean white quartz. Extending 80 feet long and 50 feet high, Grays is also one of the largest in the area. R. H. Ruchhoft, in *Kentucky's Land of the Arches,* reports that Grays Arch was well known to loggers during that era, but the subsequent regrowth of the forest hid the arch until the 1930s, when it was relocated after a summer of searching.

Return to the main trail and hike below the massive sandstone layer that forms the gorge rim. Many of the boulders along the trail are laced with unusual patterns of iron concretions in the sandstone. The concretions are harder than the surrounding sandstone, so that as the rock weathers the concretions appear in something like a bas-relief. Below the rim, evergreens are more common than above. You'll see abundant hemlock (look for the short flat needles), laurel, and rhododendron. Near the confluence with King Branch, you'll see many areas where others have camped, but remember, the forest service now asks that campers stay at least 300 feet from any developed trail or road. Camping is now prohibited within 100 feet of the cliff line or within rock shelters.

Turn up King Branch, and then up a side branch. After ascending two sets of wooden stairs, reach the signed junction with the Rush Ridge Trail (DBNF 227) at 2.2 miles. You can take a shortcut here by following Rush Ridge to the right for 1.5 miles back to the trailhead. To complete the longer loop, stay left on the Rough Trail, which soon begins to earn its name. Reach a steep drop-off at the end of a long, graceful rockhouse. Next there is a high rockhouse on the right,

which fills the end of a box canyon. The trail goes directly down to the bottom of the box canyon, where there are some blazes. Do not follow any of the false trails on the left side of the canyon wall. Though these look as well-traveled as the main trail, they lead to precarious ledges.

The descent eases somewhat as the trail approaches Rush Branch. The overused campsites next to the creek should be avoided in favor of less visible and impacted sites. The climb out of Rush Branch is tough at the start, but becomes easier close to the ridgetop. During the climb, you can see that there are two main rock layers that form rockhouses in the canyon. The most obvious layer is the one that forms the rim and Grays Arch. But there is also a similar layer closer to the valley floor. True to form, on this climb you can see a small rockhouse in it. As you approach the rim, a short side trail will lead you right to a larger rockhouse in the upper layer.

At 3.4 miles, reach the junction with the Pinch-Em-Tight Trail (DBNF 223), which is also part of the Sheltowee Trace Trail. This is your second chance for a shortcut. A right turn will lead you back to the parking area in 1.9 miles. This trail's unusual name comes from a gap to the north of the trail that was so narrow, anyone passing through was pinched. To continue on the longer loop, keep left on the combined Rough and Sheltowee Trace Trails, and follow some level trail across the ridgetop. The ridgetop supports a pine-oak forest, common in many of the drier ridgetops in the Red River Gorge Geological Area. Many of these pines are white pine. They are easy to recognize, since the needles occur in clusters of five.

Part of the ridgetop was burned in a 1999 arson-caused fire. Pines are resistant to all but the most intense fires, so many of the older trees survived the burn. Most of the

A rockhouse in Red River Gorge

plants growing in the understory did not. The race to repopulate this habitat is fierce, and new growth in the burn looks much thicker than that under the undisturbed forest.

Beyond the burn, the Rough Trail soon begins the descent toward Chimney Top Creek. You'll rock-hop the Right Fork, then the main fork, before reaching the split between the Sheltowee Trace and Rough Trails at 4.7 miles. From the junction, the STT leads left along Chimney Top Creek 1.3 miles to KY 715 along the Red River. Your loop keeps right, crosses back to right side of the creek, and reaches a signed junction with the Koomer Ridge Trail (DBNF 220) at 4.9 miles. From this point, the Rough Trail leads left 0.6 mile to Chimney Top Road and 2.4 miles to KY 715. Your route goes right to follow the Koomer Ridge Trail.

The area around Chimney Top Creek has what many campers look for in a backcountry site. Water is close by, there are many smooth, level areas, and the pine- and hemlock-shrouded slopes are as beautiful as one could want. However, some of these sites are badly worn and the forest service asks that campers stay at least 300 feet from the trail.

The Koomer Ridge Trail leaves Chimney Top Creek on the right bank with a sharp switchback to the right. The climb toward the rim is steep at first, then moderates. Along the way you pass a small rock tower that has a bowling-ball-sized hole through its base. The trail climbs one more steep pitch before reaching the ridgetop at an area where some have made a dry camp. At 6.2 miles, reach the signed junction with the Buck Trail (DBNF 226). From here the Koomer Ridge Trail goes left 1 mile to the Koomer Ridge Campground. Go right here on the Buck Trail to continue on the loop.

The Buck Trail descends to make your second visit to the Right Fork of Chimney Top Creek. Turn right, and follow the right bank of the creek for about 0.1 mile in an area infrequently blazed. There are several old campsites here. Cross the creek and begin a steady climb. Pass below a high, overhanging rock tower, beyond which the trail becomes steeper.

At 7.7 miles, reach the junction with the Pinch-Em-Tight and Sheltowee Trace Trails. To the right is the end of your second shortcut leading 0.2 mile back to the Rough Trail. Go left at the junction and enjoy some easy ridgetop walking. Watch to the left of the trail for a potential campsite and a side trail to an overlook.

At 9.1 miles, reach the signed junction with the Rush Ridge Trail and the end of your first shortcut. Keep left to reach the gravel Tunnel Ridge Road at 9.3 miles. Then turn right to reach the Grays Arch Trailhead, and the end of the loop, at 9.4 miles.

Other Hiking Options

1. Short and Sweet. A trip to Grays Arch and back is an easy 2.2-mile round trip.

2. The D. Boon Hut Trail (DBNF 209) is a 0.7-mile trail leading to a protected rock shelter containing a small hut perhaps used by Daniel Boone.

3. The loop can be cut short by taking either the Rush Ridge Trail, for a 3.7-mile loop, or the Pinch-Em-Tight Trail, for a 5.3-mile loop.

4. The main loop can also be accessed from KY 77 by hiking 1.3 miles on the west end of the Rough Trail.

28

Swift Camp Creek–Wildcat Loop

Total Distance: The loop is 5.5 miles on the Swift Camp Creek (DBNF 219) and Wildcat (DBNF 228) Trails, and includes a short return hike on KY 715.

Hiking Time: About 3 hours

Location: Clifty Wilderness Area, Stanton Ranger District, about 12 miles north of Slade

Maps: USGS Pomerton; DBNF Red River Gorge Geological Area

While most of the hiking trails in the main area of Red River Gorge are ideal for day hiking, the longer trails of the adjacent Clifty Wilderness are perfect for backpackers seeking extended escapes. Here hikers can flee the often-crowded trails in the main gorge, and enjoy the solitude and peace found only far from the trailhead.

Getting There

From Exit 40 from the Mountain Parkway, drive 1.3 miles west on KY 15 to the community of Pine Ridge. Turn right on KY 715 and drive north. In 3.0 miles pass the Wildcat Trailhead, and pass the Angels Windows Trailhead in another 1.1 miles. In another 0.3 mile reach the gravel Swift Camp Creek Trailhead and park.

The Hike

Trails in the Clifty Wilderness occur both north and south of the Red River, with no current connection between the two. Swift Camp Creek–Wildcat is the only loop in the south half of the wilderness. It is suitable for day hiking or for novice backpackers.

The Swift Camp Creek Trail (DBNF 219) starts across KY 715 from the south end of the trailhead parking area. Like all trails in the wilderness, it is marked with white diamond paint blazes. The trail parallels the road for a short distance before reaching a trailside register. After signing in, drop into the head of White Branch, where an unmarked side trail from the Angel Windows Parking area joins from the right at 0.3 mile. Just beyond, the ground is covered with big-leaf magnolia leaves.

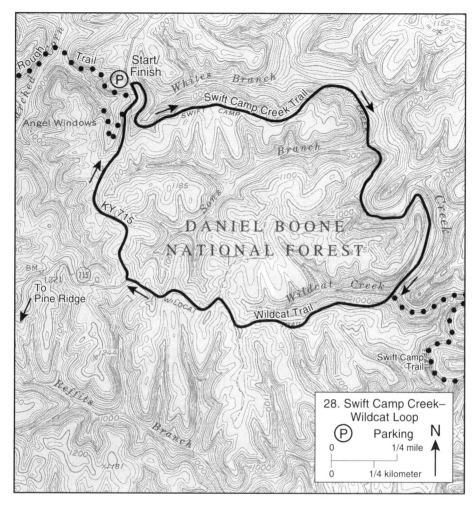

The trail continues along a wide ridge through a forest of pine, maple, beech, and oak familiar to gorge hikers. When the trail turns right off the ridge to descend into the valley of Sons Branch, the forest changes quickly. Where water is more abundant, and sunlight less so, hemlock, laurel, and rhododendron are the most common trees.

The trail crosses many side branches of Sons Branch in the upper reaches. As you descend farther into the valley, the trail passes shallow rockhouses in the cliffs and overhanging boulders large enough to make

their own "boulder houses." At 1.6 miles, the trail reaches Swift Camp Creek on the north bank of Sons Branch.

Many campers have used campsites located at the confluence, but these sites are now closed. The forest service now asks that campers stay 300 feet from any developed trail or road. Camping is not permitted within 100 feet of the base of cliff lines, or within rock shelters. There are other sites along Swift Camp Creek that are open to camping.

From the confluence, be sure to watch for white arrows to guide you down the next

Swift Camp Creek

section. Wriggle around two huge boulders in Sons Branch, then zigzag up and over a small bluff to end up beside Swift Camp Creek. The trail along the creek will be tougher than what you've experienced so far, and it is infrequently blazed. Instead of winding along the narrow creek bottom, the trail stays along the midslope above the creek's west bank.

Still there are cliff bands and small rockhouses and glimpses of the creek to entertain you. At 2.4 miles, there is a false trail on the right leading up to a rockhouse along a small branch. Swift Camp Creek Trail next takes a sharp turn to the left and switchbacks down to seasonal "Red Falls." At the falls, another small branch pours over the lip of a rusty iron-stained layer of sandstone.

You'll pass two more potential campsites between the trail and the creek before making an easy rock-hop over Wildcat Branch at 3.1 miles. From the Branch, climb to the signed junction with the Wildcat Trail (DBNF 228) at 3.2 miles. The sign indicates that Rock Bridge Picnic Area is 4.5 miles, and KY 715 is 2.9 miles via Swift Camp Creek Trail or 1.8 miles via Wildcat Trail. Turn right here to follow the Wildcat Trail.

You've got a steady 0.5-mile climb ahead before the trail levels out along the ridgetop at a closed campsite. The rest of the trail will follow long-abandoned dirt roads back to KY 715. There is an unmarked junction at 4.1 miles with an old road leading to the south. Its companion road to the north, just beyond, is hardly recognizable. Next, there is another road junction on the left leading to a private cemetery that is not part of the Wilderness Area. The dirt road beyond this junction is in better shape. Stay on the road until it reaches KY 715 at 4.5 miles. It is not necessary to make the left turn just before the road that keeps hikers on the Wildcat Trail until it reaches the Wildcat Trailhead.

Follow the Wildcat Trail to the end only if you have left a car at the Wildcat Trailhead.

From KY 715, turn right on the paved road and walk to the Angel Windows Trailhead at 5.2 miles. You can make the 0.5-mile round trip to the Windows on DBNF Trail 218, or continue straight to the Swift Camp Creek Trailhead at 5.5 miles.

The Clifty Wilderness was the second wilderness area to be designated in Kentucky. In 1985, the U.S. Congress protected almost all of the Red River Gorge east and north of KY 715 with this designation. At 12,646 acres, Clifty is almost three times as large as the state's other wilderness at Beaver Creek in the Somerset Ranger District. Designation as wilderness protects the area against activities such as logging, mining, or road building. Motorized vehicles and mechanical vehicles, such as mountain bikes, are also prohibited. The goal of wilderness management is to minimize human impact on the land and to allow the area to remain in a condition where people are only temporary visitors and they leave no impact on the land. The DBNF manages these areas at a more primitive level, so that these trails tend to be a bit more rugged and challenging than other hiking areas in the forest.

Other Hiking Options

1. Short and Sweet. The Angel Windows Trail (DBNF 218) is a 0.5-mile out-and-back hike to the Windows, which are a pair of small arches at the end of a narrow ridge. This would be a great hike when blackberries are in bloom.

2. The Sky Bridge Trail (DBNF 214) and Whistling Arch Trail (DBNF 234) are 0.9-mile and 0.2-mile walks easily accessible from KY 715 just north of the Swift Camp Creek Trailhead. Long, delicate Sky Bridge is one of the signature features of the Red River Gorge. The arch, and the views from it, shouldn't be missed.

3. An alternate, and longer, way to approach the loop is from Rock Bridge Road and Picnic Area and the south end of the Swift Camp Creek Trail. From the picnic area, the Wildcat Branch Trail is about a 4.5-mile walk.

4. The east end of the Rough Trail (DBNF 221) is also located at the Swift Camp Creek Trailhead. It is about 2.0 miles from the Trailhead to Chimney Top Road.

29

Gladie Creek Loop

Total Distance: A 9.2-mile loop on the Bison Way (DBNF 210), Sheltowee Trace (DBNF 100), Lost Branch (DBNF 239), and Osborne Bend (DBNF 240) Trails. Horses use part of the Lost Branch and Osborne Bend Trails. The loop includes a short walk on KY 715 between the two trailheads. It will be necessary to ford Gladie Creek if the water is high.

Hiking Time: About 5 hours

Location: Clifty Wilderness, Stanton Ranger District, about 11 miles northeast of Slade

Maps: USGS Slade; DBNF Red River Gorge Geological Area

The Clifty Wilderness north of the Red River is the focus of a current effort to expand the trail system in the wilderness. The Stanton Ranger District and a group of dedicated volunteers called the Red River Gorge Trail Crew are working to rehabilitate some long-abandoned trails around Osborne Bend. As of 2001, the group has reopened Trails 239, 240, and 241. These trails, when complete, will give hikers the long loops through the wilderness that make backpacking so rewarding.

Getting There

From Exit 40 from the Mountain Parkway, drive 1.3 miles west of KY 15 to the community of Pine Ridge. Turn right on KY 715 to the north. Drive 10.3 miles and park just beyond the bridge over Gladie Creek, at the signed trailhead. If you have two cars, leave the other one 1.4 miles back on KY 715 at a small turnout at the mouth of Sal Branch. The west end of Trail 240 is not yet marked with signs, but the trail can be seen emerging from the woods.

The Hike

Your loop starts on the first of the new trails in the Clifty Wilderness system. The Bison Way Trail (DBNF 210) connects the parking area near the Gladie Creek Bridge with the Sheltowee Trace Trail. The trail begins in a hardwood forest, interspersed with hemlock groves, typical of ridge areas in the Red River Gorge. Avoid a false trail that leads left where the trail makes a switchback to the right. The trail descends wooden steps to

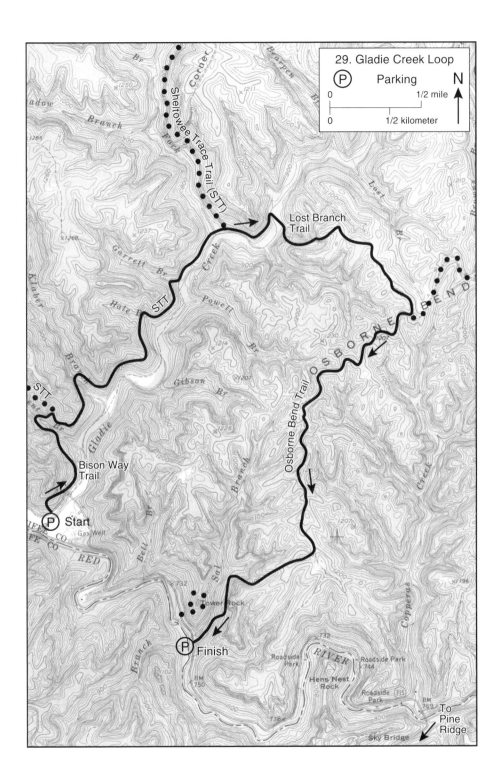

29. Gladie Creek Loop

Ⓟ Parking   N

0   1/2 mile

0   1/2 kilometer

Sheltowee Trace Trail (STT)

Lost Branch Trail

STT

OSBORNE BEND

Osborne Bend Trail

STT

Bison Way Trail

Ⓟ Start

Ⓟ Finish

To Pine Ridge

Sky Bridge

The historic Gladie Cabin

make a bridged crossing of Sargent Branch just before intersecting the Sheltowee Trace Trail at 0.6 mile.

Turn right on the wide Sheltowee Trace. Avoid another well-used false trail to the right and enter a grove of hemlocks. Notice how little vegetation grows underneath these trees. Hemlock needles, and the needles of other conifers, are highly acidic and so change the chemistry of the soil when they decompose. Conifers and a few other plants such as Christmas fern can grow in the acid soil, but many other plants cannot. The lack of underbrush allows the conifers and their allies to prosper, and not coincidentally attracts campers who much prefer open conifer groves to the brushy campsites in hardwood areas.

The trail next makes an easy crossing of Klaber Branch after a short, but steep, descent. At 1.8 miles, there is another false trail, presumably to a good fishing spot, to the right. The trail stays along contour, too high above the creek for summer viewing. Look for the large leaves of big-leaf magnolia. In summer, the light gray backs of these leaves provide the only break in the dense green carpet of the forest floor. You can tell big-leaf magnolia from other similar magnolias both by the size of the leaf and by looking for a small notch in the base of the leaf where it connects to the stem. Big-leaf and Fraser magnolias have this notch; other magnolias do not.

At 2.3 miles is a side trail to the left up to a nice campsite on a small bench. Water is just beyond at another small branch. At 3.0 miles, reach the huge sandy campsite at the confluence of Salt Fork and Gladie Creek. Don't be fooled by the wide, deep pool in the creek below the campsite. In most places the creek is less wide and more shallow. Rock-hop over Salt Fork and climb over the nose of a small ridge to the junction with the Lost Branch Trail at 3.3 miles. While the STT turns left and north at the junction, Lost

Branch goes right. Follow the white-blazed trail down to Gladie Creek, where it intersects a well-used horse trail along the river.

In 2001, the trail across the creek was difficult to follow. The absence of good blazing opportunities means that it is likely to remain so. A right turn at the 3.3-mile junction leads off the trail to a ford that will take you to a point opposite the large campsite at the confluence with Salt Fork. Instead, go left at the junction about 300 feet to the river to follow the correct trail. Ford the river to a point directly across on the far bank. If all goes well, you'll find a few blazes and a small campsite in the small stream valley on the far side.

The trail exits the valley with a sharp right turn and begins a steep climb. The trail climbs up a steep, rock-strewn mud slope, pockmarked with hoof prints and sprinkled with horse droppings. It's hard to imagine this steep narrow track was once a road, but soon irrefutable evidence appears. A long-abandoned sedan lies broken in two just off the trail. The car's snazzy red paint job, still intact, is a hint of its age—since Detroit can't seem to make a long-lasting car paint these days.

Soon the trail reaches the top of Osborne Bend Ridge and begins a level walk to a T-junction with the Osborne Bend Trail (DBNF 240) at 4.7 miles. The left branch turns east along Osborne Bend, taking most of the horse traffic with it. Though signed as Trail 239 in 2001, this is part of Trail 240. Your route goes right and follows the Osborne Bend Trail toward Tower Rock. The trail stays along the crest of this narrow ridge, except to make a few slight detours.

At 6.7 miles, blazes indicate a junction with an abandoned trail to the left. Soon you begin a steep descent toward Sal Branch. At the end of the step descent, turn left and travel above Sal Branch. Pass a concrete shed high above an overused campsite. Reach the unsigned end of the trail and KY 715 at 7.7 miles. If you were unable to leave a car here, you must walk 1.5 miles right on KY 715 to the Gladie Creek Parking Area.

Other Hiking Options

1. Short and Sweet. The Tower Rock Trail (DBNF 229) is one of the Red River Gorge's finest short walks. The 1.0-mile semi-loop climbs to the base of Tower Rock and then circles it. The entire loop offers views up the magnificent tower, which was the site of some of the gorge's earliest rock-climbing activity. Even if there are no climbers, see if you can spot some of the routes they use.

2. The Bison Way and Sheltowee Trace Trails can also be combined into 3.9-mile hike between trailheads that are 1.2 miles apart.

3. From the concrete bridge over the Red River at the eastern edge of the wilderness you can now combine the east leg of the Osborne Bend Trail with the new Brewers Shute Trail (DBNF 241) for about a 4-mile loop.

30

Sheltowee Trace and Tater Knob Loop

Total Distance: The 14.7-mile loop uses the Cave Run, Tater Knob Connector, Buck Creek, Sheltowee Trace, Buckskin, and Hog Pen Trails.

Hiking Time: This is a moderate overnight backpack or an 8-hour day hike

Location: Cave Run Lake–Pioneer Weapons Hunting Area, Morehead Ranger District, about 12 miles south of Salt Lick

Maps: USGS Salt Lick; Daniel Boone National Forest Cave Run Lake

The hiking trails around Cave Run Lake are some of the best and most extensive in the entire Daniel Boone National Forest. Here are trails both scenic enough for short journeys and long enough for overnight trips. This compact area has plenty of variety. There are hikes along the lakeshore, trails hugging the ridgetops, tremendous vistas, and opportunities for solitude.

Getting There

From the junction of US 60 and KY 211 drive 3.7 miles south on KY 211. Turn left on DBNF Road 129, which becomes Zilpo Scenic Byway. Drive 8.3 miles to a turnout at the gated end of DBNF Road 1058. Be sure not to block the gate. You can also access the loop by driving 0.5 mile farther on Zilpo Road and parking below the Tater Knob Tower. There are also other access points from Zilpo Road and at the Clear Creek Campground.

The Hike

The Sheltowee Trace–Tater Knob Loop explores the heart of the Cave Run Lake trail system. This loop is too long for most day hikers, but the area offers many other shorter options. Backpackers will enjoy the loop for its diversity, challenge, and scenery.

From the pullout at the end of gated DBNF Road 1058, look for the north end of the blue-blazed Cave Run Trail (DBNF 112) about 20 feet north of Zilpo Scenic Byway. Despite the proximity to the road, both deer and wild turkey are easily seen on this trail. The trail stays within 100 feet of the road for the first 0.4 mile, where it crosses the

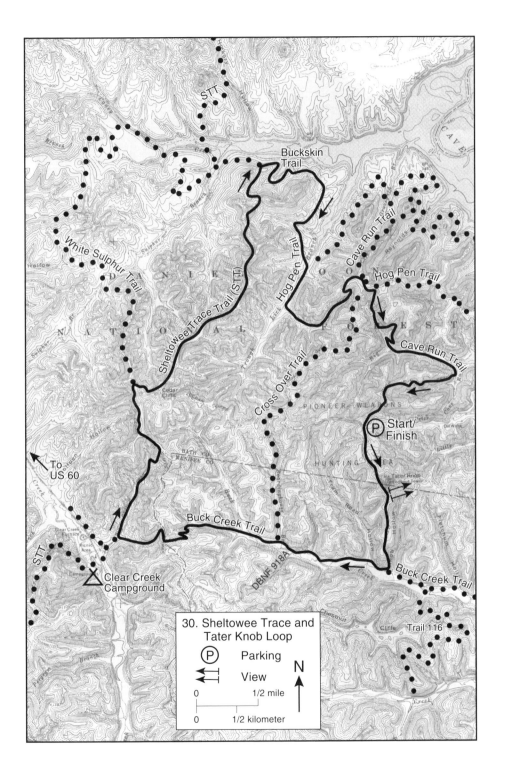

STT

Buckskin
Trail

Cave Run Trail

White Sulphur Trail

Hog Pen Trail

Hog Pen Trail

Sheltowee Trace Trail (STT)

Cave Run Trail

Cross Over Trail

Start/
Finish

To
US 60

STT

Buck Creek Trail

Clear Creek
Campground

DBNF 918A

Buck Creek Trail

Trail 116

30. Sheltowee Trace and
Tater Knob Loop

(P) Parking

View N

0   1/2 mile

0   1/2 kilometer

highway. Pass a roadside interpretive sign for the Tater Knob Fire Tower and reach the side trail to the tower at 0.7 mile.

Tater Knob Tower is a 1,000-foot long side trip up stairs and ladders. Only the shell of the lookout remains, but the views of the unbroken forest are as breathtaking as ever. Tater Knob was known until the 1930s for the small spring at its base. Then in 1934 the Civilian Conservation Corps went to work. To ferry supplies to the tower site nine men built a road (now the Tater Knob Connector Trail) to the site from Buck Creek in only six days. Think about that kind of productivity next time you're stuck in traffic behind one of those seemingly endless road construction projects. A new cab was added to the tower in 1959. The tower was manned until the mid-1970s, and was the last manned tower on the forest. It remains only one of two serviceable towers left in the forest.

From the tower, take the white-blazed Tater Knob Connector Trail (DBNF 104) south. The trail begins by following the ridge crest, but soon drops off the left side to arrive at a junction with the Buck Creek Trail (DBNF 118) at 1.4 miles. The orange-blazed Buck Creek Trail is an old road (formerly DBNF Road 1056). Turn right onto Buck Creek and enjoy some easy walking along the north side of the creek. You'll note that the Pioneer Weapons Wildlife Management Area supports a healthy wildlife population; flocks of turkey as large as 12 birds have been spotted along the trail. The trail near the creek can be wet, and there is one small stream that must be rock-hopped. Pass a large flat campsite to the left just before reaching a locked gate across the road at the junction with DBNF Road 918A at 2.2 miles.

Beyond Road 918A, the Buck Creek Trail has signs restricting use to foot travel only. The Crossover Trail (DBNF 107) splits

right to go up Boardinghouse Gulch. At 2.6 miles, make the first of several creek crossings. At the head of the creek, climb four switchbacks to reach Zilpo Road at 3.4 miles. From Zilpo Road descend steeply through some erosion gullies to a flat area that could be used as a campsite. Reach the junction with the Sheltowee Trace Trail at 4.0 miles.

To the left the Sheltowee Trace Trail leads 0.3 mile to the Clear Creek Campground, an alternate starting point for this loop. Your route keeps right and follows the turtle blazes of the Sheltowee Trace Trail. In 300 feet, hop over a small creek and reach another connector trail leading left to Clear Creek. Go right and follow the creek through a forest of maple, oak, beech, and sycamore. After climbing again to the ridgetop on switchbacks, reach the junction with the Buck Branch Connector at 4.8 miles. The connector leads right to a parking area on Zilpo Road. Next, turn right when the trail intersects an old dirt road on the ridgetop. Pass a small pond on your left, then turn left off the road at a point only 150 feet from Zilpo Road.

The trail next passes a research exclosure. Deer are fenced out of this area so that scientists can gather data on the effects of deer grazing by comparing the differences between forest plots where deer have, and have not, grazed. At 5.5 miles, reach the junction with the White Sulphur Horse Trail (DBNF 115). Keep right at this junction and stay on the Sheltowee Trace Trail. Beyond the junction is some prime ridgetop walking along the border of the Pioneer Weapons Wildlife Management Area. In the first saddle along the ridge one last connector trail leads back to Zilpo Road on the right. At 6.3 and 7.3 miles are open areas that have been used as campsites. The trail makes a few detours off the ridge crest to avoid climbs to

The view from Tater Knob

viewless knobs, but mostly you are free to enjoy that top-of-the-world feeling.

At 7.8 miles you reach a confusing junction. Two false trails to the right merge to form an unofficial shortcut down to Trough Lick Branch and the Buckskin Trail. Two other false trails also lead north and south along the ridge crest to the tops of small knobs. Follow the Sheltowee Trace Trail, which makes a sharp left downhill, and crosses the head of a small branch. At 8.4 miles, reach the official junction with the Buckskin Trail (DBNF 113). The Sheltowee Trace Trail turns left to reach Cave Run Dam in 5.5 miles. Your loop turns right onto the yellow-blazed Buckskin Trail. At 8.6 and 8.7 miles cross small streams above enticing lakeshore campsites. The trail continues through groves of hemlock and crosses several small branches. Just after passing the east end of the unofficial shortcut trail, reach the junction with the Hog Pen Trail (DBNF 106) at 9.9 miles.

Turn right onto the orange-blazed Hog Pen Trail and walk up Trough Lick Branch. The lower part of this trail is muddy and overgrown, but once the trail reaches its former start at 10.6 miles, and begins the climb toward the Crossover Trail, conditions improve dramatically. The climb is well graded even through the remarkable steep valley. Once you gain the ridge there is a dry campsite just short of a grassy, abandoned logging road. Pass a wildlife opening with a small pond to reach a four-way junction with the Cave Run Trail at 11.6 miles (DBNF 112).

Turn right at this junction onto the blue-blazed Cave Run Trail. Soon cross gravel DBNF Road 1225. The southern pine beetle has attacked the short-leaf pines on this ridgetop. You can tell the beetle-infested trees by the holes left behind by the boring insects. The valley of Big Cave Run is again remarkably steep, but your trail uses plenty of switchbacks to moderate the descent.

Sheltowee Trace and Tater Knob Loop

At 13.2 miles, reach the junction with the white-blazed connector trail that leads left 0.25 mile to the Buckskin Trail. To complete the loop, keep right and climb two pairs of switchbacks to reach the ridge crest. You'll cross one old logging road and then follow the crest, often on outcrops of bare limestone. At 14.7 miles close the loop when the trail intersects DBNF Road 1058, just short of Zilpo Road.

The Cave Run Dam on the Licking River was completed by the U.S. Army Corps of Engineers in 1969. The Corps transferred management of the area surrounding the 8,270-acre lake to the Daniel Boone National Forest. By the late 1970s, the forest began developing the area by replacing the former Cedar Cliffs Trail with paved Zilpo Road. The trail system was expanded from 20 miles in the late 1970s to cover over 50 miles today. There are now campgrounds at Zilpo, Clear Creek Lake, and Twin Knobs with a combined 400 campsites, in addition to the horse camp at White Sulphur.

The Pioneer Weapons Wildlife Management Area consists of 7,480 acres south of Cave Run Lake that are comanaged by the forest and Kentucky Department of Fish and Wildlife Resources. In the Pioneer Weapons Area, hunters are limited to primitive weapons such as bows or black-powder guns. Wild turkey and white-tailed deer are the primary game. All trails in the Pioneer Weapons Area are open to horses and mountain bikes. OHVs are prohibited on all the hiking trails around Cave Run Lake.

Other Hiking Options

1. Short and Sweet. To hike to the Tater Knob Tower and back is about a 0.5-mile round trip.

2. The Leatherwood Loop Trail (DBNF 116A) is a new 3.3-mile loop off Leatherwood Road (DBNF Road 129) in the south part of the trail system.

3. On the north side of Cave Run Lake, the Caney Loop (DBNF 1226) and Sheltowee Trace Trails can be combined into an 8.8-mile loop.

Daniel Boone Country–North

31

Carter Caves Cross-Country Trail (4C's)

Total Distance: A 7.8-mile loop hike that is also partly in the Tygart State Forest

Hiking Time: About 4 hours

Location: Carter Caves State Resort Park, about 7 miles northeast of Olive Hill

Maps: USGS Wesleyville, Tygarts Valley, Grahn, and Olive Hill; Carter Caves Hiking Trails

Carter Caves is one of the state's oldest and most popular parks. Though the caves are the park's biggest draws, there are also exciting backcountry trails that visit stately arches and rockhouses reminiscent of Red River Gorge or the Big South Fork.

Getting There

From Exit 161 off I-64, drive east on US 60 to the intersection with KY 182. Turn north on KY 182 and drive 2.8 miles north to the park entrance. Turn left into the park and drive 1.0 mile to the welcome center.

The Hike

The 4C's Trail explores both the front-country highlights and quiet backcountry of 1,800-acre Carter Caves State Resort Park. If you add in the very short side trip to Raven Rock, you will pass three sandstone arches in addition to crossing a state nature preserve and crossing the outlet of Smoky Valley Lake. This hike can be done as a long day hike, or you can make it an easy overnight hike by using the Johnson Homeplace Backcountry Campsite. Overnight campers will need to get a permit from the park welcome center.

From the far end of the welcome center parking area, walk toward X Cave. In 150 feet, reach the start of both the 4C's and the Horn Hollow Trails. The trails split in another 100 feet, at a point just above the cave. Beyond, the 4C's is marked with white and orange blazes and an occasional "4C's" diamond.

At 0.5 mile the trail crosses below a small, intermittent pour-over waterfall. At 0.8

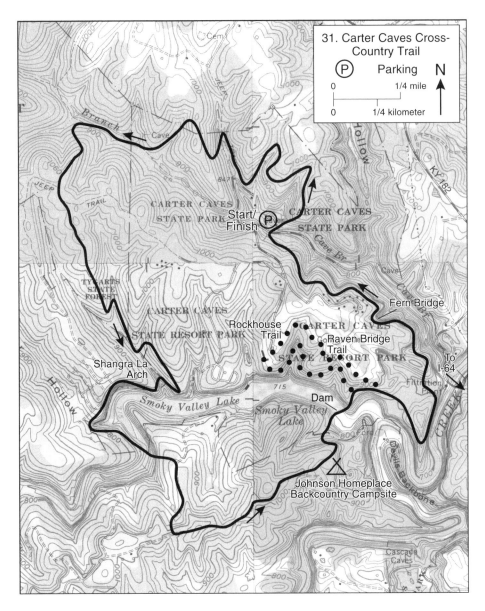

31. Carter Caves Cross-Country Trail

Ⓟ Parking   N

0   1/4 mile

0   1/4 kilometer

Start/Finish Ⓟ

Fern Bridge

Rockhouse Trail

Raven Bridge Trail

Shangra La Arch

Smoky Valley Lake

Dam

Smoky Valley Lake

To I-64

Johnson Homeplace Backcountry Campsite

mile, the trail intersects an old jeep road. To the left the road leads 500 feet to the paved picnic shelter road. To the right the trail enters the Carter Caves State Nature Preserve. Two small tracts, totaling 146 acres, within the park are managed as preserves to protect the federally endangered Indiana Bat and two plants rare in Kentucky, the mountain maple and Canadian yew.

Reach a mowed area in a meadow at 1.3 miles. To the left the park maintenance area is only 500 feet away. To the right the trail passes through a meadow blessed with plentiful sunlight. Queen Ann's lace, butterfly milkweed, thistle, and black-eyed Susan are some of the summer flowers you may find here. At the end of the meadow the road splits. A yellow-blazed trail leads right to the closed Indiana bat cave. The 4C's trail takes the left branch.

At 1.5 miles, leave the nature preserve in a stream bottom at an intersection with the Kiser Trail. Here a sign also indicates that the 4C's was once part of the Jenny Wiley Trail. From the stream climb to an old road by a campsite on the ridgetop. At 1.9 miles cross a maintained gravel road. Just beyond the road is a junction with the now-abandoned Simon Kenton Trail, which used to connect with the Jenny Wiley Trail. From this point on, the 4C's Trail will have white blazes only.

The 4C's Trail next turns right onto an old dirt road that it follows through a hardwood forest dominated by oak, maple, and beech trees. This is a good spot to look for animals both fast and slow of foot. White-tailed deer and box turtles are both common. Soon turn off the ridgetop and make another intersection with the yellow-blazed Kiser Trail at 2.5 miles.

Come to Shangra La Arch at 3.0 miles. The arch seems more like a long natural tunnel. It is roughly 50 feet long but only 6 feet high and 8 feet wide. The top of the arch is formed from a thick layer of massive sandstone. You can see from the debris at the base of the arch that the sandstone layers below the arch were much thinner. Just below the arch there is a small, wet-weather waterfall. Beyond the arch, sneak between the cliff and a huge boulder, and then walk along the base of the cliffs.

At 3.1 miles, reach an unsigned trail junction with two side trails to Smoky Valley Lake. The more worn of the trails on the left leads to the paved access road to a boat ramp; the 4C's Trail makes a sharp right at

the junction and follows the lakeshore below a cliff band. Cross two small side streams before reaching Smoky Creek at 3.8 miles. The creek must be forded when water is high, but probably can be rock-hopped at drier times. In 2001, the state trail crew was building a swinging bridge over the creek upstream of the current crossing. When complete this bridge will provide a dry crossing, but will lengthen the trail by about 0.5 mile.

The current route climbs a steep, rocky road along the park boundary beyond the crossing. Ignore two forks to the right. About 75 feet past the second fork, you arrive at a T-junction with a dirt road. Go past an old stock pond on the left, and then begin to descend again down the nose of a small ridge. Then turn right off the old road. The trail alternates through open, grassy areas and patches of mixed pine and hardwood forest, which has a thick cover of ground cedar. Pass a small rockhouse to the right of the trail and arrive at the Johnson Homeplace Backcountry Campsite at 5.1 miles.

The campsite has a grassy, flat area for tents and a small rock shelter, but no water or latrine. To stay at the campsite it is necessary to get a permit from the park welcome center. From the campsite the 4C's Trail descends toward the outlet of Smoky Valley Lake. When you reach the cascades at the base of the spillway of the dam, turn sharp left, cross the creek, and climb toward the dam. On the far side of the dam, reach a swinging bridge over the main spillway at 5.7 miles.

Turn left after crossing the spillway and begin a short, but steep climb to the base of the bluff line. Pass two tiny arches before climbing a flight of stairs that offers good views of Smoky Valley Lake. At 5.9 miles reach a signed junction with the red-blazed Rockhouse Trail. Go right at this junction to

A fallen tree in Box Canyon

reach a junction with the blue-blazed Raven Bridge Trail. Just 100 feet to the left, and barely out of sight, is Raven Bridge. This short side trail leads to a classic stone arch that formed in a narrow neck of a sandstone ridge.

The 4C's Trail continues right from the junction with the Raven Bridge Trail. The trail follows just below the rim along contour. Notice how many of the trees along the way have grown to diameters of 3 feet or more. Some of these trees must be survivors of the early logging days. At 6.9 miles, reach the wooden walkway under Fern Bridge.

Fern is the largest of the bridges along the loop, stretching nearly 150 feet long and towering 84 feet high. The bridge formed from rock that has separated from the main cliff face, similar to Split Bow Arch in the Big South Fork. Someday this could be a double arch. There is another alcove behind the arch that may also separate from

the main cliff band along a joint set where you can see water slowly dripping.

Beyond the arch climb up sets of both wooden and stone steps to reach a junction with the side trail to the cottages in 300 feet. Keep right at this junction and walk along the rim while enjoying some more huge trees. Cross two wooden bridges before descending to the park road at the entrance to Saltpeter Cave. Reach the parking area and close the loop at 7.8 miles.

Carter Cave State Resort Park offers a full range of services. There is a lodge, dining room, cottages, and campground. You can also boat or fish on Smoky Valley Lake. In addition to the guided cave tours, rangers also lead canoe trips on Tygarts Creek.

No one should visit this park without taking one of the cave tours. Tours of Cascade, X, and Saltpetre caves are offered frequently in the summer. Some summer tours of Bat Cave also may be scheduled. You must buy tickets for the tours beforehand at the welcome center. All tours are guided, charge a small fee, and take close to an hour. The happy coincidence of caves and arches in the area is in part the result of the stratigraphy of the geology here. The top rock layer is the Pennsylvanian Lee sandstone, the same rock type that forms the rock arches at the Big South Fork and Red River Gorge. Below the Lee are the Chester and St. Genevieve limestones, which are the hosts for the caves. The park contains at least six major caves, plus some smaller ones surrounding Cascade Cave.

Other Hiking Options

1. Short and Sweet. The Box Canyon Trail is a 0.8-mile semi-loop that starts near the entry to Cascade Cave. Though most folks use it to pass time waiting for their cave tour, it is a worthy destination in its own right. The sheer walls and alcoves in the canyon are the highlights of the scenery.

2. The Raven Bridge Trail leads 0.7 mile to Raven Bridge from Caveland Lodge.

3. The Horn Hollow Trail is a 2.5-mile loop that starts from the park welcome center.

4. The Three Bridges Trail is a 3.3-mile loop that passes Fern, Raven, and Smoky bridges. The last 2 miles of this loop follows the 4C's Trail.

5. The Kiser Hollow Multiuse Trail is a 10-mile loop through the park and Tygarts State Forest that begins at the riding stables. The trail was constructed in 2000 and is administered by Carter Caves State Park.

32

Michael Tygart Loop Trail

Total Distance: A 10.1-mile semi-loop trail that uses a short section of a gravel road and a paved road.

Hiking Time: About 5 hours

Location: Greenbo Lake State Resort Park, about 19 miles north of Grayson

Maps: USGS Old Town and Argillite; Greenbo Lake State Resort Park Trails Guide

Greenbo Lake State Park is known primarily for the fishing and boating on 225-acre Greenbo Lake. But the park has a lot to offer hikers, include a rare long loop with backcountry camping options for overnight trips.

Getting There

From Exit 172 off I-64 in Grayson, drive 15.1 miles north on KY 1 to KY 1711. Turn left onto KY 1711 and drive 2.7 miles to Buffalo Furnace Cemetery. Turn right at the cemetery and drive 0.8 mile to Jesse Stuart Lodge. Park in the far end of the lodge parking area.

The Hike

The Michael Tygart Loop Trail is one of the rare Kentucky state park hiking trails that is long enough for overnight trips. The loop is both diverse and scenic, visiting forests, creeks, and Greenbo Lake. Day hikers can shorten the loop to 7.5 miles by starting near Buffalo Cemetery.

Start the hike by the large signboard at the far end of the Jesse Stuart Lodge parking area. The trail begins as a wide gravel road, and you'll see both yellow blazes and interpretive markers for the interpretive Fern Valley Trail. At 0.2 mile the trails split. The Fern Valley Trail goes right and the Tygart Trail goes left.

From the split, cross a small stream and turn left off the dirt road where a sign indicates that mountain bikes are prohibited from the trail. Here the forest is mostly hardwood; American beech, sugar maple, and

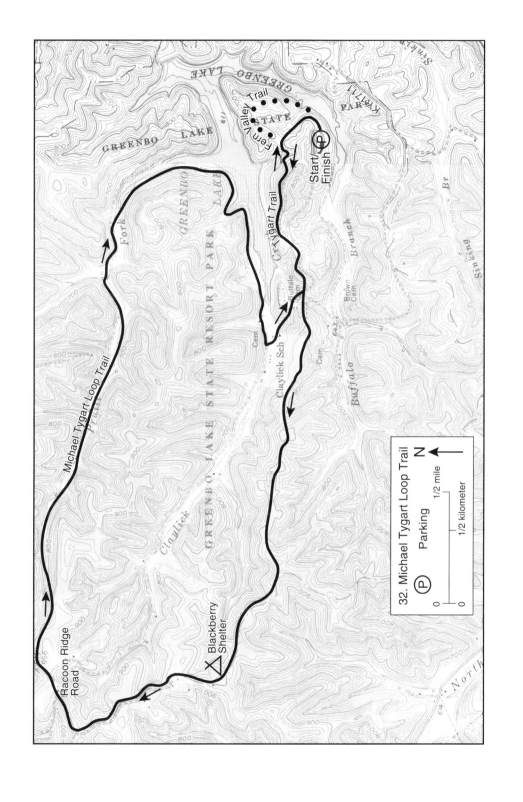

GREENBO LAKE

Fern Valley Trail

STATE

KENTUCKY

PARK

Sinking Br

Senkri

Start/
Finish

GREENBO LAKE

Br

Tygart Trail

Fork

GREENBO LAKE STATE RESORT PARK

Buffalo

Buffalo

Brown
Cem

Branch

Michael Tygart Loop Trail

Pruitt

Cem

Claylick Sch

Cem

643

Claylick

Buffalo

Blackberry
Shelter

Racoon Ridge
Road

956

North

32. Michael Tygart Loop Trail

Ⓟ Parking

N

| 0 | 1/2 mile |
| 0 | 1/2 kilometer |

oaks are the most common trees. At 1.3 miles, reach a thick stand of pine trees and cross the paved road to the campground and boat dock near the split with the road to Jesse Stuart Lodge.

Just beyond the road is the Buffalo Furnace Cemetery, which was established in 1851. Family names here include Kidd, Burton, and Kilburn. Buffalo Furnace smelted iron from 1818 until 1856. The remains of the furnace are along the park entrance road beside Buffalo Branch. You may also spot deer, who like to feed at the edge of the cemetery. From the cemetery, climb up the crest of a small ridge, and then keep to the ridge crest under an open hardwood forest with scattered pines. At 2.0 miles, come to a side trail leading right to some small pits where iron ore was mined in the 1800s to feed Buffalo Furnace. These long, shallow pits look like short sections of long-abandoned rail lines. The side trail will rejoin the main trail, so you don't have to retrace your steps if you visit the pits.

At 2.5 miles, come to the first of three old mileposts along the trail. This is the 6-mile post. You'll later see 5- and 3-mile posts, which give the distance to the park marina. The trail remains on the ridgetop until it joins an old road in an area filled with blackberry and sumac. A slight detour to the right side of the ridge brings you to Blackberry Shelter at 3.0 miles. Other shelters indicated on the trail signs here were part of the Jenny Wiley Trail system and have been abandoned. Blackberry is a three-sided Adirondack shelter similar to those used along the famous Appalachian Trail. Though the structure is in good shape, careless travelers have left their garbage behind. There is no drinking water or latrine at the shelter. To use the shelter overnight you must register at the front desk of Jesse Stuart Lodge.

Beyond the shelter, the Tygart Trail, marked with yellow blazes, splits right from the dirt road (marked with blue blazes) and parallels it about 50 feet to the right. The trail leaves the ridge crest to the right and crosses a very old road, then under a power line. The trail shadows a gravel road, and makes another power-line crossing in thick pines, before reaching gravel Raccoon Ridge Road at 4.2 miles. Turn right onto the gravel road and ignore the first side road leading right. At 4.7 miles turn right off the road near the 4-mile signpost. The trail passes a field on the right, then turns left to descend steeply off the ridge crest to reach Pruitt Fork Creek.

The dark, moist forest alongside Pruitt Fork Creek can produce prodigious numbers of mosquitoes, so it's a good idea to have some repellent, or you'll have to move fast in the summer here. Besides the pesky bugs, the creek supports prolific understory vegetation, including Christmas fern, ground cedar, poison ivy, sassafras, and tulip poplar. In pre-park times several families lived along the creek and you may see relics of their homes. But the lush forest is rapidly reclaiming these signs of habitation. Occasionally in summer, the dense bottom growth totally blocks views of the creek. At 6.2 miles make an easy crossing to the left bank of Pruitt Creek. You'll cross one side branch before returning to the right bank at 6.6 miles.

Just beyond will be the first views of Greenbo Lake and a large campsite. Lucky hikers can enjoy some bird-watching and may even spot a great blue heron here. Beyond the campsite, the Tygart Trail follows the lakeshore closely, offering you nearly constant views and allowing you to keep in touch with how the bass are biting. Since you left the mosquitoes behind at Pruitt Fork Creek, a quick swim stop is no

Buffalo Iron Furnace

problem. Watch the lakeshore trees carefully for signs of beaver.

At 8.2 miles reach the accessible fishing pier located in another pine grove. Walk along the park road past both the marina and the campground road back to the road junction near Buffalo Furnace Cemetery at 8.8 miles. At the junction, turn left onto the trail and retrace the first 1.3 miles of the hike back to the parking area.

In addition to the hiking trails and the lodge, the park offers camping and picnic areas, a dining room, tennis courts, and boat and canoe rentals. The Jesse Stuart Lodge is named for the famous Greenup County native and Kentucky poet laureate, who lived just north of the park.

Other Hiking Options

1. Short and Sweet. The Fern Valley Trail is a 1.1-mile interpretive loop that also starts at the Jesse Stuart Lodge. You can check out the interpretive guide from the front desk of the lodge.

2. The Jesse Stuart State Nature Preserve is located just 6 miles north of the park, near Greenup on KY 1. The preserve contains about 3 miles of trails.

IV

Bluegrass Heartland

33

Main Trail

Total Distance: A 1.7-mile loop for hikers

Hiking Time: About 1 hour

Location: Boone County Cliffs State Nature Preserve, about 6 miles west of Burlington

Maps: USGS Rising Sun

This 74-acre pocket preserve is known for its prolific spring wildflower displays, festive fall foliage, and rocky cliffs formed from glacial conglomerate. But at any time of year it is a pleasant walk and a welcome escape into serene woodlands. This small space packs a powerful biological punch. More than 300 species of flowers, ferns, trees, and shrubs have been recorded in the preserve. More than 90 species of birds have been sighted here.

Getting There

From Exit 181 off I-75 take KY 18 for 10.7 miles west through Burlington. Turn left at a sign for Middle Creek Road. Drive for 1.7 miles east on this narrow, twisty paved road to the gravel trailhead on the north side of the road.

The Hike

The Main Trail begins at the west side of the parking area, is marked with orange blazes, and follows a well-defined footpath. Be sure to observe the signs instructing you to stay on the trail to preserve fragile plant habitats. In a short distance from the parking area the trail splits into a loop that will encircle the headwaters of this tributary of Middle Creek. Go right at the split to follow the loop counterclockwise. At 0.2 mile the trail climbs to an outcrop of conglomerate where a short side trail leads left to an overlook above the creek. These outcrops are your best chance to observe the preserve's namesake cliffs.

A conglomerate is a type of rock composed of fragments of other rock that have been recemented together. Conglomerates can form by several processes; one common conglomerate forms from the debris left behind by glaciers. The fragments in glacial conglomerates consist of pieces of various rock types that have been eroded from the previous path of the glacier. Some of the fragments in this conglomerate originated as far north as Canada. The matrix, or the material that holds the fragments together, is usually the very small remains of rocks that have been pulverized by the glacier. At the Boone County Cliffs, the conglomerate is composed of small fragments in a muddy brown matrix. The rock was deposited 700,000 years ago, during the last glacial period—very recently in geologic time.

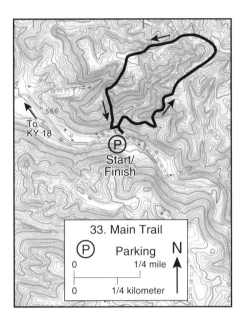

At 0.3 mile, reach the north end of the closed East Boundary Trail. The mature open forest contains sugar maple, beech, basswood, white oak, white ash, and slippery elm trees. The smooth gray bark of mature beech trees can be too much for vandals to resist. One small ridgetop grove is marred by carvings of names and initials left by thoughtless visitors. Beechnuts are an important food source for bear, deer, squirrels, and wild turkeys and were an important food for some Native Americans. Beech leaves have large curved teeth and are deeply furrowed. Perhaps the best time to learn to recognize the leaves is in the winter. When most trees have dropped all their leaves, many young beeches keep their wrinkled brown ones.

At 0.8 mile, the trail crosses the head of the small creek, still following the ridge crest. Leave the ridgetop at 1.5 miles and descend toward Middle Creek. The trail ends at the west end of the parking area after descending nearly to the road and crossing the stream.

The Kentucky State Nature Preserves Commission was created in 1976 to help protect the state's natural heritage. The commission seeks to find, acquire, and manage lands containing rare native species, rare natural communities, and special natural features. Through extensive survey work, the commission has helped many landowners protect significant natural sites. The commission manages 41 preserves, some in conjunction with either the Nature Conservancy or the Kentucky Department of Parks. While some preserves are too sensitive to be opened to the general public, others such as Boone County Cliffs and Bad Branch provide environmental education and recreation opportunities as well as established hiking trails.

The first 46 acres of Boone County Cliffs was purchased by the Nature Conservancy in 1974, when it became the Kentucky chapter's first preserve. Two important and sensitive species of salamanders live in the small creek on the property.

Other Hiking Options

1. Short and Sweet. A round-trip hike to the conglomerate cliffs and overlook is only 0.5 mile. There are no other hiking trails at the preserve. The former East Boundary Trail is permanently closed due to erosion problems.

2. The 107-acre Dinsmore Woods State Nature Preserve is located on KY 18 just west of the junction with Middle Creek Road. The preserve is open to day use only and has a short hiking trail. Hikers may park in the county parking lot across the road from the preserve.

34

Big Bone Creek and Bison Trace Trails

Total Distance: A 0.9-mile loop, part of which is handicapped accessible

Hiking Time: About 45 minutes

Location: Big Bone Lick State Park, about 8 miles west of Walton

Maps: USGS Union and Rising Sun; Big Bone Lick State Park Map

Big Bone Lick State Park offers hikers a pair of features unique to state parks in this region. First, there is a diorama showing how so many fossilized bones of prehistoric creatures came to be found in one place at Big Bone Lick. Second, there is a chance to observe some modern wildlife in the pen that contains middle Kentucky's only public bison herd. The opportunity to combine these two treats on an easy hiking trail is too good to pass up.

Getting There

Turn off I-75 at Exit 171. Follow KY 1292 west 5.4 miles to a four-way junction with US 127/42 and KY 338. Continue west on KY 338 for 3.2 miles to reach the signed entrance to Big Bone Lick State Park. Enter the park and drive 0.3 mile. Turn right on the road to the park museum. You'll reach the trailhead in 0.5 mile at a parking area for the museum.

The Hike

If you're like most hikers, you want to be on the trail as soon as possible after reaching a trailhead. But at Big Bone Lick, some patience will be rewarded, especially if you take the time to visit the park museum to educate yourself on the role that this site has played in the development of American paleontology. In 2001, the museum entry fee was only $1. The displays of arrowheads, a bison skeleton, and a mastodon head are well worth the price.

Start hiking at the large signboard for the Big Bone Creek Trail in front of the

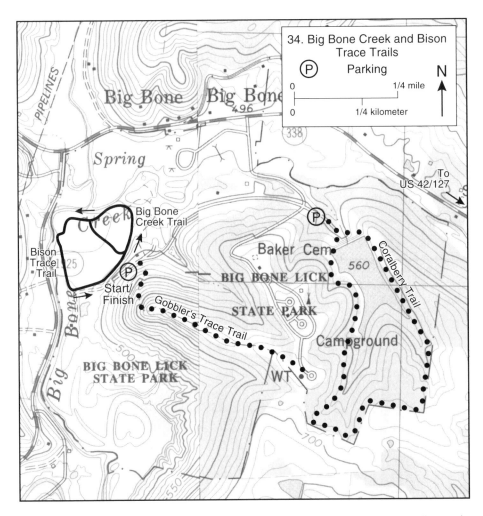

museum. You'll want to take the side trail over to the bog diorama, where full-scale models of mastodons, mammoths, and sloths are shown in the predicaments that led to the preservation of so many bones at this site. Where the trail forks below the diorama, go right to follow the longer loop around. The connector trail to the left cuts directly to the bison fence in 0.2 mile.

Other side trails off the main trail lead to displays about the culture of the native Shawnee people, the history of salt making at Big Bone Lick, and the geology and

paleontology of the park. At 0.4 mile, reach the fence around the bison coral, and the far end of the connector trail. The Big Bone Creek Trail to this point is paved and is wheelchair accessible.

The park's bison herd is a living symbol of both the area's close and distant pasts. Bison of today are similar to, but not exactly the same as, the bison that were trapped in the salt licks in prehistoric time. But these are the same animals that were still found on the American frontier as late as the 1700s. Wild bison were exterminated by hunting across the eastern United States, but recently small herds have been returned to public areas such as Big Bone Lick and the Land between the Lakes. The Big Bone bison herd has been a remarkable success. In 2001, the herd numbered 14 animals, and included several of the small cinnamon-colored calves. The bison graze in two plots that total 19 acres and are supplemented with feed and salt blocks. Since the project started in 1990, the population has grown enough so that some bison were exported to the Salato Wildlife Center (formerly called the State Game Farm).

Though less active at midday, these rugged grazers will feed continuously. Bison add an extra layer of fur to keep warm in winter, then shed the layer by summertime. If any of the animals look especially shaggy, don't worry about their health; they may just be shedding their winter coats.

Start on the Bison Trace Trail by following the mowed path around the corral. This path will eventually lead to a dirt road that takes hikers past the entrance to the main corral. Beyond the main corral, the road turns to gravel, and then to pavement, before you close the loop by the museum at 0.9 mile.

Big Bone Lick is known as the birthplace of American vertebrate paleontology and was one of the country's most important fossil sites. The first recorded visit was in 1739 by French soldiers, who wrote that huge bones were found scattered all over the ground. The bones of giant mammoths, mastodons, ground sloths, and bison were found in huge quantities. The animals were originally attracted to the site by the salty mineral springs. The bones date from the ice age 12,000 to 20,000 years ago, a time of much colder temperatures when the region was covered by boreal spruce forests, much like the climate of today's Canada or today's 6,000-foot-high mountains in the Smokies. These animals were driven south by advancing ice sheets, which reached approximately the present location of the Ohio River.

Scientists aren't now sure if the animals simply became trapped in the boggy ground around the springs or if some already dead animals were washed together by small streams to concentrate the deposits of bones. In either case, the bones must have been quickly covered, because they were preserved under layers of dirt before they decomposed.

The first major collection of bones occurred in 1765 by a party led by George Croghan. In those times before the scientific value of leaving fossils in place was realized, the bones were simply hauled off the site, perhaps to be studied in a faraway museum. Both Thomas Jefferson and Benjamin Franklin acquired bones collected from Big Bone Lick. However, in the late 1700s the primary value of the site was for salt making from the mineral-laden springs. By the early 1800s some developers touted the curative properties of the mineral springs. Health spas thrived at Big Bone Lick until the Civil War.

Though major fossil collections had been made at the site beginning in the 1800s, it was not until 1962 that a systematic paleontological excavation was carried out. From 1962 to 1966 the University of Nebraska State Museum worked at the site with several partners, including the Kentucky State Department of Parks. An archeological dig at the site, designed to study the activities of late Archaic Indians was carried out at the park in 1982 by the University of Kentucky Department of Anthropology. The park's junior curator program recently excavated artifacts dating back to the 1760s at the site of one of the old bathhouses.

Other Hiking Options

1. Short and Sweet. A quick trip via the connector trail to the bison corral is only a 0.6-mile round trip.

2. The Gobblers Trace Trail is a useful 0.6-mile connection between the park campground and museum. This trail also connects to the Coralberry Trail via an unmarked trail that leads east from the water tower along the park boundary fence.

3. The Coralberry Trail is a 2.0-mile loop that leaves from the lake access parking area. Because the trail is difficult to follow, it should only be attempted by experienced or adventurous hikers. Many trails used by fisherman lead directly around the lake.

35

Scotts Gap Loop Trail

Total Distance: A 3.5-mile loop on a hiking trail. Mountain bikes are prohibited from all park trails. Pets must be leashed at all times.

Location: Jefferson County Memorial Forest, south of Louisville, in Fairdale

Maps: USGS Valley Station; Jefferson County Memorial Forest Scott Gap Loop Trail Map

The Jefferson County Memorial Forest is a remarkable 5,400-acre area located just outside the I-265 beltway south of Louisville. The forest is dedicated to the area's war veterans, and is used for a variety of public educational and recreation programs. There are trails in four sections of the forest, three of which are open to the general public. The Scotts Gap Loop is a special delight because of its prolific spring and summer wildflower display and for the historic Plymouth half-buried along the route.

Getting There

From Exit 3 on I-265 (Gene Snyder Parkway), drive south 0.7 mile on Stonecrest Road to Blevins Gap Road. Turn right on Blevins Gap Road and drive 3.2 miles southwest to Scotts Gap Road. Turn left on Scotts Gap Road and drive 0.9 mile to the trailhead, which is located just beyond the western end of the signed Siltstone Ridge Trail. The small parking area is located on the west side of the road.

The Hike

From the far right end of the parking area hike through a gate and begin climbing Miller Hill. The trail is well marked with red paint blazes. Watch carefully to avoid the prolific poison ivy along the start of the trail. The three-leaved menace is in stiff competition here with the benign five-leaved Virginia creeper, which is also an important ground cover. At 0.1 mile, reach the start of the loop and turn right to follow the loop clockwise. Reaching the crest of the ridge earns

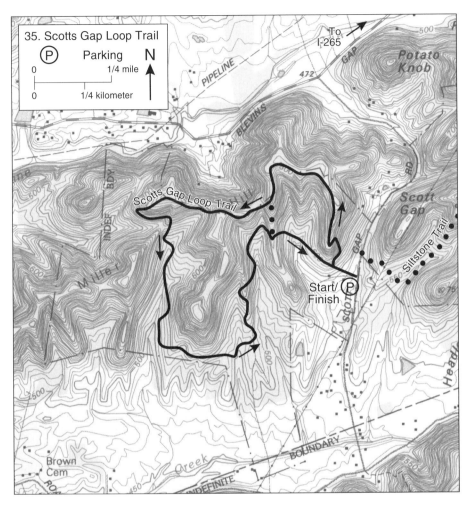

the small reward of a tree-shrouded view. The ridgetop is covered in hardwood, including sugar maple and redbud. Purple redbud blossoms compete with the blossoms of dogwoods and some other domesticated trees to be the first sign of approaching spring. The buds appear well before the smooth, heart-shaped leaves. Later the trees produce a long stringbean-shaped fruit. Some of the common spring wildflowers that you might see along the trail include mayapple, fire pink, wild geranium, chickweed, spring beauty, red trillium,

bluets, rue anemone, hepatica, foamflower, and blue violet.

At 0.8 mile, reach a signed junction with a shortcut trail leading left. The main trail continues along the crest of Miller Hill, but does not appear too heavily used and may be a bit brushy. Look for zigzag spiderwort and the light blue heads of common fleabane here. At 1.4 miles, drop off the right side of the ridge onto a drier slope covered in oak trees. Look here for the bright orange heads of butterfly milkweed. According to Randy Seymour, in *Wildflowers of Mammoth*

A small ravine along the Mitch McConnell Loop Trail

Cave National Park, the roots of this plant were used by Native Americans to treat respiratory diseases and the plant was also used to treat cuts, bruises, and sores.

The trail then begins to follow a tributary of Brier Creek. True to form, there are some briers and nettles mixed with Christmas fern and mayapple. This stretch is a favorite of box turtles, who favor the trail's easy terrain over other cross-country routes. After leaving this branch and swinging around the base of Miller Hill, at 2.5 miles you come to one of the trail's most amazing sites. In a deep but narrow draw, half buried in decades of debris, is the body of an old Plymouth automobile. At one time this small stream must have been accessible by car, and probably marked the edge of some farmer's field. Looking at the area now, it is just as easy to believe the car fell here from the sky.

After leaving the vehicle behind, climb up and over a small ridge, then follow up another small branch of Brier Creek. Cross two log bridges along the trail in small draws that again have a few nettles. At 3.1 miles, reach the other end of the 0.2-mile connector trail at an unsigned junction. Keep right to avoid repeating your loop. At 3.4 miles, reach the end of the loop and descend to the trailhead at 3.5 miles.

The Jefferson County Memorial Forest is open for day use only. The Scotts Gap Loop was closed for nearly a year after a powerful windstorm lashed the area in May 1998 and felled many trees at the top of Miller Hill.

Other Hiking Options

1. Short and Sweet. Using the connector trail to short-circuit the main loop is a 1.4-mile trip.

2. The most popular hike in the forest is probably the 6.2-mile Siltstone Trail between Scotts Gap and the forest Welcome Center near Holsclaw Hill. The entire trail requires either a car shuttle, or a 12.4-mile round trip. Shorter variations include using the Tulip Tree Trail and park road for a 1-mile loop, or exiting the trail at Jefferson Hill Road (2 miles from the Welcome Center) or Bearcamp Road (3 miles from the Welcome Center). However, there is no parking at these other road crossings.

3. The third park hiking area is the Paul Yost Recreation Area, which contains the Mitch McConnell Loop Trail. This 5.6-mile loop has several short connectors that make shorter trips possible. The McConnell Trail is intertwined with a horse trail, and separating these routes can be difficult.

36

Tioga Falls National Recreation Trail

Total Distance: A 2.0-mile loop on a foot trail

Hiking Time: About 1.5 hours

Location: U.S. Army Center and Fort Knox, about 6 miles north of Fort Knox

Maps: USGS Fort Knox; Tioga Falls National Recreation Trail

The Fort Knox Military Reservation contains two National Recreation trails possessing very different characters. The Tioga Falls Trail is a loop on foot trails leading to Tioga Falls. The Bridges to the Past Trail is an abandoned paved road that dead-ends at the boundary of the military reservation. Both are fairly heavily used, but offer quick and convenient escapes into the woods. Both are also interpretive trails. You should call ahead to the Fort Knox Hunt Control Office to get the interpretive brochures and to find out when the trails may be closed due to hunting season or military training.

Getting There

From the junction of US 31 West and KY 44 just south of Louisville, drive 4.5 miles south on US 31 West. Make a left turn onto a narrow paved road at a sign for Fort Duffield and Bridges to the Past. Follow the road to the large parking area for Bridges to the Past and Tioga Falls. From the parking area, the left fork is the Bridges to the Past Trail and the right fork is Railroad Trestle Road.

The Hike

The Tioga Falls Trail begins in back of the large signboard at the end of the parking area, to the right of the railroad trestle. Follow the foot trail for 0.1 mile, then cross a small stream on a footbridge. For its first half, the Tioga Falls Trail follows the route of the old Muldraugh Road through a thin strip between the railroad on the left and a paved road on the right. At 0.4 mile, join the railroad tracks and walk alongside them for

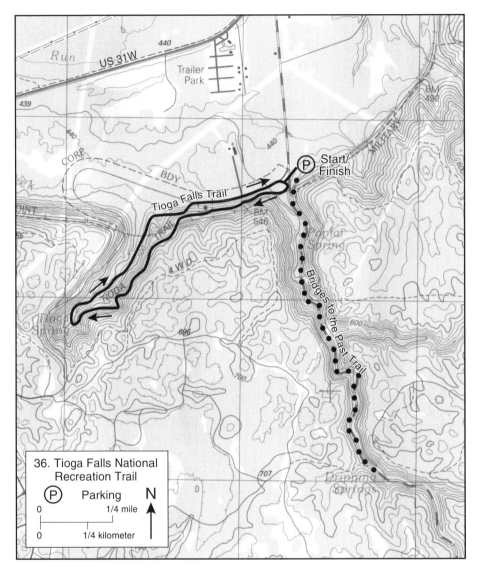

36. Tioga Falls National Recreation Trail

P Parking

N

0   1/4 mile

0   1/4 kilometer

100 feet before exiting into the woods on the left. Exercise caution around the tracks, as the rail line is still active. The forest here is mostly hardwood, with red maple, sugar maple, tulip poplar, beech, shagbark hickory, and sycamore. If you look closely you can see where the forest has survived fire, tornado, and windstorms in recent years.

Beyond the tracks the trail is a little hillier; you'll climb over one small ridge before descending to Tioga Falls at 1.0 mile. The falls has two parts: an upper drop of 30 feet and a lower drop over a ledge of around 10 feet. Both sets of falls are undercut; you should avoid the temptation to climb to the top. Well above the falls is the site of the 1800s-era Tioga Falls Hotel, a popular summer retreat

Tioga Falls

for wealthy southerners. Unfortunately, nothing remains of this once-fine structure. Immediately downstream of the trail is another smaller series of cascades. This small stream was once dammed to provide a swimming area for hotel guests.

Though many visitors fail to realize it, by crossing the stream and continuing on the trail, they can loop back to the trailhead rather than retracing their route. A sign across the creek warns that the trail is steep and rough, but it will not give most experienced hikers any trouble. At 1.1 miles, recross Tioga Creek on a very old log bridge. At 1.2 miles there is an old springhouse to the right of the trail. Pass underneath the trestle over Tioga Creek at 1.5 miles. This 130-foot-high and 700-foot-long structure (even larger than the trestle near the parking area) is more than 100 years old. Just beyond you'll begin to follow an abandoned section of Railroad Trestle Road that is blocked by a huge berm at 1.8 miles. Beyond the berm, follow the main road past a private residence, and past the entrance to the River of Life Church, back to the parking area at 2.0 miles.

The trestle at the parking area was built in 1873. It stands 85 feet high and is 578 feet long. It has served a variety of railroads and is still used by the Paducah and Louisville Railroad. The old L & N Turnpike under the trestle was a major transportation route between Louisville and Nashville from 1838 until the Old Dixie Highway was built to take travelers out of the range of the military exercises. The old Dixie Highway, which includes the last 0.5-mile of the Tioga Falls Trail, served until 1942, when US 31 West was built.

Fort Knox is a 109,000-acre military base. It is perhaps best known as home of the Gold Vault, where the U.S. government stores its supply of gold bullion (sorry, no free samples, or tours). But it is also the primary training site for the army's armored divisions and home to the 1st Armor Brigade and 16th Cavalry Regiment. The base has 59,000 acres potentially open for recreation, including hunting and fishing and the two trails described above. Access to these recreation areas is through the Hunt Control Office, which you should contact before visiting. Birders should also enjoy this area. A 1998 survey identified 54 different species!

Other Hiking Options

1. Short and Sweet. The Bridges to the Past Trail along the historic L & N Turnpike is a 1.1-mile abandoned paved road that ends at the military reservation boundary near Siebolt Cave and Dripping Springs. This is also a self-guided interpretive trail and is fully handicapped accessible.

2. At Fort Duffield, near West Point, mountain bikers have constructed 8 miles of single-track trails.

37

Otter Creek Trail

Total Distance: This 8.2-mile loop on trail shared with mountain bikes includes the side trip to Morgan's Cave.

Hiking Time: About 4.5 hours

Location: Otter Creek Park, about 15 miles south of Louisville

Maps: USGS Rock Haven; Otter Creek Park Trail Map

Though not as close to Louisville as one might expect for a city park, Otter Creek is a wonderful resource for hikers, mountain bikers, and nature lovers from all over the state. The park contains almost 15 miles of trails spread over 2,600 acres. Otter Creek is heavily used, but you may still have some of the park to yourself. The longest hike in the park follows the Otter Creek Trail in an 8.2-mile loop, which includes a side trip to Morgan's Cave, a visit to North Point Overlook, and a quiet stroll along Otter Creek. The many trail junctions mean that you'll need to watch your map carefully.

Getting There

From the junction of KY 44 and US 31 West, south of Louisville, drive south on US 31 West for 7.7 miles to the junction with KY 1638. Turn right on KY 1638 and drive 2.8 miles to the park entrance. Turn right again and drive 0.9 mile to stop at the park office to pick up a trail map. Then drive another 0.4 mile to reach trailhead parking at the nature center, where trail maps may also be available.

The Hike

From the nature center, start north across the parking area on the Otter Creek Trail. You'll immediately come to a junction where the Valley Overlook Trail branches to the right. Next, cross the campground road and walk through shrubby hardwood and open pine forests. You'll cross under a power line, and then cross a closed paved road near the campground, before reaching the side trail to Morgan's Cave at 1.0 mile.

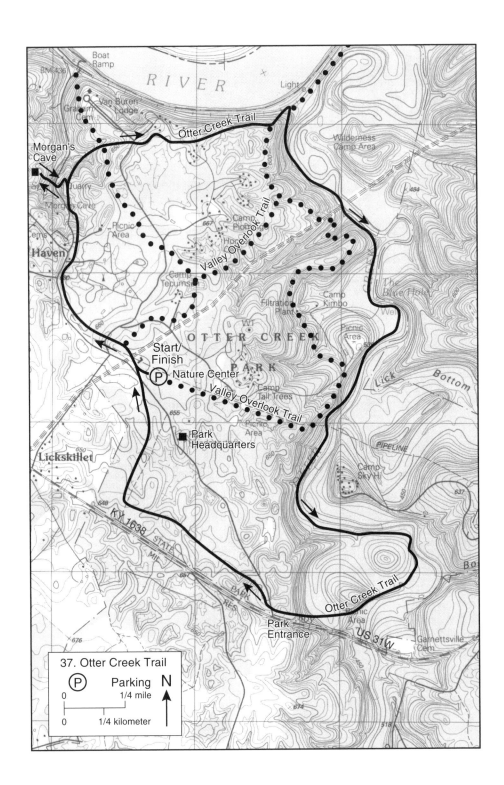

R I V E R

Boat Ramp

BM 436

Graham Cem

Van Buren Lodge

Otter Creek Trail

Light

Wilderness Camp Area

Morgan's Cave

Morgan's Cave

Quarry

Haven

Picnic Area

Cems

667

Camp Piomora

Valley Overlook Trail

484

Camp Tecumseh

Filtration Plant

Camp Kimbo

The Blue Hole

Picnic Area

OTTER CREEK

Wt

P A R K

Lick Bottom

Start/Finish

Nature Center

Valley Overlook Trail

Camp Tall Trees

655

Park Headquarters

Picnic Area

PIPELINE

Lickskillet

650

648

KY 1638

657

Camp Sky Hi

637

STATE

676

PARK

RES

Otter Creek Trail

Park Entrance

US 31W

Garnettsville Cem

674

518

Bo

37. Otter Creek Trail

(P) Parking   N

0   1/4 mile

0   1/4 kilometer

To visit Morgan's Cave, turn left at the junction and descend a set of log stairs past an old roadside quarry. Turn right briefly on the park road, and then make another left turn to descend a set of log ladders. Cross an unnamed creek, and look for a path to the right of where a small tributary enters the creek. At 1.2 miles, reach the gated entrance to this small limestone cave. Morgan's Cave is formed in a rock called the St. Louis limestone, which formed during the Mississippian Period. Limestone of this age is common across the United States, but it is known by many other names such as the Redwall in Grand Canyon National Park, the Paha Sapa in the Black Hills of the Dakotas, or the Madison of the Rocky Mountains in Montana. Morgan's Cave can be toured for a fee by prior arrangement with Otter Creek Park.

Return to the junction of the side trail and Otter Creek Trail at 1.4 miles, and continue north around the loop. You'll pass two other side trails leading left to the quarry. Many of the trees here are sugar maples. You can tell sugar maple from red maple by looking at the leaf in between the three major lobes. If the notch between the lobes is V-shaped, it is a red maple. If the notch is smooth and rounded like a "U" it is a sugar maple. To remind yourself, look for the "U" in sugar in between the lobes.

At 1.8 miles, come to an offset four-way junction. The right branch is a 0.9-mile connector to the Valley Overlook Trail. Go left and come to the other branch in 100 feet. Here the left branch leads to the park conference center. Turn right on the Otter Creek Trail to North Point Overlook.

Next, cross the park's cabin road and a power line right-of-way. The bedrock here is still limestone, and you can spot small sinkholes along the trail, evidence of the same type of karst activity that likely produced Morgan's Cave. The trail then begins to hug

the line of bluffs high above the Ohio River and offers some nice views down to it. Enjoy these views, since the North Point Overlook itself (reached at 2.5 miles) is partly obscured by the rapidly growing forest. If you hear distant booms, and see no likely thunderclouds, you're probably hearing the troops at Fort Knox on maneuver. Still, this is an ideal rest stop, especially since the hardest part of the hike is just ahead.

From North Point begin the steep, but short, descent down to Otter Creek. Though many previous hikers have cut the switchbacks in the trail, leaving a slippery route straight down the fall line, the easiest and safest route is to follow the trail, which zigzags down a gentler route. Though this trail is open to mountain bikes it is undoubtedly unridable for all but the most skilled and daring cyclists. At 2.6 miles reach Otter Creek and a junction with a side trail that leads left 0.7 mile to the mouth of Otter Creek at the Ohio River. Your route from this junction leads right, upstream along the wide track of an old road. For the next 3.3 miles the trail follows its namesake creek. Many side trails branch that from the main route lead to fishing holes or follow other old roads. If you find yourself leaving the creek bottom before you see the Garnettsville Trailhead, then you're on the wrong path.

At the upper end, Otter Creek looks sluggish, like a backwater of the Ohio River. As you progress downstream, the creek gains life, picking up current and rolling over small riffles. According to park employees, water quality is fine for swimming and swimming is allowed. Occasionally the valley limestone along the trail will form small cliffs. The trail appears to be a favorite with both deer and mountain bikers. Reach a signed junction at 3.6 miles, near Blue Hole, with a trail leading 0.3 mile to Camp Sycamore. The Otter Creek Trail will

Quillim's Cave

continue south along Otter Creek until reaching a signed junction with a side trail to the Garnettsville Picnic Area at 5.9 miles.

Turn right at this junction and begin a gradual climb. Pass a cinderblock structure before descending to cross a dry creek on a wooden bridge. Cross the park access road at 6.4 miles. Beyond the park road, the trees are mostly evergreens such as pine and cedar. The cedar seems grow best at the edge of the pine forest. These pines were planted in the early days of the park to reforest abandoned farmlands and stabilize soil. You'll cross a small meadow before reaching the park road near the disk golf course. Close the loop at the nature center at 8.2 miles.

Otter Creek was originally purchased by the U.S. government at the same time that it began acquiring lands for the Fort Knox Military Reservation. During the early 1930s this land consisted of overused and eroded farmlands. Later, crews from the Civilian Conservation Corps worked to convert the land into a park by building roads and structures. The U.S. government donated the park to the City of Louisville in 1947 in gratitude for the city's support of Fort Knox in World War II.

Mountain bikes are allowed on all park trails during dry weather. Bike traffic is normally not heavy and has not degraded the trails.

The park has recently renamed its trails and is in the process of replacing older colored blazes with new signposts.

Other Hiking Options

1. Short and Sweet. The hike from Conference Center Lodge Road to North Point and back is a 1.4-mile round trip

2. You can combine the north legs of the Otter Creek and Valley Overlook Trails with the connector between them to make a 2.5-mile loop that also visits North Point.

3. The Valley Overlook Trail makes a 3.9-mile loop from the nature center that stays on the park uplands.

38

Millennium Trail

Total Distance: A 13.7-mile loop on a foot trail that uses short sections of gravel roads

Hiking Time: All day

Location: Bernheim Arboretum and Research Forest, 6 miles south of Shepherdsville

Maps: USGS Samuels and Shepherdsville; Bernheim Trail System

Bernheim Forest has long been known to hikers for its beautiful, short interpretive trails. But forest hikers get to remember the turn of the millennium in a big way any time they set out on the forest's new Millennium Trail, a long excursion through parts of the forest recently opened to the general public. Surprisingly, the new trail doesn't connect with any of the older, shorter foot trails. The route isn't entirely new, though; it follows sections of forest roads for three short stretches.

Getting There

From Exit 112 on I-65, drive east 1.1 miles to the entrance to Bernheim Forest. If you are not an Arboretum member, and it is a weekend, you will need to pay an admission fee of $5 per vehicle. Drive 2.1 miles to the visitors center, where you must register for the Millennium Trail, to get a copy of the trail map. Then, take Guerilla Hollow Road to where it splits to make a loop. The start of the Millennium Trail is not signed, but it is located where a cable gate blocks an old two-track road. You can park in a small area just ahead on the right side of the road.

The Hike

The trail begins at the chain gate across the old road. In 250 feet you'll see a grass-covered road enter from the left; this is your return route. Follow the yellow circular trail markers into a small meadow at 0.3 mile, then cross the inlet to Lake Nevin on a wooden bridge at 0.4 mile. Next the trail joins the paved Tom's Town Walk-Bike Path,

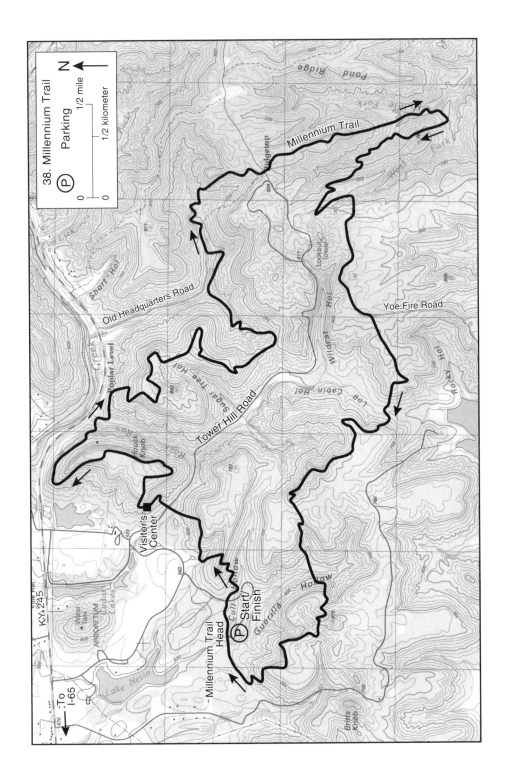

38. Millennium Trail

Ⓟ Parking

N

0   1/2 kilometer
0   1/2 mile

a favorite of local fitness walkers, at a right turn. Leave the road at 0.7 mile on another right turn.

Cross Guerilla Hollow Road at 0.8 mile, just at the head of the loop in the road. You will pass the Magruder Family Cemetery, and a more modest cemetery for the family's slaves, before reaching a gate in the deer fence at 1.1 miles. Descend along the fence and cross the paved Tower Hill Road at 1.7 miles. This is the recommended starting point for a half-day hike on the Millennium Trail to the junction of the Tower Hill and Old Headquarters roads. The half-day hike is 5.4 miles one-way.

There are mile markers every 2 miles along the Millennium Trail. Though I reached the signed 2-mile mark at almost exactly 2.0 miles when measuring this trail, I found the distances between miles 2 and 4, and between miles 4 and 6, to both be 2.2 miles. I'll use my distances in this description, which has the odd consequence that you may come to landmarks over 4, 6, 8, 10, or 12 miles out before you come to the mile markers.

At 2.5 miles, reach the edge of an overgrown meadow and leave it by following an old two-track road. Leave this road just before it reaches a power line a short distance from KY 245. Cross under the power line at 3.3 miles, and then cross a small streambed before recrossing the power line right-of-way. Begin a steady climb to a side trail to a picnic area at 4.0 miles. The 400-foot side trail leads to a 1940s-era table, and a new one constructed in 2000. The site honors Robert Paul, who was the first executive director of Bernheim Forest.

At 4.9 miles, reach Jackson Cemetery. This small fenced cemetery contains graves dating back to the 1800s. Beyond the cemetery, two false trails split off to the right. Ignore these, and continue a long descent

that brings you along gravel Old Headquarters Road. Join the road at 6.2 miles, then turn off it to the left at 6.4 miles.

At 7.1 miles, reach an important signed intersection with two gravel roads at a place called "Ridgetop." Here Old Headquarters Road meets Tower Hill Road. This is also the end of the half-day segment of the Millennium Trail. West on Tower Hill Road leads back to the Arboretum. Your route crosses Tower Hill Road and follows a long, narrow ridge to the south. By 8.0 miles, the ridge has ended and you cross a small stream, and then climb beside it. Leave the creek bottom at 9.0 miles.

At 9.6 miles, reach a four-way junction with two gravel roads. At the junction, cross Wilson Fire Road and continue straight ahead on Yoe Fire Road. Enjoy this well-deserved level stretch until the trail turns right off the road at 10.2 miles. Step carefully through a healthy patch of poison ivy. At 10.9 miles the trail crosses the head of Log Cabin Hollow, then climbs up and follows the crest of a ridge. Two false trails will lead off the main path, so be sure to keep watch for the yellow blazes.

At 12.4 miles, cross Guerilla Hollow. Cross through a gate in the deer fence at 13.4 miles, then turn right to follow an old two-track road. Turn left away from the deer fence at 13.6 miles, before finally reaching the end of the loop at 13.7 miles.

Bernheim Arboretum and Research Forest has a long and distinguished history. This is one of the rare protected pieces of land in what is known as the Kentucky Knobs, the series of hills that border the Bluegrass region. Though the hills are not especially high, a full day of climbing up and over them will tire out all but the fittest hikers.

The 14,000-acre site was purchased in 1929 by Isaac W. Bernheim, a German immigrant who made his fortune distilling

Along the trail in Bernheim Forest

whiskey with the brand I. W. Harper. Whiskey making is still important to the area; the modern Jim Beam distillery is just north of the forest off KY 245. Bernheim was grateful for his success and bought the logged-and farmed-out land for the people of Kentucky to make a park and arboretum.

Twelve thousand acres of the property are used in the research forest. Current projects include studies of decline in population of frogs and toads, the impact of non-native cowbirds on songbirds, and surveys of insects, snakes, and small mammals. Berheim's forests are more diverse than they first may appear to the casual hiker. Researchers have identified six distinct forest types on the property. Sycamore, sweet gum, and tulip poplar dominate the rich riparian areas along streams. On moist slopes where the bedrock is limestone, beech and sugar maple are the dominant trees, and wildflowers can be especially abundant. Three types of oak forests cover the remaining drier or steeper slopes or cover areas with more acid soils. Some ridgetops, where conditions are especially harsh, may be covered in Virginia pine.

Other Hiking Options

Most of the other trails at Bernheim are short loops that are ideal for nature study.

1. Short and Sweet. To exit the loop where it crosses Guerilla Hollow Road and return to the parking area would be about a 1-mile loop.

2. Four trails with a total length of 2.7 miles leave from the visitors center. Three of these trails have interpretive signs.

3. Nine trails with a total length of 7.9 miles leave from various points along Tower Hill Road. Three of these trails have interpretive signs.

4. Both the Guerilla Hollow (1.2 miles) and Tom's Town Walk-Bike (0.7 mile) Trails leave from Guerilla Hollow Road.

39

Lakeshore and Scenic Overlook Trails

Total Distance: The Lakeshore and Scenic Overlook loops can be combined for a total of 3.8 miles of hiking. These trails are also open to mountain bikes.

Hiking Time: About 2 hours

Location: Green River Lake State Park, 5 miles south of Campbellsville

Maps: USGS Campbellsville; Green River Lake State Park Trail Guide

Green River Lake State Park has an intricate web of well-used trails. The Lakeshore and Scenic Overlook Trails both leave from the same trailhead and can be hiked independently, but since both loops are short, most hikers will combine them into a longer hike.

Getting There

From US 55 south of Campbellsville, turn east onto KY 1061. Drive 1.5 miles and turn left onto State Park Road. Drive 1.3 miles to the hiker-biker parking area across from Thornton Children's Foundation Camp Kentahten.

The Hike

With the exception of the Windy Ridge Trail near the park campground, the trails at Green River Lake are relatively new. And as with many new things, not all the bugs are worked out of these trails. There are many "unofficial " routes out there, and even the established trails are not well signed, so hikers must pay careful attention to their route. There is a virtual maze of unsigned trail junctions around the trailhead, so getting started can be daunting for the first-time hiker.

The easiest way to get to the lake is to walk the Lakeshore Trail clockwise. From the parking area, take the main trail that leaves just to the left of the signboard. In 150 feet, reach an unsigned T-junction with the Marina–Main Trail and turn right. Turn left off the Marina–Main Trail at the next unsigned junction in another 150 feet. Ignore the tangled web of trails to your right and

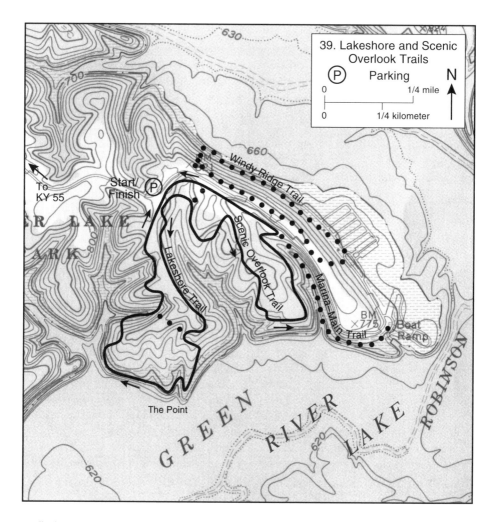

walk down the Lakeshore Trail. The loop is entirely within a hardwood forest typical of central Kentucky. Oak, hickory, maple, and beech are among the dominant hardwoods, and cedar is especially common near the trailhead. The understory is open, probably perfect conditions for watching spring wildflowers. At 0.2 mile, pass a rejuvenated red maple with many vertical branches sprouting from low horizontal branches. The bark on the new shoots is smooth and shiny, while the trunk and older branches are deeply furrowed and shaggy.

At 0.5 mile, reach the signed junction with the Beginner's Bypass Trail on the right. This 0.25-mile trail skips the descent to the lake, and the climb back from it, that might tax inexperienced hikers or bike riders. Beyond the junction, the trail leads down the nose of a small ridge toward Green River Lake. At 0.7 mile, reach the lake in an open shaded area perfect for a lunch break. You can see much of the lakeshore from this spot. Spotted wintergreen and pipsisewa are among the summer flowers that grow here.

Lakeshore and Scenic Overlook Trails

Continue walking along the lakeshore and reach "the Point" at 0.8 mile. From the Point both the Green River Dam and Dike are clearly visible. Both were built in the mid-1960s by the U.S. Army Corps of Engineers for flood control along the Green River. The dam is an earth- and rock-fill structure 140 feet high. The Point offers easier access to the lake than your first stop and may be a better swimming hole.

From the Point, the trail begins a steady climb back to the parking area. Pass one side trail to the left, which leads to a view above the lake. Mountain bikers have built several low jumps along this section of trail. At 1.5 miles reach a signed junction with the west end of the Beginner's Bypass. While the bypass continues straight, and an old road leads right, your trail bears left at this junction. Soon the trail passes the overturned shell of a large farm spreader, evidence that these ridgetops were once cultivated fields.

At 1.8 miles, the trail splits as it reaches the edge of the maze of trails near the trailhead. You should pass both ends of Eddie's Loop leading left in quick succession, and unsigned junctions with the Rex Trail and Marina–Main Trail, before reaching the trailhead at 1.9 mile.

Of course you can end your hike here, or it is possible to extend your walk another 1.9 miles around the Scenic Overlook Trail. To hike this second loop, return to the first trail junction 150 feet from the trailhead. This time turn left and follow the unsigned Marina–Main Trail. At 0.1 mile, turn right onto the signed Fox Hollow Trail. You'll come to an unsigned junction at 0.3 miles. Here the Fox Hollow Trail goes left to lead to the Marina–Main Trail in a grassy field alongside the park road. Your route follows the Scenic Overlook Trail to the right.

The trail winds through old fields now overgrown with cedar trees, ground cedar,

and Christmas ferns. Enter a hardwood forest in about 0.5 mile, and reach a wooded bluff above the lakeshore at 1.0 mile. Hike along the top of the bluff a short distance, and then turn left to follow a small inlet of the lake, which turns into a small stream. If your group is quiet and careful, you might see the deer or wild turkey that frequent this stretch of woods. Park personnel also report spotting foxes on their nightly patrols.

Pass a small spring before reaching a T-junction with the unsigned Marina–Main Trail at 1.4 miles. Turn left and follow the trail out of the woods and onto the mowed area alongside the park road. At 1.7 miles a mowed side trail leads left. This path leads to the Fox Hollow Trail, and the junction you encountered at 0.3 mile. Keep alongside the road until the trail leaves the mowed area at 1.8 miles. Once back in the woods, keep right at the next intersection and reach the trailhead at 1.9 miles.

Green River Lake State Park offers camping, boating, fishing, and swimming in addition to 28 miles of trails. The 8,200-acre lake is owned by the Army Corps of Engineers, which leases 20,500 acres around the shore to the Kentucky Department of Fish and Wildlife Resources for a Wildlife Management Area. In addition to the hiking, hunting, and fishing activities in the area, there are three other developed recreation areas around the lake managed by the Corps.

The trails at Green River Lake were built in the late 1990s with the help of the local mountain bike club. The North and Marina–Main Trails were built on old roads; the rest were newly constructed. The park plans to install more trail signs and replace existing ones with carsonite posts. It seems the original signs were held together by glue with a taste that squirrels found irresistible.

Other Hiking Options

1. Short and Sweet. Both loops are 1.9 miles long, and each can be done alone.

2. The 1.3-mile Windy Ridge Loop is open to hikers only. It leaves from the first bathhouse at the campground.

3. There are 28 miles of multiuse trails at the park. The rest of the park trail system is open to horses, but mountain biking appears to be the dominant use in the park.

4. There is also a hiking trail in the Green River Wildlife Management Area south of the Pikes Ridge Recreation Area, off KY 76. The Corps also maintains three shorter trails in recreation areas along the lake.

V

Cave Country

40

Echo River Loop

Total Distance: This is a 2.5-mile loop on hiking trails.

Hiking Time: About 1.5 hours

Location: Mammoth Cave National Park, the hike starts at the MCNP visitors center.

Maps: USGS Mammoth Cave; National Geographic/Trails Illustrated Mammoth Cave National Park

The most popular surface trails at Mammoth Cave National Park are those that leave from the park visitors center. A number of scenic loops lead to Green River and back. By following the River Styx, Echo River Spring, and Mammoth Dome Trails, hikers can see the surface expression of many of the features they might later see close up inside the cave.

Getting There

The loop starts at the park visitors center. To reach the visitors center from I-65, take Exit 48 and follow South Entrance Road for 7 miles to the parking area.

The Hike

Though the main trail corridor from the visitors center past the Historic Entrance of Mammoth Cave down to the Green River is heavily used, the rest of this loop is not. Many people walk part of the loop while waiting for cave tours to start, but the crowds really start to thin out once you're more than a half-mile down the trail. Those who have the time to continue around the loop can learn firsthand about the relationship of the park's surface features to the remarkable cave that lies beneath the trails.

From the visitors center, follow the paved route down to the Historic Entrance of Mammoth Cave. Many of the park cave tours start with this walk, so the route can be crowded. The first thing you'll notice at the entrance is a rush of the 54-degree air that pours from the cave. In summer, the feeling is like standing in front of a huge natural air conditioner.

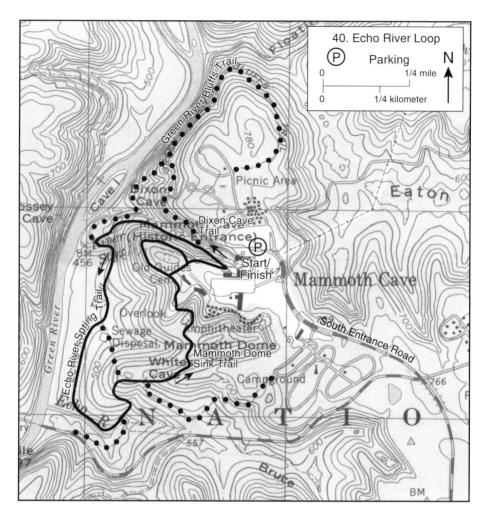

Two trails leave from the Historic Entrance. The Dixon Cave Trail starts to the right, while your route, the River Styx Trail, splits left and follows a wide gravel road toward the river. At the river, reach a junction with the Green River Bluffs Trail that enters to the right. Straight ahead, a spur trail leads to an overlook above the river next to beech and sycamore trees that have reached 4 feet in diameter. At rare quiet times you might also see deer browsing nearby. To the left at this junction is the Echo River Spring Trail. Take the Echo River

Spring Trail to an immediate fork. The right side of the fork follows a boardwalk to an overlook above River Styx Spring. This low-roofed cave and modest water flow look far too small to be an outlet to the world's longest known cave system. The blue water pouring from the spring contrasts to the pasty green water of the Green River.

Return from the boardwalk, and turn onto the Echo River Spring Trail. The trail climbs the slope above the boardwalk and mingles among limestone bluffs on the hillside. The forest here is open, and the understory

The Historic Entrance to Mammoth Cave

grassy, giving the area the look of a clean, well-kept park. Pass a trail sign indicating that Echo River Spring is 0.9 mile ahead. Next reach a clearing with an old stone building where deer often browse. At the far end of the clearing an unnamed trail climbs left to the Mammoth Dome Sink Trail.

The Echo River Spring Trail exits straight across the clearing and follows the flat bottomland along the river. At the next junction, Echo Spring is 0.1 mile to the right, and the trail ends in 0.4 mile at the Green River Ferry. Echo Spring is much different from the River Styx Spring and is worth the side trip. The water seems to boil straight from the ground, instead of pouring from the mouth of a cave.

Return to the junction, and take the Mammoth Dome Sink Trail. This well-maintained gravel path climbs steadily away from the river past low bluffs until it reaches a junction with the spur trail to the campground, where the park service has installed a rest bench. Turn left at the junction, and soon come to the gated entry to Whites Cave nestled in the face of a shallow limestone bluff. The trail next loops around the nose of narrow ridge, where you might notice some unusual plants such as bedstraw and prickly pear cactus, which here is found far from its usual dry habitats.

At the next junction, the left fork is the top of the unnamed trail down to the stone building on the Echo River Spring Trail. The right fork leads into Mammoth Dome Sink. The throat of the sink is choked with fallen timber, and the floor is covered with water-loving ferns. Sinks are the surface expressions of karst terrain, where the bedrock limestone has been leached away. This sink feeds magnificent Mammoth Dome, which is the final climatic climb of the Historic Cave Tour. Water entering the sink flows directly into the throat of the sinkhole and

down into Mammoth Dome. Through time, this water wears away the rock through erosion and by dissolution, forming the tall, cylindrical Dome.

Loop around the sink to rejoin the main trail. Next, a side trail leads left to a bench beside an overlook that is being gradually reclaimed by the forest. To the right you'll pass some cabins and another pumphouse. The trail next intersects the handicapped-accessible Heritage Trail. To enjoy the view from Sunset Point, turn left and follow the loop. Beyond Sunset Point, take the wooden boardwalk to the Old Guides Cemetery at the start of the Heritage Loop. The cemetery began as a burial plot for slaves, and then became used for guides, who were mostly African Americans in the early years. Many famous guides and cave explorers, including Stephen Bishop, who was born into slavery, are buried here. In some families, three generations rest in this spot.

To return to the visitors center from the cemetery, take the wooden walkway past an overlook above the Historic Entrance, walk behind the Mammoth Cave Hotel, and over the concrete bridge.

Mammoth Cave was probably rediscovered by white settlers in the late 1700s. By the War of 1812, the cave was the site of an important saltpeter mining operation. Later the cave was used and explored primarily for commercial tourism. By the early 1900s public support for a national park at Mammoth Cave was building. The U.S. Congress authorized the park in 1926. In 1928 the Kentucky legislature began efforts to purchase land. In 1941 Mammoth Cave National Park was formally dedicated.

The trail system at Mammoth Cave has changed significantly over the years. There are now 6 miles of hiking trails in the frontcountry area by the visitors center, and 55 miles in the backcountry area north of the

Green River. While most visitors come to see the cave, few can truly appreciate it without at least a short walk on the cave's roof.

In addition to protecting the cave, the park is also an important home to many wild animals. Sixty-five species of reptiles, including the northern copperhead and timber rattlesnake, have been found in the park. There are 43 mammal species here also. Besides the common possum, raccoon, squirrels, chipmunks, and white-tailed deer, you may also see signs of foxes, coyotes, or even bobcats. More than 200 species of birds have been sighted in the park. The list includes America's national symbol, the bald eagle. The Green River supports an unusual diversity of fish. The park is also an important home to many species of freshwater mussels. Seven different mussels on the national endangered species list are found in the Green River.

Other Hiking Options

1. Short and Sweet. The Heritage Trail is a short handicapped-accessible trail that leaves from the park visitors center

2. From the visitors center, you can also make a loop with the Dixon Cave and Green River Bluffs Trails that is about 2.5 miles long. This loop also passes the Historic Entrance, and emerges from the woods near the picnic area across the main parking area.

41

White Oak Trail

Total Distance: A 5.0-mile round-trip hike on a trail shared with horses

Hiking Time: About 2.5 hours

Location: Mammoth Cave National Park, about 14 miles northeast of the MCNP visitor center

Maps: USGS Mammoth Cave; National Geographic/Trails Illustrated Mammoth Cave National Park

The White Oak Trail follows the route of the long-abandoned Dennison Ferry Road. This trail is an easy backpacking trip, or a moderate day hike. Because this is the only trail in the northeast part of the park, it is little used, especially by horses. If you plan on camping in the park backcountry, you must get a free permit at the park visitor center. You must camp in designated sites. The NPS limits backcountry sites to one party per night.

Getting There

From the park visitors center, drive south to Green River Ferry Road. Cross the river on the ferry, which operates from 6 AM to 9:55 PM, and follow North Entrance Road out of the park to KY 1827. Turn right on KY 1827, and drive 4.3 miles to signed Dennison Ferry Road. Turn right and follow the main road for 1.7 miles, until it turns to gravel beside a private house. Continue for another 0.3 mile to reach the signed trailhead at a gate across the trail.

You can also reach the trailhead by driving 4.5 miles east on gravel Little Jordan Road (also called Ugly Creek Road) from North Entrance Road. However, Little Jordan Road is narrow, twisting, and slow.

The Hike

Even in a backcountry as uncrowded as that of Mammoth Cave, it is nice to know of a few special trails that others seldom visit. The White Oak Trail is the only trail in the northeast corner of the park, and it sees

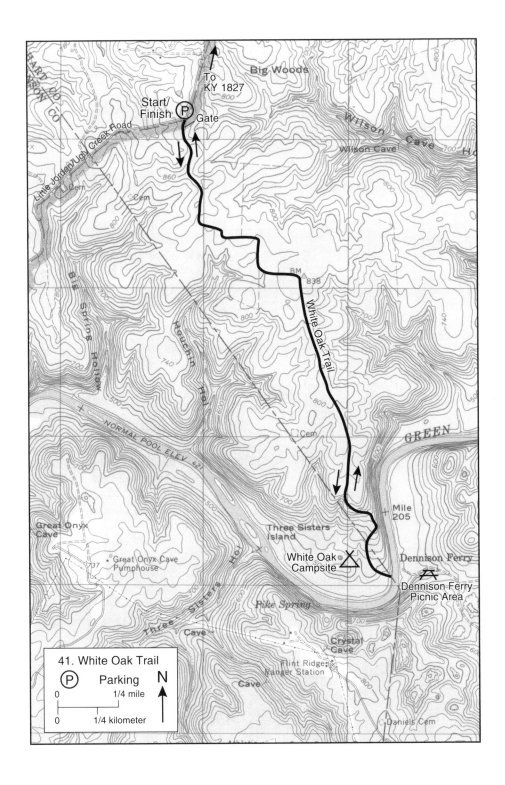

To
KY 1827

Big Woods

Start/
Finish   P
          Gate

HARD CO
SON CO

Wilson Cave
Wilson Cave

Little Jordan/Ugly Creek Road

Cem
Cem

White Oak Trail

BM
838

Big Spring Hollow

Houchin Hol

Cem

GREEN

NORMAL POOL ELEV 42

Mile
205

Great Onyx
Cave

Great Onyx Cave
Pumphouse

Three Sisters
Island

White Oak
Campsite

Dennison Ferry

Dennison Ferry
Picnic Area

Three Sisters Hol

Pike Spring

Cave

Crystal
Cave

Flint Ridge
Ranger Station

Cave

Daniels Cem

41. White Oak Trail
P   Parking   N
0   1/4 mile

0   1/4 kilometer

Backcountry camping in Mammoth Cave National Park

very little use. As an added bonus, at the end of the trail is a backcountry campsite, one of only 12 in the entire park.

Cross the gate and begin hiking south on the old road. The trail is not blazed, but there are no other roads along the way that can be confused with the main trail. Most of the trail is in the hardwood forests typical of the ridgetops in the park, but in areas where the forest is reclaiming old fields, cedars dominate the landscape. There is abundant poison ivy along the way, particularly near the start, so make sure to watch your step if you venture off the trail.

At 0.3 mile, the remains of a wooden shed lie on the left of the trail. Only two sides of the structure remain upright. It will not be long before the forces of time and weather topple it entirely. At 1.0 mile, notice a faint old road leading to the left where the trail makes a prominent right turn. If you look a few feet into the fork of the split, you can find

a 1930s U.S. Geological Survey benchmark, which gives your elevation at 838 feet.

At 1.7 miles, enter a grove of dense cedars and pass an old chimney on the right of the trail. At Mammoth Cave, cedars are the first trees to occupy abandoned farms or other clearings such as this old homestead. This old farmhouse probably burned not long after it was abandoned.

At 2.0 miles, begin a steady descent toward the Green River. You'll pass the very faint trace of a road leading right toward Three Sister Island, then reach an overlook at the top of some bluffs above the river. From this vantage point, the color of the river looks little different from the bright green of the younger vegetation along it. Reach the White Oak Campsite, and the end of the trail at 2.5 miles. The campsite occupies a small bluff just above the river. You'll find the standard fire ring, hitching posts, and tent pad.

White Oak Trail

On the opposite bank is the Dennison Ferry Picnic Area and boat launch site. Occasionally the solitude of this campsite is broken by the clatter of boats being dragged down to the put-in. One popular trip in the park during summer is the 7-mile paddle between Dennison Ferry and the Green River Ferry. Most paddlers use an outfitter for the shuttle to the launch from the Green River Ferry. Boats can be rented from outfitters also. Keep in mind that there is no longer a ferry at this site, and that there is no water or overnight camping allowed at the picnic area.

Mammoth Cave National Park receives more than 2 million visitors per year. And though most are attracted to the park by the cave, only 500,000 of those choose to take a cave tour. A much smaller number will walk one of the front-country trails near the visitors center. Only a tinier number still will visit the park backcountry. But at over 52,000 acres, Mammoth Cave represents the only large block of protected land in the region. With much of the land undisturbed since the creation of the park in the 1920s, the successional forests are now maturing, and they harbor a rich hoard of diverse plant and animal life. More than 866 species of plants have been documented in the park, including 21 considered by the Kentucky State Nature Preserves Commission as threatened, endangered, or of special concern. Seymour, in *Wildflowers of Mammoth Cave National Park,* has documented almost 200 species of flowering plants along the roads and trails. In addition, 65 species of trees, 30 species of shrubs, and 5 species of vines have been cataloged.

Not all the land in the backcountry of Mammoth Cave was cut for timber and planting. Just to the west of the White Oak Trail at Big Woods is one of the larger stands of old-growth forest remaining in Kentucky.

Other Hiking Options

1. Short and Sweet. The park contains four other isolated trails, all on the south side of the Green River. The Turnhole Bend Nature Trail is a 0.5-mile loop off West Entrance Road. The trail passes two huge sinkholes and an elevated platform with an overlook above the Green River at the Turnhole. The trail was rehabilitated in 2000 by the Youth Conservation Corps and park trail crews.

2. The Cedar Sink Trail is a 1.9-mile round-trip hike into the depths of a sinkhole even larger than those at Turnhole Bend. There is a wooden platform above the rim for those who may not want to climb down and out of the hole. This is also one of the better wildflower trails in the park front country. Look for false Solomon's seal, tall bellwort, bush clover, mist flower, ironweed, mountain mint, and black-eyed Susan among the summer flowers.

3. The Sloan's Crossing Nature Trail is a 0.4-mile handicapped-accessible trail around the pond.

4. The Sand Cave Trail leads 0.2 mile to the entrance to Sand Cave.

42

Raymer Hollow Loop

Total Distance: The hike is an 8.5-mile loop on trails shared with horses. It includes short walks on the Maple Springs and Good Spring Church roads.

Hiking Time: About 4.5 hours

Location: Mammoth Cave National Park, about 5 miles north of the MCNP visitor center

Maps: USGS Rhoda and National Geographic/Trails Illustrated Mammoth Cave National Park

The Raymer Hollow Loop visits one of the most historic parts of the backcountry area at Mammoth Cave. The loop passes Good Spring Church, Sand Spring Cemetery, and passes long-abandoned homesites. This is a moderate loop for day hikers. It can also be an easy loop for backpackers staying at the Raymer Hollow Campsite who will walk an extra 0.4 mile each way to the campsite. If you plan on camping in the park backcountry, you must get a free permit at the park visitors center. You must camp in designated sites. The NPS limits backcountry sites to one party per night. Since the NPS plans to make some changes to the hiking trails over the next few years, you should stop by the visitors center to ask about your route.

Getting There

From the park visitors center, drive south to Green River Ferry Road. Cross the river on the ferry, which operates from 6 AM to 9:55 PM, and follow North Entrance Road for 1.9 miles to the south end of the Maple Springs Loop. Follow the Maple Springs Loop for 1.0 mile, past the group camp and Sal Hollow Trailhead, to the main parking area at the Maple Springs Trailhead.

The Hike

Watch and listen for wild turkey near the trailhead; flocks as large as 15 birds have been seen here. The birds have flourished in the park since their 1983 reintroduction. Start at the main trailhead at Maple Springs, directly opposite the south entrance to the parking area. The trail begins as a graveled path. Pass a well to the right, and reach the

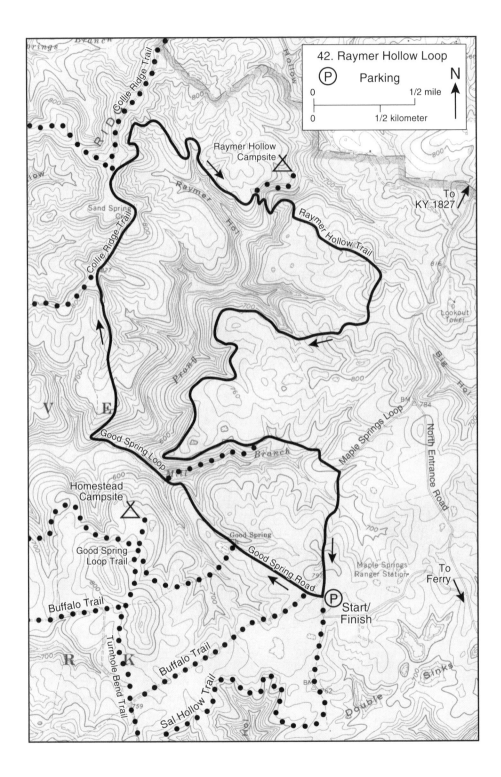

42. Raymer Hollow Loop

P Parking   N

0 _____ 1/2 mile
0 _____ 1/2 kilometer

Collie Ridge Trail

Raymer Hollow
Campsite

To
KY 1827

Raymer Hollow Trail

Collie Ridge Trail

Sand Spring

Lookout
Tower

Raymer Hol

Prong

Big Hol

Maple Springs Loop

BM 784

North Entrance Road

Good Spring Loop

Branch

Homestead
Campsite

Good Spring
Loop Trail

Good Spring

Maple Springs
Ranger Station

To
Ferry

Good Spring Road

Buffalo Trail

P Start/
Finish

Turnhole Bend Trail

Buffalo Trail

Double Sinks

Sal Hollow Trail

Good Spring Church

intersection with the gravel road to Good Spring Church at 0.1 mile. Here the Buffalo Trail, also a gravel road, splits off to the left. The NPS has opened the Buffalo, Sal Hollow, and Turnhole Bend (south of the Buffalo Trail only) Trails to mountain bikes on an experimental basis, so you may see some riders here. Keep straight on Good Spring Road and follow it to the church at 0.5 mile.

Good Spring Church is a simple, white wooden frame structure that was built in 1842. It is rarely used for services, but the cemetery behind the church is well maintained by the NPS. Two branches of the Good Spring Trail leave from the church road. To the left, near an interpretive sign, the south loop leaves toward Turnhole Bend and Bluffs campsite. If you are heading this way note that the former Waterfall Campsite has been replaced by the Homestead Campsite, which is located near the junction with the Turnhole Bend Trail. Your loop leaves to the right of the church and heads toward Raymer Hollow and Collie Ridge.

The trail follows an old road past the church. A few blue blazes guide you past a split in the main road. Horse traffic on the loop is moderate, but expect to encounter some muddy sections on the flats and eroded trail on the hills. You'll pass many traces of old roads along the way, evidence of how densely settled this area was back in the 1920s, before the establishment of the national park. The trail descends gradually to a low, arched bridge over Mill Branch at 0.9 mile. On the far side of the branch, a sign indicates that a connector trail leads right to the Raymer Hollow Trail. This connector leads 0.25 mile up the old Mill Branch Road to connect to the Raymer Hollow Trail.

The main loop continues downstream from the bridge. In the 1930s the Civilian Conservation Corps maintained a small quarry near here to provide limestone for building. At 1.3 miles, cross the dry bed of the Dry Prong of Buffalo Creek, and soon begin hiking on a 1994 relocation that is marked by scattered blue blazes. The new trail crosses the wide stream bottom, then begins to slab up the right side of an unnamed ridge. The old Good Spring Shortcut Trail found on older maps near here is now abandoned. Pass old roads branching left, then right, before reaching the Collie Ridge Trail at 2.3 miles.

At this junction, the Collie Ridge Trail and the Good Spring Trail loop lead left, while your route turns right along Collie Ridge toward the Raymer Hollow Trail. The trail follows a dirt road to reach the Sand Spring Cemetery at 2.7 miles. The most recent grave here is that of a Korean War veteran, Elmer Elmore, who maintained the cemetery for many years. Some of Elmore's kin are buried here with him, but most of the other headstones are old and illegible. Past the cemetery, reach a four-way junction at a rest area with hitching posts at 2.9 miles.

At this junction, the left fork follows an old road toward the Wet Prong of Buffalo Creek, and the straight fork follows Collie Ridge to the Lincoln Trailhead. Take the Raymer Hollow Trail, which begins here on the right. The trail crosses two small branches at the head of Raymer Hollow and then follows the edge of the plateau rim. Just before reaching the side trail to Raymer Hollow Campsite, pass an old homesite that is now grown over with eastern red cedar. Though no buildings remain, you may find some other artifacts scattered through the trees. Remember that any artifacts in the park are protected by law and cannot be removed. Please leave them for the enjoyment of other visitors.

At 3.9 miles, reach the side trail to Raymer Hollow Campsite. The side trail leads 0.4 mile to the site, which is located above a reliable water flow in upper Raymer Hollow. From the good condition of the trail here, it appears that few horses take this side trip. Return to the Raymer Hollow Trail

from the campsite and descend to cross the hollow at 4.1 miles.

The trail then makes a long loop around a side branch of the Raymer Hollow, then returns to trace the rim above the Dry Prong. The woods here are typical second-growth forests, with many oak, maple, hickory, beech, and pine trees. Pass a large rock pile on the left side of the trail at 6.0 miles, and a large sinkhole at 7.1 miles. At 7.3 miles reach the upper end of the shortcut trail down to the Good Spring Loop, which you first reached at 0.9 mile. Returning to the trailhead via the new shortcut trial is slightly shorter, but requires climbing into and out of Mill Branch. Keep left and on the main loop, which by now follows an old dirt road.

Cross one small creek and reach paved Maple Springs Loop Road at 7.9 miles. To return to the trailhead at 8.5 miles, turn right on the road.

Other Hiking Options

1. Short and Sweet. There are few satisfying short loops among the backcountry trails at Mammoth Cave. One option is to hike from the Maple Springs Trailhead to the new connector trail and back via the Raymer Hollow Trail. This loop would be 2.4 miles around, with half the distance on roads.

2. Also from Maple Springs hikers can make a 2.7-mile loop using the Buffalo, Turnhole Bend, and Good Spring Trails.

3. The Good Spring Loop is a 7.9-mile route past backcountry sites at Bluffs, Collie Ridge, and Homestead that can be used for day or overnight hikes.

4. The Sal Hollow Trail can be combined with either the Buffalo or Good Spring Trails to form an 11.5-mile day hiking or backpacking loop. The park has recently relocated two sections of the trail near the Green River and plans a third relocation near the Sal Hollow backcountry site.

43

First Creek–McCoy Hollow Loop

Total Distance: This 14.7-mile loop on the First Creek, McCoy Hollow, and Wet Prong of Buffalo Trails is shared with horses. In high water, the Wet Prong of Buffalo Creek may be impassable.

Hiking Time: The loop can be done in a full 8 hours, but is best as an overnight trip.

Location: Mammoth Cave National Park, 13 miles north of the MCNP visitors center

Maps: USGS Rhoda; National Geographic/Trails Illustrated Mammoth Cave National Park

First Creek is the gem of the backcountry trails north of the Green River in Mammoth Cave National Park. The loop has plenty of scenery, lots of campsites, and is big enough to give hikers that national park-caliber backcountry feel. Best of all, the horses that frequent the Mammoth Cave backcountry rarely use the loop. If you plan on camping in the park backcountry, you must get a free permit at the park visitors center. You must camp in designated sites. The NPS limits backcountry sites to one party per night. Since the NPS plans to make some changes to the hiking trails over the next few years, you should stop by the visitors center to ask about your route.

Getting There

From the visitors center, drive south to the Green River Ferry Road. Cross the river on the ferry, which operates from 6 AM to 9:55 PM, and follow North Entrance Road out of the park to KY 1827. Turn left onto KY 1827 and drive 1.9 miles to KY 728. Then go 0.2 mile farther to paved Ollie Ridge Road. Follow Ollie Ridge Road for 2.8 miles, and turn left on gravel Houchins Ferry Road. The First Creek Trailhead is 0.1 mile down the gravel road.

You can also access this trailhead, and the trailhead near Temple Hill, via Brownsville and Houchins Ferry over the Green River. Keep in mind that this ferry only operates from 9:30 AM to 5:15 PM.

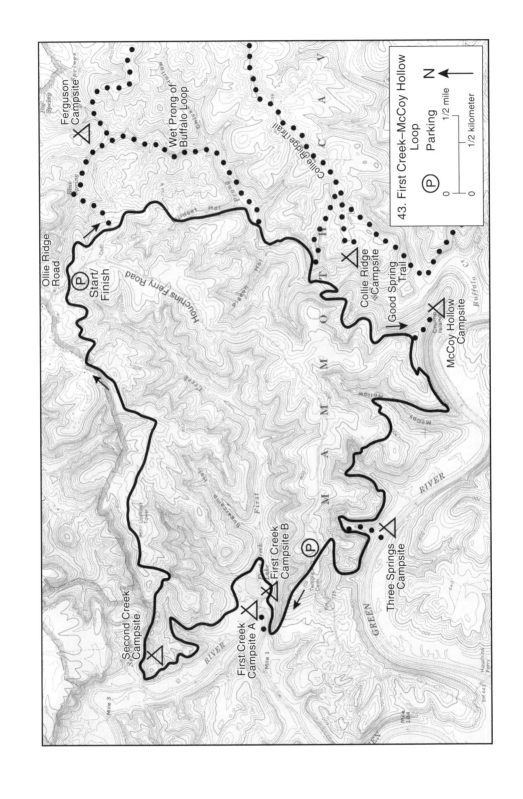

43. First Creek–McCoy Hollow Loop

The Hike

If you are day hiking the loop, you can start at either trailhead along Houchins Ferry Road. But if you plan to stay overnight, start at the northern trailhead, off Ollie Ridge Road, so that the campsites at First Creek Lake or Three Springs are close to halfway around the loop.

To hike the loop clockwise, begin on the Wet Prong of Buffalo Trail. The trail follows an open ridgetop through hardwood forest. Wet Prong gets a lot of horse traffic, so expect some muddy spots and rough footing. Reach a junction at 0.6 mile where the Wet Prong splits into a loop. The left fork follows an old road past Blue Springs, and the side trail to the new Ferguson Campsite, toward Collie Ridge, while your route leads right.

The trail continues a short distance along the sandstone-capped ridge. Look carefully for trefoil, mistflower, aster, Indian tobacco, and goldenrod growing beside the trail. The trail then leaves the ridge to join Wildcat Hollow. Make several crossings of the branch, which is normally dry by summer, then follow the right bank on a trail wide enough to be an old roadbed. At 2.1 miles cross the Wet Prong. In low water, this crossing is an easy rock-hop, but in high water hikers should be prepared to wade or ford the creek.

Just beyond the crossing is the south end of the Wet Prong of Buffalo Loop at a spacious rest area. The Wet Prong Loop takes the left fork up the Wet Prong. To continue on the First Creek Loop, take the right fork toward McCoy Hollow. Traverse above the left bank of the Wet Prong on a slope broken by many low bluffs of limestone.

At 2.7 miles, reach the junction with the connector trail to Collie Ridge. The connector turns left, while the McCoy Hollow Trail begins to the right. The McCoy Hollow and First Creek Trails are marked by blue blazes,

while some park connector trails are marked with red blazes. The McCoy Hollow Trail crosses the Wet Prong where most of its water now flows underground, then makes a short but steep climb on switchbacks. As soon as the trail begins to traverse among outcrops of rust-colored sandstone, it is time to bring out your wildflower book. Even in the heat of summer, spiderwort, squawroot, and tall bellwort decorate the forest floor.

Pass a large sinkhole to the left of the trail before reaching the signed junction with the orange-blazed side trail to McCoy Hollow Campsite at 4.5 miles. The campsite is 0.2 mile on the side trail. Unlike most of the backcountry sites in the park, McCoy Hollow does not have a nearby water source. Hikers can use water from the Green River, as long as it is boiled, filtered, or treated with iodine. But otherwise it is a pleasant site located on a narrow ridge between the Wet Prong and the Green River. Beyond the campsite, the McCoy Hollow Trail reaches an intricate series of low sandstone cliffs, an area called Devils Den by Seymour. Lucky hikers may spot a rare type of alumroot growing among the rocky cliffs. This member of the saxifrage family is only found growing on outcrops of this type of rock in Mammoth Cave National Park.

Past Devils Den, traverse along the base of the cliff bands. Here you can readily see concretions, quartz pebbles, and cross beds in the sandstone that forms the cliffs. While the individual beds are flat, within some beds you can see much smaller layers that are steeply dipping; these are the cross beds. The trail next reaches the narrow end of the ridge above McCoy Hollow and switchbacks down into it. After a long traverse along the creek, cross it and climb up and over another small ridge. At 6.5 miles, cross a shallow, unnamed creek in a grove

The McCoy Hollow campsite

of sycamore. You can always tell this tree by its thin peeling bark that makes the tree look "sick."

These sunny slopes remain good habitat for summer flowers, including the rare spider lily. This lily shoots up a thick green stalk that can display up to six showy petals. Remember that this and all plants in the park are protected, and that it is illegal to remove them. Next, cross a small flowing creek and reach the signed junction with the orange-blazed 0.1-mile side trail to Three Springs Campsite at 7.5 miles. Water for the campsite can be found in the creek back up the trail. The site is a pleasant setting on a small bluff above the river.

Beyond the campsite, pass a 50-foot-high limestone cliff, capped with a wide shelf-like overhang. Just beyond is a clear view of the Green River to the left of the trail. Pass a wide-open rest area at the base of the climb to Houchins Ferry Road at 7.8 miles.

Reach gravel Houchins Ferry Road, and the end of the McCoy Hollow Trail, at 8.2

miles. There is a parking area here, along with a register and trail signs. Cross the road, and start down the blue-blazed First Creek Trail. The trail follows a ridge a short distance then drops down to First Creek Lake. Along the way, watch for bedstraw and the purple blooms of mistflower. At the bottom of the descent, at 9.3 miles, reach the junction with the orange-blazed side trail to First Creek Campsite A, located alongside the outlet creek for the lake.

The side trail leads over a wooden bridge above the creek to Campsite A in 0.1 mile. This site replaces the former sites 1 and 2. It is tucked into a shady grove of trees on a small bluff above the lake. The lake is spring-fed, and may be partly dry in midsummer. The side trail continues past the lake to rejoin the main trail at 10.4 miles. It offers a substantial shortcut to the main trail.

The main trail reaches the orange-blazed side trail to Campsite B at 9.4 miles. This side trail leads to the new campsite, and view of the lake, in 0.1 mile. Here water is available from the outlet of the lake.

The First Creek Trail continues past Campsite B through a marshy bottomland around the lake. Look for purple Joe-pye weed on stalks up to 6 feet high. At 9.7 miles, cross an inlet to the lake and keep left, crossing an old road in another 100 feet. Continue around the lake to reach another inlet at 10.1 miles. Go sharp left here, and reach the far end of the shortcut trail from Campsite A at 10.4 miles.

Now that you've finally circled the lake, keep right on the blue-blazed trail, and walk northwest above the Nolin River. Reach a trail sign at 11.4 miles and begin to climb above Second Creek. At 11.6 miles, reach the orange-blazed side trail to the new Second Creek Campsite. The side trail leads 0.2 mile to the site, which is now located on the nose of a small ridge above the creek.

From the Second Creek Campsite junction, prepare for your last climb of the loop. When you reach another side trail at 11.8 miles, which leads to a now-overgrown overlook, all the significant climbs on the loop are behind you. The trail now traverses a long, broad ridge capped with sandstone. To the left of the trail, you'll even spot a small rockhouse that might remind you of hiking in the Big South Fork or at Red River Gorge.

At 12.6 miles intersect an old dirt road, and begin the start of a new relocation. The First Creek Trail formerly crossed this road and followed a route along the edge of the rim above Sugarcamp Hollow. The right fork of the road is unmaintained and leads to an abandoned fire tower site. The trail now turns left here and follows the road. In 2001, there were two blazes in the first 50 feet of the relocation, and then none until you reach the end of the relocation at 14.0 miles. The NPS plans to completely blaze the relocation. The walking is easy on the road. Flowers such as wild potato vine take advantage of the road's break in the canopy to capture sunlight unavailable deep in the forest. You'll see two more blazes, and the end of the abandoned foot trail, just before the road ends at a locked gate at the park boundary. Just short of the gate, the blue-blazed trail branches right and becomes a footpath again. The trail traverses the head of First Creek Hollow to reach the trailhead at 14.7 miles.

Other Hiking Options

1. Short and Sweet. The hike to First Creek Lake and back from Temple Hill is 2.2 miles round-trip.

2. The Wet Prong of Buffalo Loop from the First Creek Trailhead is 4.7 miles around.

44

Historic Cave Tour

Total Distance: This guided cave tour covers about 2 miles of the cave. You must pick up a tour ticket at the park visitors center. Contact the park for the current tour schedule and fee information.

Hiking Time: This tour takes about 2 hours, and can include up to 120 people.

Location: The tour starts at the Mammoth Cave National Park visitors center.

Maps: The Mammoth Cave National Park Brochure has a 1984 National Geographic illustration that shows most of the tour route.

Cave tours are the reason Mammoth Cave is part of the national park system. No one should visit the park without taking one. The Historic Tour enters the cave at the Historic Entrance and explores many of the huge open passages that made the cave famous in the days long before it was known to be the world's longest. The tour visits remains of a War of 1812 mining operation in the cave, and finishes with a climatic climb up a steel tower in Mammoth Dome. These passages are generally large. However, for many, Fat Man's Misery and Tall Man's Misery are the most memorable parts of the trip.

You must purchase a ticket to go on any cave tour in the park. You can order tickets through the park website at www. nps.gov/maca, www.reservationsnps.gov, or by phone at 1-800-967-2283. Same-day or advance tickets can also be bought at the ticket counter at the visitors center. Cave tours often are sold out on weekends or during the busy summer season, so it is best to make your reservations early.

Getting There
To reach the visitors center from I-65, take Exit 48, and follow South Entrance Road for 7 miles to the parking area.

The Hike
The Historic Cave Tour begins in the breezeway outside the main entrance to the visitors center. You should be ready at least 5 minutes before the scheduled starting

time. Keep in mind that the only bathroom along the route is at Great Relief Hall. Temperatures inside the cave average 54 degrees, which can feel uncomfortably cold for those used to summer heat. A jacket and long pants are usually enough to stay warm. It shouldn't be necessary to remind hikers to wear sensible shoes.

Your tour guide will lead the group down the paved walkway to the Historic Entrance. Your first stop will be a talk about safety, for both you and the cave. If your tour is full, you will need to stay near the front to hear what the guide will say once you are in the cave. You will next enter the cave down a long set of stairs. The initial passages are very large, resembling slightly flattened tubes with a level floor. The first room you come to is called the Rotunda. Here are the remains of niter mines that operated during the War of 1812. Miners collected calcium nitrate from the cave, mixed it with water, pumped it out, and treated it to produce potassium nitrate. The nitrate was critical to the war effort; it is one of the main ingredients in gunpowder. You can see much of the miner's equipment in a lower level of the room, and you will have already passed many of the hollow logs that they built to bring water into the mine and to pump the niter out.

From the Rotunda, the tour follows another large passage called Broadway. The gentle meanders of this wide passage seem very similar to the meanders of a gentle river. The main passages in Mammoth Cave formed as surface water flowed into the cave system and was concentrated in underground rivers that cut their way downward until reaching the level of the Green River. The main passageways were once as much as 80 feet high, but have been partially filled by breakdown from the cave roof and sediment from the underground rivers.

Well before the rediscovery of the cave in the late 1700s, Native Americans used Mammoth Cave. From a period between 4,000 and 2,000 years ago, they explored as much as 12 miles of cave passages using only reed torches. They apparently removed gypsum and other salt crystals, for reasons not yet completely understood. Several bodies, including one left as the result of a rock fall from mining, have been found in the cave. Archaeologists have learned much about the diet of these early visitors from the feces they left behind.

The tour makes a right turn off Broadway at Giants Coffin into the narrow passage called Dante's Gateway. It then descends through the middle level of 70-foot-high Sidesaddle Pit and continues along a boardwalk at the edge of Bottomless Pit. Beyond the pits are the narrow, winding passages of Fat Man's Misery and the lower passages of Tall Man's Misery. These passages were enlarged by early cave operators, whose clients must have been smaller than modern visitors. Besides their smaller size, the meanders in these passages are more pronounced and more closely spaced. The shape of these passages are similar to many of the slot canyons of the Colorado Plateau, where the passages are carved by infrequent flooding, rather than the gradual erosion of steady streams. If you look above in the passages, you can see that some of the walls are overhanging, and in other places, rocks have fallen from the roof or walls to become wedged in the narrow openings.

At the end of the "misery," come to the welcome space of Great Relief Hall, where you are 310 feet below the surface. Just beyond this room, at River Hall, a passage leads down to the Echo River. The park service once led underground boat tours on the river, but this was found to disturb the endangered Mammoth Cave shrimp, so the tours were discontinued. The cave is home to 130 different animals, and several of these are endangered, including the cave shrimp and several species of bats.

The climax of the Historic Tour is the climb up the steel tower inside of Mammoth Dome. At the lower part of the Dome you'll see the flowstone and stalactites that are the only cave formations on this tour route. The Dome is a complex arrangement of vertical shafts nearly 200 feet high, with smooth, fluted walls. A stairway spirals up the side, offering close-up views of the entire height. If you walked the Echo River hike, you've seen the huge sinkhole that is the surface expression of Mammoth Dome.

The top of the Dome leads to a small, undistinguished passage that would give explorers approaching Mammoth Dome no indication that the wonders of the Dome might lie ahead. This passage leads into larger Audubon Avenue and then joins the inbound route at the Rotunda Room. Turn left at the Rotunda Room to exit the cave and return to the visitors center.

After the War of 1812, exploration of Mammoth Cave was rather haphazard until Franklin Gorin bought the cave in 1838. He turned guiding and exploration of the cave over to his slave Stephen Bishop. Bishop became the first and foremost of a long line of cave explorers. He was the first to push beyond the easy walking passages, the first to cross the feared bottomless pit (he used only a wooden ladder) and he discovered the Echo River. His explorations extended the length of known cave from 4 to 27 miles.

In 1908 the German engineer Max Kemper teamed with Bishop's grand-nephew Ed to produce the first high-quality map of the cave. Their map showed 35 miles of passages, and it is still a convenient guide

for modern cavers. In the late 1910s and early 1920s G. D. Morrison bought the southern end of Mammoth Cave and blasted the New and Frozen Niagara Entrances to the cave. Shortly afterward Mammoth Cave National Park was authorized and land acquisition began.

Meanwhile serious exploration of a number of caves was also ongoing underneath Flint Ridge, just to the east of Mammoth Cave. Dedicated explorers were able to tie together the many originally separate caves into a network nearly as long as Mammoth itself. Through the 1960s and early 1970s explorers worked to find the connection between the Flint Ridge system and Mammoth Cave. In 1972, they were successful; the Mammoth Cave–Flint Ridge system was then the longest in the world at 144 miles.

Through dedicated exploration and linkages with other caves, Mammoth is now the world's longest cave at 350 miles, with no signs of stopping soon. The world's second-largest cave, Optimistceskaya in Russia, is nearly 150 miles behind. Jewel Cave National Monument in South Dakota is the United States' second-longest, with 125 miles of passages.

Other Caving Options

1. Short and Sweet. If you have arrived without a reservation at a crowded time, you'll end up on the self-guided Discovery Tour, a half-hour, 0.75-mile route that overlaps part of the Historic Tour.

2. The Mobility Impaired Tour enters the cave by elevator near the Snowball Dining Room and explores 0.5 mile of the cave in 75 minutes.

3. The Trog Tour treats children ages 8 to 12 to a 2.5-hour adventure including crawling through cave passages. Some special clothing is needed, and the tour is limited to 12 people.

4. The Mammoth Passage Tour visits the "Main Cave" and parts of the Historic Tour. It lasts 75 minutes and covers 0.75 mile.

5. The Making of Mammoth Tour explores the geology of Mammoth Cave. It overlaps much of the Historic Tour and covers 2.5 miles in 2.5 hours.

6. The Violet City (3 hours, 3 miles) and Great Onyx (2¼ hours, 1 mile) tours explore Mammoth and Great Onyx caves by lantern. The Violet City Lantern Tour is rated strenuous and is closed to those under 6 years old.

45

Grand Avenue Tour

Total Distance: This guided cave tour covers about 4.5 miles of the cave. You must pick up a tour ticket at the park visitors center. Contact the park for the current tour schedule and fee information.

Hiking Time: This tour takes about 4 hours, and can include up to 120 people. The tour was formerly called the half-day tour.

Location: The tour meets at the Mammoth Cave National Park visitors center.

Maps: The Mammoth Cave National Park Brochure has a 1984 National Geographic illustration that shows most of the tour route.

The Grand Avenue Tour explores Mammoth Cave between the Carmichael and Frozen Niagara Entrances. This long walk features a lunch stop at the underground Snowball Dining Room, the climb up Kentucky's version of Mount McKinley, and finishes with a visit to the fantastic formations at Frozen Niagara.

You must purchase a ticket to go on any cave tour in the park. You can order tickets through the park website at www.nps.gov/maca, www.reservationsnps.gov, or by phone at 1-800-967-2283. Same-day or advance tickets can also be bought at the ticket counter at the visitors center. Cave tours often are sold out on weekends or during the busy summer season, so it is best to make your reservations early.

Getting There

To reach the visitors center from I-65, take Exit 48 and follow South Entrance Road for 7 miles to the parking area. The tour starts at the Mammoth Cave National Park visitors center.

The Hike

The Grand Avenue Tour begins with a bus ride to the cave's Carmichael Entrance. You should be ready at least 5 minutes before the scheduled starting time. Temperatures inside the cave average 54 degrees, which can feel uncomfortably cold for those used to summer heat. A jacket and long pants are usually enough to stay comfortable. It shouldn't be necessary to remind hikers to wear sensible shoes. You can buy lunch along the route or bring it with you in a small pack.

After a brief safety talk at the Carmichael Entrance, you'll descend a narrow man-made passage down stairs to enter the cave at Sandstone Avenue. You soon turn into a larger passage called Cleaveland Avenue (named for a geologist, not the president). The roof of this passage is coated with crystals of gypsum, a soft white mineral formed from calcium and sulfate. Native American explorers entered the cave 4,000 to 2,000 years ago to collect this and other minerals for reasons still not fully understood.

You'll pass signs of previous explorers, who may not have been as sensitive to the ideals of cave preservation as modern visitors. Writing on the walls or leaving trash behind was acceptable in the early years while the cave was privately owned. Now, however, the cave is fully protected and any damage to the cave is punishable by fines or even jail.

The tour's longest stop is at the Snowball Dining Room. Here you can buy a boxed lunch, drinks, snacks, and soup if you need to warm up. There may be some bats in this room to entertain you. The room is named for the abundant white gypsum "snowballs" that coat the ceiling. The Snowball Room is also your last chance to use the bathroom. Be prepared to go the next 3 hours without facilities.

Beyond the Snowball Room, the huge passage of Cleaveland Avenue begins to change. You'll enter a more complicated multilevel passage called Boone Avenue, even though the famous Kentucky explorer never saw Mammoth Cave. Boone Avenue is a long narrow slot much like an underground version of the sandstone slot canyons of the Colorado Plateau. Past Boone Avenue is Kentucky Avenue and

then the climb up Mount McKinley. The climb is necessary because the formerly smooth and level (for a cave) floor has been buried here by piles of rock fallen from the roof. Here you can see that although the cave passages were originally carved by water, collapse of rock from the roof of the cave has played a major part in shaping the modern structure of Mammoth Cave.

Though the climb is a challenge for many cave visitors, it will not be a problem for trail-tested hikers. There are many switchbacks, and although the grade is steep and climbs 92 feet, there are no obstacles to climb over. But, unfortunately, Mount McKinley is only the first of three climbs on the trip. The 87-foot climb up Heart Attack Hill on Aero Bridge follows in quick succession.

Your next stop will likely be at Grand Central Station, near where the Frozen Niagara tour joins the route from the start at the New Entrance. These next passages require some bending and stooping to pass. Make the final ascent of the tour up Big Break. Once this climb is behind you, you may begin to see some cave crickets on the walls or ceiling. These unusual creatures use long feelers to move about the cave. They are very sensitive, so avoid touching them or taking up-close flash photos.

After the Travertine Tour joins the route, you begin to see some of the formations that have made this part of the cave so famous. You will descend to the bottom of the Drapery Room, the base of a large dome with walls covered in red travertine. There is some cave bacon here; the red-stripped form of flowstone must have been named by an awfully hungry explorer.

For their own protection many of the formations are fenced off from the walkways. The climax of the tour is at Frozen Niagara, a 70-foot-high flowstone formation that visitors climb past on a broad stairway. The tour leaves the cave by the Frozen Niagara Entrance and returns to the visitors center by bus.

Mammoth Cave is developed in limestone of Mississippian age. Three different formations, named the St. Louis, SS. Genevieve, and Girkin, host part of the cave. Overlying the limestone is the sandstone and conglomerate of the Pennsylvanian age Caseyville Formation. These rocks are very similar to those forming the ridgetops in the Big South Fork or Red River Gorge. No cave is formed in them.

The cave was formed as the flow of surface water begins its long journey toward sea level. At Mammoth Cave, the quickest route to the sea is via the Green River. On the surface, water will first follow small streams, and then larger ones, until reaching the river. When streams flow over limestone, small cracks and other points of weakness in the rock are eroded by stream action and slowly dissolved as water flows across the rock. Naturally occurring rainwater is slightly acidic, and can react with and very slowly dissolve limestone. The surfaces between rock layers, called bedding planes, are one weak area that may initially divert water from a surface to a subsurface passage.

"Karst" is the term geologists use to describe limestone areas where water flow is underground. Sinkholes, which connect the surface to underground passageways, are the characteristic surface feature of karst landscapes. As you see at Mammoth Dome, a sinkhole can collect surface water and feed it directly into a cave system. Once underground, the water at Mammoth Cave tends to flow along a single rock layer. This results in the tubular shape of many of the passages. The floor of the cave is scoured and dissolved by flowing water, while the sides of the cave are opened by the same processes, but at a slower rate. The roof of the cave may

be covered by water only during rare floods. The roof is expanded by breakdown of blocks onto the floor of the cave.

As the Green River has gradually cut its way down into the plateau around Mammoth Cave, the base level for water flow has also dropped. There are five different levels in the cave, each corresponding roughly to the outside factors that have controlled the rate of erosion of the Green River. The lowest level of Mammoth Cave now contains several major rivers that are still working to expand the cave.

Above the lowest levels, and on most of the tourist routes, Mammoth Cave is a dry cave. While this makes for comfortable cave tours, it does not make for spectacular cave formations. In areas where the cave is capped by sandstone, little groundwater leaks into the cave to form the drapery and flowstone and other decorative features. These formations are formed from travertine, a mineral identical in composition, but different in structure, to calcite, the basic building block of limestone rocks. Travertine forms when the waters that have dissolved limestone are exposed to the atmosphere in a cave. When the water reaches the cave opening, some of the dissolved carbonate from the limestone is deposited on the cave walls as travertine. So if there is little groundwater flow into a cave, there will be few travertine formations. The origin of other cave formations such as gypsum and nitrate is less understood.

Other Caving Options

1. Short and Sweet. Visitors can see most of the cave formations along this route on either the Travertine (75 minutes and 0.25 mile) or Frozen Niagara (2 hours, 0.75 mile) tours.

2. If the Grand Avenue Tour was not enough adventure for you, try the Wild Cave

Tour. This 6-hour, 5.5 mile epic travels some of the route used by Grand Avenue, but then ventures off the tourist routes to slither through tight and tiny passages that will test your fear of claustrophobia. This tour requires special gear, is offered only once a day, and is limited to 14 people, so make your reservations well in advance. The tour is limited to those 18 or older, or 16-to-18-year-olds accompanied by an adult. You must check in 30 minutes prior to the scheduled start of this tour.

3. The Introduction to Caving Tour (3 hours) is designed to teach responsible caving techniques to those over 10 years old. Those 10 to 15 years old must be accompanied by an adult. This tour requires special gear, is offered only once a day, and is limited to 20 people, so make your reservations well in advance.

VI

Lakes and Rivers

46

Backcountry Loop

Total Distance: 4.2 miles of loops on hiking trails

Hiking Time: About 2.5 hours

Location: John James Audubon State Park, near Henderson

Maps: USGS Evansville South, IND-KY; John James Audubon State Park Guide Map

John James Audubon State Park honors the legacy of one of the country's most renowned early naturalists with a 692-acre park in Henderson, the artist's home from 1810–1819. Here Audubon did much of the work that led to his breakthrough publication *Birds of America,* still regarded as one of the world's masterpieces of wildlife art. The park also contains a 325-acre state nature preserve centered around Wilderness Lake, which is laced by eight hiking trails that cover 5.7 miles. This hike picks the best of those trails and combines them into a series of loops.

Getting There

From the north end of Pennyrile Parkway on the outskirts of Henderson, drive 1.5 miles north on US 41. Turn right onto the park entrance road, and park in front of the park office.

The Hike

Your first stop at the park should be a visit to the John James Audubon Museum and Nature Center. The museum contains some of the artist's original work along with a detailed series of displays about his life and his contributions to both the arts and conservation. In 2001, the museum fee was $4 for adults, $2.50 for children 6–12, and free for those under 6. The CCC-era museum and park office are two of the prettiest buildings in the Kentucky state park system. The graceful turrets of the museum building are a masterpiece of stonework.

The park trails begin in back of the museum and nature center. Begin on the

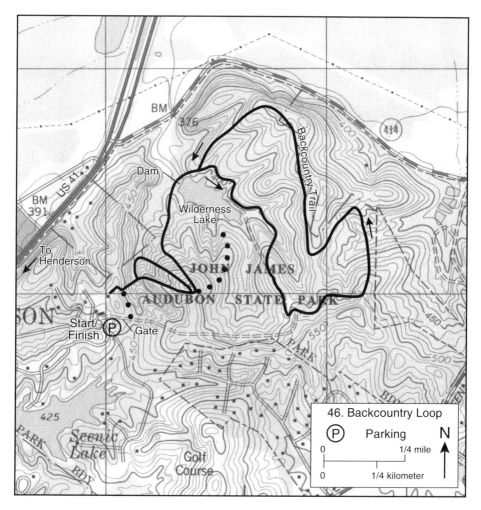

Museum Trail, an interpretive trail constructed as part of an Eagle Scout project. Signs along the trail identify white ash, black locust, and hackberry trees. At the first junction, the Museum Trail splits left to make a short loop, while your main route goes right on the Kentucky Coffee Tree Trail. The dense ground cover along this trail includes Virginia creeper, mayapple, and a variety of ferns.

Arrive at a second signed junction at 0.2 mile where the Kentucky Coffee Tree Trail merges with the Woodpecker Trail, which enters from the right. Unless you want to get a taste of what stinging nettles feel like, avoid touching the plants around the sign. Go left at this junction, and cross a small wooden bridge. Go left again when the trail splits. The Kentucky Coffee Tree Trail follows a tiny stream before beginning the climb to a small ridge. On the ridgetop, the trail rejoins the Woodpecker Trail and an old dirt road. Turn left onto the road, and reach a stone shelter at 0.8 mile. The small shelter has benches and a fireplace. Beyond the shelter, a side trail leads 0.2 mile down to the shore of Wilderness Lake. Your route will offer more open views of the lake than

A stone warming hut along the trail

this side trail, which is clogged with poison ivy and saw briers near the shore.

From the shelter, turn left onto the Wilderness Lake Trail, and descend gradually down flights of wooden steps to the dam across Wilderness Lake. The lake's clear waters harbor a healthy population of very vocal frogs. The dam site and the trail along it are cleared by the park. At the second wooden bridge over an arm of the lake, reach the signed junction with the Backcountry Trail at 1.2 miles. The Backcountry Trail, combined with the remainder of the Wilderness Lake Trail, forms a 2.2-mile loop from this point. You should hike the Wilderness Lake leg first by continuing to circle the lake.

Cross a few more wooden bridges, where raccoons have left their mark, as you traverse the sunny north shore of the lake. At 1.6 miles, the trail joins paved Warbler Road, which is blocked to vehicle traffic at the park office. Pass one false trail leading left before turning left onto the Backcountry

Trail at 1.8 miles. A carsonite post and shallow wooden stairs mark the start of this trail.

The Backcountry Trail is marked by scattered red blazes but is easy to follow through the dense hardwood canopy of the nature preserve. Note how little sunlight makes it to the forest floor along much of the trail, and as a result, how sparse the undergrowth is here. Only on the tops of some of the ridges does the canopy thin, and understory plants, including poison ivy, flourish.

The Backcountry Trail returns to Wilderness Lake at 3.2 miles. Head back home across the dam and up to the stone shelter at 3.6 miles. From the shelter you can continue to retrace your route back, or follow the Woodpecker Trail to cover some new terrain on a shorter route. From the shelter, the Woodpecker Trail leads down a ridge crest through a dense growth of ferns. The largest trees here are American beeches, whose smooth bark has proved too great a temptation for vandals who have carved into the trees.

Pass two intersections with the Kentucky Coffee Tree Trail, each on either side of a short wooden bridge, before reaching a T-junction with an old dirt road. This road is part of the King Benson Trail. Turn right on it, and climb to reach the museum and nature center at 4.2 miles.

John James Audubon State Park is known as a sanctuary for the birds so beloved by Audubon. More than 200 species have been cataloged in the park. But the mature second-growth forest is also a sanctuary for hundreds of species of flowers, herbs, and shrubs. Some of the most striking spring blooms are bloodroot, Dutchman's breeches, bluebell, trout lily, trillium, blue-eyed Mary, and phlox.

John James Audubon moved to Henderson in 1810 from Louisville, where he had been operating a store with a partner. Their Louisville store was profitable enough for the two men to live on, but his partner felt that the growing city of Henderson offered more opportunity than they could find in an established town. Audubon had already begun sketching, painting, and studying birds while in Louisville, and he knew that Henderson was located along a major flyway beside the Ohio River. He realized that the new location would give him access to new and unusual birds, so he agreed to make the move.

During his time in Henderson, Audubon had already developed some of the traits that would later make him famous. He had begun banding birds to study their nesting habits. At this time he also refined his unique style of painting by posing mounted specimens against their natural backgrounds and painting them life sized. But the Henderson area was still too unsettled to support the partners' store. Audubon spent much of his time roaming the woods and sketching. He also built a small steam

mill in Henderson, but that too was far ahead of his time. By 1819 bankruptcy had left Audubon with only the clothes on his back, his gun, and his original drawings. He then left Kentucky for a life of teaching, painting, and battles with the world of publishing.

The publication of his most famous work, *Birds of America,* took 14 years to complete. Each of the 435 engraved plates were colored by hand. The book was published in magnificent volumes, each 30 inches by 40 inches, to accommodate the life-size portraits. During his career, the artist described 23 species of birds previously unknown. He died in New York in 1851.

The remains of Audubon's mill burned in 1913, and with it the last traces of Audubon in Henderson almost disappeared. But local citizens began buying and donating land toward a park effort. By the 1930s labor from the Civilian Conservation Corps and the Works Project Administration was available, and the park was developed. The museum and park offices were built, the trail system was constructed, and streams were dammed for fishing lakes.

The park also contains a nine-hole golf course, cottages, camping and picnic areas, a fishing lake, and boat rentals. The nature center has a wildlife observation room, a hands-on discovery center, and rooms for instructional programs.

Other Hiking Options

1. Short and Sweet. The hike to Wilderness Lake and back can be done in a direct out-and-back route totaling 2 miles.

2. The King Benson Trail is a 0.3-mile loop that starts at the far end of the office parking area at the gate across Warbler Road.

3. The 0.9-mile Eagle Glen Pet Trail leaves from the back end of the parking area for the museum and nature center.

47

Macedonia Trail

Total Distance: A 3.6-mile loop on hiking trails

Hiking Time: About 2 hours

Location: Pennyrile State Forest, about· 9 miles south of Dawson Springs

Maps: USGS Dawson Springs SW; Pennyrile State Resort Park Visitor's Guide

The Pennyrile State Forest and Pennyrile Forest State Resort Park hide one of the state's most underappreciated outdoor recreation areas. Here lies a paradise of trails for hikers and mountain bikers just waiting to be discovered. The Macedonia trails are a set of three loops designed to let hikers pick the length of trail that best suits their time and ability.

Getting There

From the junction of KY 62 and KY 109 in Dawson Springs, drive 6.8 miles south on KY 109 to a junction with KY 398. Drive 1.1 miles on KY 109 to the trailhead, which is located by Macedonia Cemetery.

The Hike

The Macedonia Trail consists of three loops, each of which makes for a slightly longer hike. All three loops begin at the signed trailhead on the east side of KY 398, across from Macedonia Cemetery. Your route will extend through all three loops, but it is easy to make a shorter hike. In the thick pines just beyond the trailhead the trail immediately leads to loop 1. Turn right here to follow the loops clockwise. Look for young sassafras, Virginia creeper, Christmas fern, and poison ivy growing below the pines.

Keep your tree book handy here; you'll see Virginia, loblolly, shortleaf, and pitch pines at various points along the route. The pines are mostly non-native trees. These fast growers were planted in the 1940s, shortly after the state acquired the land. This well-worn parcel of land was then in danger of

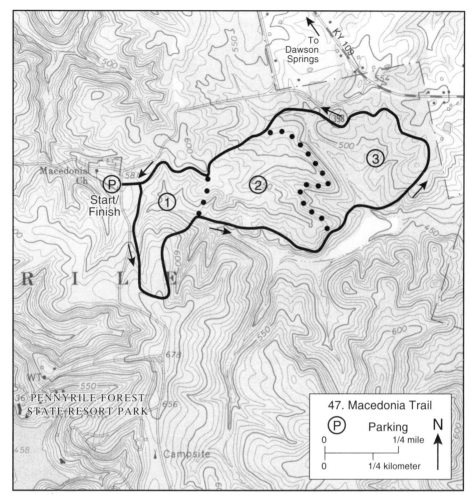

severe erosion. The pines stabilized the soil until the native oak-hickory forest could be reestablished. Now the pines are being decimated by the southern pine beetle, which has invaded most of the stands. The Pennyrile State Forest may be forced to thin some of these stands to reduce fire hazard. The demise of the mature pines will also let much more sunlight through the tree canopy and will make for shrubbier trails.

You'll soon leave the pines for a more typical hardwood forest that provides food and shelter enough for a small deer herd.

Loop 1 circles the headwaters of a small stream, which may be reduced to a series of shallow pools by early summer. At 0.9 mile reach a signed junction with red-blazed loop 2 and turn right. Soon a collapsed chimney formed of blocks of native sandstone will mark the site of an old homesite. The encroaching forest now means that deer, rather than people, make their homes here. The trail follows the course of a small stream with a set of sandstone ledges looming above. If you find yourself looking down the ledges at a set of crude ladders,

The author's measuring wheel along the Pennyroyal Trail

rather than looking up at the ladders, you've been led astray by an informal mountain bike route. The Macedonia Trails have good footways and are well blazed, but there are a number of intersecting roads and trails, so you must pay attention to the blazes.

You'll next turn from the stream and reach the junction with the yellow-blazed loop 3 at 1.4 miles. Loop 3 then enters another grove of pines before descending into a dry branch. You'll briefly join a very old road, and then branch left from it before approaching the forest boundary, where you can spot cleared fields through the trees. When the trail joins another old road, be ready to make a left turn from it before crossing a dry creek on a partially collapsed bridge.

At 2.9 miles your path intersects with the far end of loop 2 at a signed junction where you should keep right. The far end of loop 1 comes in at 3.1 miles. Keep right here also and in a few hundred yards reach a faint side trail leading left to the heavily overgrown Collins Cemetery. Dr. Morgan Collins and E. B. Owen are buried here along with at least six others. Finally, the trail reaches the pine grove near the trailhead and closes the loop at 3.6 miles.

The connector between loops 1 and 2 is only 0.1 mile, making loop 1 only 1.5 miles around. The connector between loops 2 and 3 is 0.7 mile, making loop 2 only 2.8 miles around. This connector is less used than the other trails, and hikers should be prepared for poison ivy.

The name Pennyrile comes from the small pennyroyal plant, a member of the mint family. The name, in its various spellings, has spread from the plant to encompass the entire region of low rolling hills in south-central Kentucky.

Pennyrile State Forest consists of 15,331 wooded acres acquired by the U.S. government during the depression. During the 1930s the Works Progress Administration built the cabins, lodge and other buildings that are now part of the state park. The Commonwealth of Kentucky acquired the land in 1954. Nearby Pennyrile State Resort Park also contains a network of hiking trails. The park has a 68-site campground, a lodge, and a lake for fishing and boating.

Other Hiking Options

1. Short and Sweet. Loop 1 is only 1.5 miles around, and Loop 2 is only 2.8 miles.

2. There are seven short hiking trails in Pennyrile State Park. The main route is the 2.4-mile loop around Pennyrile Lake on the Lake Trail. Hikers could extend this loop, or make shorter loops by using the Pennyroyal or Cane Creek Trails that connect to the Lake Trail. The Indian Bluff, Clifty Creek, Camper's Trace, and Thompson Hollow Trails are all about 0.25 mile long.

3. Pennyrile State Resort Park is also the southern end of the new 13.5-mile Pennyrile Nature Trail, which connects the park to Dawson Springs. The trail between Indian Bluff and Road 20 will be rerouted as the result of a planned expansion of the golf course at Pennyrile State Park. Until this expansion is complete, hikers should use Road 20 as the southern end of the trail. The trail land south of Road 20 will be transferred from the forest to the park when the expansion begins.

4. Pennyrile State Forest also contains four loop routes for mountain bikes that mostly follow maintained gravel forest roads.

48

Canal Loop B

Total Distance: A 2.9-mile loop via Connector B on trails shared with mountain bikes.

Hiking Time: About 1.5 hours

Location: Land between the Lakes National Recreation Area, 2 miles north of the North Welcome Station

Maps: USGS Birmingham Point; Land between the Lakes National Recreation Area Hike and Bike Trail Map

The Canal Loop trails are some of the most convenient and most popular trails at the Land between the Lakes (LBL), probably because it is so easy for hikers to find a loop exactly the length they want. Not only can you easily find a quiet walk nestled in deep forest, but the location close by Kentucky Lake, Lake Barkley, and the canal that joins them guarantees some lake views. It's also a safe bet that you'll be walking through woods thick with deer.

Getting There

From The Trace just south of the canal between Lakes Kentucky and Barkley, turn west on Kentucky Lake Drive and drive 0.4 mile to a signed parking area. The Canal Trail begins a short distance back up the road where the road has turned left.

The Hike

There are enough hiking options at the Canal Loops that a brief orientation is in order. The main loop here is a north-south oval split down the middle by The Trace, which is the main north-south road through LBL. The north end of the loop is where The Trace Bridge crosses the canal between the lakes, and the south end of the loop is at the North Welcome Station. The loop connects to the very north end of the North/South Trail at the North Welcome Station. Then there are four connector trails (labeled A, B, C, and D from north to south) that let you short-circuit the loop. Connector C is parallel to the south end of Kentucky Lake Drive. Mountain bikers have

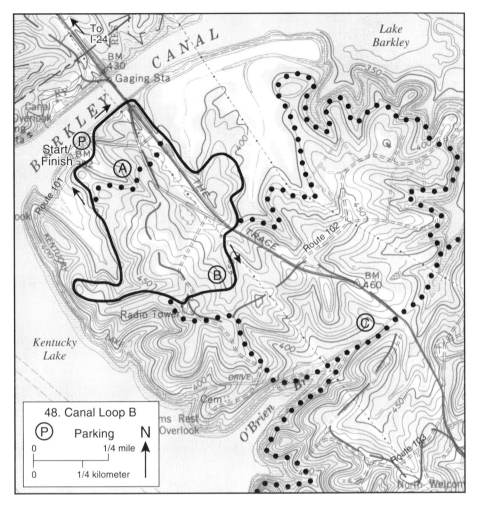

been allowed on these trails since 1997, but the trails are in better shape than many hiking trails in other areas.

For a short hike that packs in a maximum of lake views, try starting from the north end of the trails and making a loop via Connector B. From the parking area, walk north to the trail sign at the edge of Kentucky Lake Drive. Many unofficial side trails lead down to the lake on this initial stretch. Make sure you're careful to avoid poison ivy should you explore any of them. At 0.2 mile come to the end of a pre-canal

road, and cross underneath the highway bridge. The trail is marked by blue metal blazes and a few older white paint blazes.

At 0.6 mile, reach the signed east end of Connector A. If you want to cut the loop short, the yellow-blazed connector is 0.5 mile, and you will return to the trailhead in 0.9 mile. You will also notice that some of the older signs on the loop indicate that the North-South Trail once continued all the way along the west side of the Canal Loop to your trailhead, and that the east side of the loop was once called the Barkley Trail.

While this was once true, the North/South Trail now officially ends at the North Welcome Station. To continue on the loop, keep left at this junction. The trail climbs very gradually through a thick hardwood forest to the signed junction with Connector B at 1.1 miles.

Now turn right on the yellow-blazed connector trail. You'll next cross The Trace at the end of an abandoned asphalt road (be careful of fast-moving traffic here), then pass underneath a large line bringing power from the Tennessee Valley Authority (TVA) dams. On the hilltop that marks the divide between Kentucky Lake and Lake Barkley, turn left onto a gravel road and follow it for 200 feet before turning right back into the woods. The gravel road is used to service a nearby microwave tower. The tower is off limits, and no views can be had from it.

At 1.6 miles, turn right onto the blue-blazed main loop at the west end of Connector B. You'll enjoy some views of Kentucky Lake to your left through the trees. The trail here is old enough that some less-used areas have thick coatings of moss that would not have been able to grow on a newer trail or on a heavily traveled footpath. At 2.4 miles reach the west end of Connector A. At 2.9 miles you can access the parking area by a south path, just before closing the loop.

The Land between the Lakes is unique among America's National Recreation Areas. LBL occupies a wedge of land once known as "Between the Rivers" by the people who lived where the Tennessee and Cumberland rivers raced side by side to join the mighty Ohio. Early white settlers were dependent on logging, farming, and the iron industry. However, the Great Depression of the 1930s hit the area hard and many families were forced to sell their land. A New Deal program called the Resettlement Administration acquired the lands of the Hillman Land Company in 1936. In 1938, a 65,000-acre wildlife refuge was created from the Resettlement Administration lands along with TVA and U.S. Army Corps of Engineers property.

The Tennessee Valley Authority recognized the hydroelectric potential of the rivers. In 1937, plans for the construction the Kentucky Dam on the Tennessee River caused the removal of 3,500 families. This massive project allowed TVA to control flooding downstream but also resulted in the loss of farms along the fertile river bottoms to make way for the 134,000-acre lake. In 1966, the Barkley Dam across the Cumberland River and the canal joining the two lakes were competed. This dam displaced another 2,300 families.

By the 1960s it was clear that any boom times from logging or iron smelting were long gone, and with the fertile bottom lands now under water farming too would never be the same. The Wildlife Refuge lands were transferred to TVA in 1964. The plan to convert the Land between the Lakes into a recreation area required the removal of the remaining 2,300 people by the TVA, which purchased more than 96,000 acres from private holdings. TVA ultimately came into possession of 170,000 acres for LBL, stretching across Kentucky and Tennessee, property that included more than 300 miles of shoreline to devote to outdoor recreation and environmental education.

LBL now contains more than 130 miles of hiking trails, three large developed campgrounds, and six other less-developed camping areas. There are hundreds of miles of old roads to explore on a mountain bike. Some of the other attractions in the Kentucky portion of LBL include the 700-acre Elk and Bison Prairie. The 3.5-mile drive through the area costs $3 per car. In

2001, 25 elk from LBL were transferred to the Great Smoky Mountains National Park as part of a 3-year experimental reintroduction of elk into that park. The Golden Pond Visitor Center, located at the junction of The Trace and US 68/KY 80, includes displays, a gift shop, and a planetarium. Hunting for white-tailed deer, wild turkey, and small game is popular in the Recreation Area, as is fishing for crappie, bass, sauger, catfish, and bluegill.

In October 1999 the management of LBL was transferred to the United States Forest Service. The forest service is committed to maintaining current services and facilities until a new land and resource management plan is developed. The forest service does plan to upgrade part of the North/South Trail and some of the horse trails near Wrangler's campground in the next few years.

Other Hiking Options

1. Short and Sweet. Using Connector A you can walk a 1.5-mile loop.

2. Starting from the North Welcome Station and making a loop via Connector D is a 1.9-mile walk.

3. There are a total of 14 miles of trail in the Canal Loop system.

49

North/South Trail—Hillman Ferry Campground to Hatchery Hollow

Total Distance: 9.2 miles one way on a trail shared with mountain bikes; one-way hikers must leave a car for their return trip on Road 309.

Hiking Time: About 5 hours

Location: Land between the Lakes National Recreation Area, about 1 mile east of the Hillman Ferry Campground

Maps: USGS Mont and Birmingham Point; Land between the Lakes National Recreation Area Hike and Bike Trail Map

The North/South Trail is the premier hiking trail at Land between the Lakes, and the only long-distance hiking trail in western Kentucky. The trail extends 60 miles from the North Welcome Station in Kentucky to the South Welcome Station in Tennessee. It connects to LBL's second- and third-largest trail networks at the Canal Loop and Fort Henry in Tennessee. Since the North/South Trail, and The Trace, the main road through LBL, both run down the middle of the area, it is relatively easy to make a shuttle hike and avoid retracing your route if you cannot go all the way. The section of trail between Hillman Ferry Campground and Hatchery Hollow has particularly easy access and offers more lakeside views than other sections. Hikers share the entire trail north of the Golden Pond Welcome Center with mountain bikers, but as with the Canal Loop Trail, conflicts are few and the trails remain in great shape. Overnight hikers must buy a permit at one of the welcome stations or at Hillman, Piney, or Energy Lake Campgrounds. The permits cost $10 per person and are good for one year. A group permit can be arranged through the Golden Pond Welcome Center.

Getting There

From the junction of The Trace and Road 110 to Hillman Ferry Campground, drive 0.2 miles west on Road 110 to the crossing with the North/South Trail. There is minimal parking here, and it may be necessary to park at the campground entrance 0.7 mile farther west on Road 110.

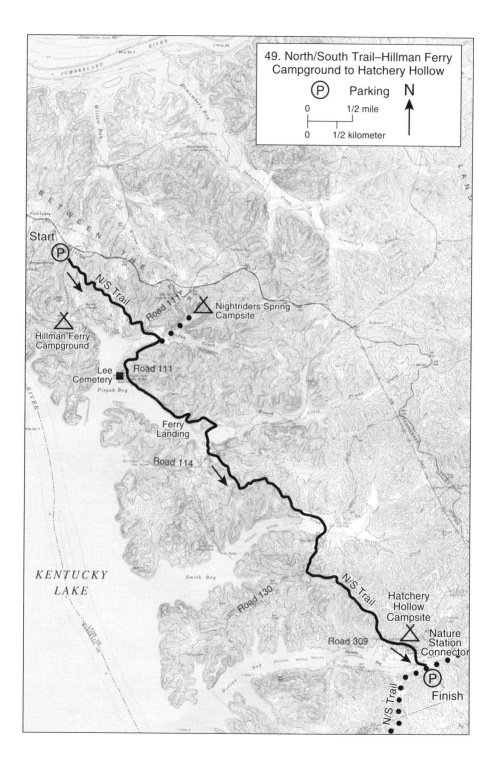

49. North/South Trail–Hillman Ferry
Campground to Hatchery Hollow

P Parking   N

0   1/2 mile

0   1/2 kilometer

Start
P

N/S Trail

Road 117

Nightriders Spring
Campsite

Hillman Ferry
Campground

Lee
Cemetery   Road 111

Pisgah Bay

Ferry
Landing

Road 114

KENTUCKY
LAKE

Smith Bay

Road 130

N/S Trail

Hatchery
Hollow
Campsite

Road 309

Nature
Station
Connector

P

N/S Trail   Finish

CUMBERLAND

RIVER

BETWEEN THE

RIVER

Campers at Pisgah Bay

To leave a car at the south end of this trip, leave The Trace west on Road 132. Then turn onto Road 309 and follow it to the crossing of the North/South Trail, just before reaching the Wildlife Restoration Center.

The Hike

The North/South Trail is marked with white metal rectangular blazes. It begins as a wide footpath. The area around the campground is prime deer habitat, so keep an eye out for those not-so-elusive whitetails. The trail follows the edge of a wide powerline cut where deer love to graze. Edges of forests and openings provide them with large quantities of the browse they love.

At 2.0 miles come to the junction with the side trail leading east 0.6 mile to Nightrider Spring and backcountry campsite. Signs indicate that Ferry Landing is 4.1 miles ahead and Hillman Ferry Campground is 2.3 miles behind. If you'd like to visit this unusual spot,

follow the side trail and make a left onto a gravel road for 100 yards before turning back into the woods. The shelter looks like a half-buried Quonset hut, but it is a dry and comfortable place to spend the night.

From the Nightrider junction, continue south to reach gravel Road 111 near modern Lee Cemetery. There is also access to Kentucky Lake here, and primitive camping is allowed. The trail beyond this point is one of the highlights of the trip. For much of the way you'll ride along the shore of Pisgah Bay past enticing campsites while enjoying constantly changing views of the bay. After crossing three small bridges, the trail crosses the marshy inlet of the bay and then joins a gravel road. The North/South Trail leaves the gravel road in a cluster of pine and cedar trees, but stays parallel to it until crossing paved Road 114 at 4.7 miles.

To the east on Road 114, The Trace is 2.4 miles. Ferry Landing is 1.0 mile west. Signs indicate that Road 130 is 2.3 miles south and Lee Cemetery Road 111 is 2.7 miles north. From this intersection the trail makes a gradual climb to a hilltop where it turns left onto dirt Road 306. From this hillside, the forest is interspersed with cultivated fields. Deer can often be found feeding nearby.

The trail next turns left onto a gravel road near Isaac Gray Cemetery. The cemetery holds the remains of two generations of Isaac Grays, and other graves are as recent as 1998. Beyond the cemetery, reach a T-junction with gravel Road 130. Turn right, and climb to the top of a small hill where the trail branches left onto a dirt road. The trail next branches left from the dirt road and follows it beside a small field. Soon the trail begins a long descent through wide-open forest to reach gravel Road 309. To the right at this junction is LBL's Wildlife Restoration Center. This building has an outside water spigot for campers. Just beyond the road is the Hatchery Hollow campsite at 9.2 miles. If you have arranged a shuttle, your car should be parked near Road 309.

Long-distance hikers should note that the northernmost spring on the North/South Trail is located just 0.9 mile north of the Hillman Ferry Campground Road at Brown's Spring. The next potential camping area to the south of Hatchery Hollow is at Sugar Jack Spring, where there is a spring and trail shelter. Sugar Jack Spring is 2.8 miles south, along Road 318, via a side trail from the North/South Trail.

Mountain bikes are allowed on the North/South Trail anywhere north of the Golden Pond Trailhead. Horses are allowed on the North/South Trail only from the junction with the side trail to the Colson Hollow Overlook Picnic Area south to the crossing of The Trace between the Cedar Pond Picnic Area and Road 201.

Other Hiking Options

1. Short and Sweet. The Hillman Heritage Trail, which leaves from near Hillman Ferry Campground, contains about 5.1 miles of trails. A hike from the trailhead near the campground entrance station to the overlook is 2.4 miles round-trip.

2. Other major trail networks in the Kentucky portion of LBL include 4.8 miles at the Energy Lake Campground.

50

Honker Lake Trail

Total Distance: A 4.5-mile loop on foot trails.

Hiking Time: About 2.5 hours

Location: Land between the Lakes National Recreation Area, about 12 miles northeast of the Golden Pond Visitors Center

Maps: USGS Mont; Land between the Lakes National Recreation Area Hike and Bike Trail Map

The Woodlands Nature Station is the Land between the Lakes' environmental education center. Two small lakes nearby are perfect for canoeing or wildlife watching. The Woodlands Nature Station is also the trailhead for five diverse hiking trails, including the Honker Lake Trail, which circles Honker Lake.

Getting There

From the junction of The Trace (the main north-south road through LBL) and Silver Trail Road (Road 133), drive 3.2 miles east on Silver Trail Road to the Woodlands Nature Station parking area. The nature station is open 9–5, so it may be wiser to park by the Center Furnace Trail or near the picnic pavilion. If you plan to visit the Woodlands Nature Station, remember that it is a fee area.

The Hike

From the picnic pavilion, follow a gravel path north for 100 yards to the point where the Nature Station Connector to the North/South Trail splits to the left along a mowed path. Your next intersection is a four-way junction. The gravel path straight ahead leads to boat rental area, and the trail to the right is part of both the Honker and Woodland Trails. Your route turns left on the Honker Trail and enters the forest where sweet gum trees are especially common. Sweet gum is easily recognized by the five long points on its leaves and its small spiny fruits that some call "porcupine eggs." Sap from the tree can be made into chewing

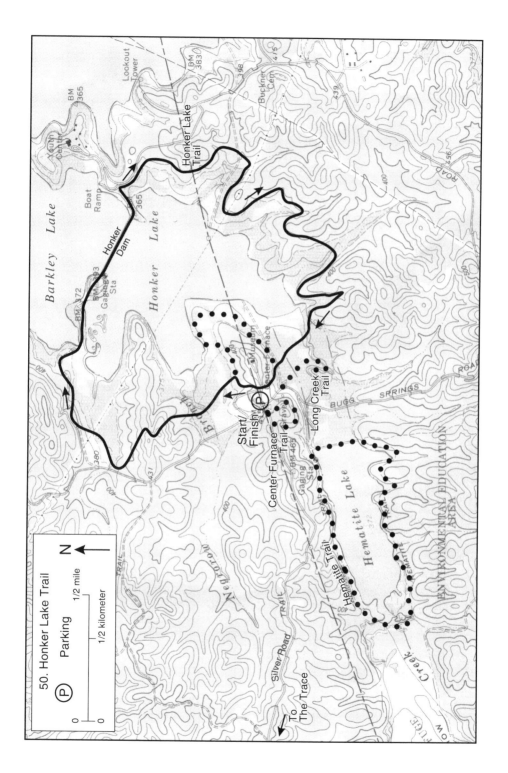

50. Honker Lake Trail

Ⓟ Parking

0   1/2 kilometer

0   1/2 mile

N ←

Honker Lake Trail

Barkley Lake

Honker Lake

Honker Dam

Boat Ramp

BM 4365

Mount Cents

Lookout Tower

BM 383

Buckner Cem

BM 372

BM 393

Gaging Sta

365

380

431

400

398

415

439

456

400

ROAD

Start/Finish

Museum

Center Furnace

Long Creek Trail

BUGG SRRINGS

ROAD

Center-Furnace Trail Loop

BM 465

Gaging Sta

Hematite Lake

372

Hematite Trail

HEMATITE TRAIL

400

ENVIRONMENTAL EDUCATION AREA

NegFurrow

TRAIL

Silver Road

To The Trace

Creek

REFUGE

FURROW

Scenic view within the Land between the Lakes

gum, but the tree is most valuable to furniture makers who prize its hard wood.

Soon the trail will cross a small creek and begin a gradual ascent of a small ridge. Just beyond the crest of the hill watch to your left for a small pit where iron ore was mined. A boulder of ore beside the trail is stained red, yellow, and brown by the various oxides of iron that comprise the raw ore. At LBL raw ore like this was heated to extremely high temperature in ovens stoked with coal, then combined with small amounts of limestone, to separate the pure iron from the other elements in the ore. If you'd like to see where the ore was converted to metal, you can hike the short Center Furnace Trail, which also begins near the Woodlands Nature Station. Iron smelting was the region's most important industry from the 1820s until the Civil War. After the war, steel production replaced traditional iron production, and there were few trees left in the region from which to make

charcoal. However, some small furnaces struggled on until 1912, when the iron industry disappeared from the region.

When the trail appears to split, keep right and head downhill. You'll then cross a small bridge and a power line right-of-way before crossing, then joining, a two-track dirt road that is within sight of Honker Lake. The lake was named for the nasal call of Canada geese. The 190-acre lake was built in 1966 to provide a nesting area for migrating geese. Here you are close to Goose Island, where the recreation area has constructed a special nesting area for these big birds.

On the other side of a small grove of pines cross a small dam. The pines were probably planted in the late 1930s to both prevent erosion and provide shelter for wildlife at a time when the land had been overused. Next reach Honker Dam. With Honker Lake on your right, and Lake Barkley on your left, the views from the dam can't be beat. This perfectly flat walk is not quite as easy walking as you might expect. The dam is obviously an extremely popular stop for wildlife, and you'll need to watch your step to avoid what they've left behind.

On the far side of the dam, turn left onto a gravel road for 500 feet past another boulder of iron ore. Look for a sign indicating a right turn onto a wide foot trail. The rest of the trail is blue blazed, and you will see several numbered interpretive stations. Two old roadways will branch left from the trail; ignore both of these and keep to the right. The trail next crosses a power line opening where white-tailed deer often browse. Several types of trees are labeled here. Watch for a black cherry tree that has reached almost 1 foot in diameter. Seldom will you see one this large.

The trail crosses two shallow sloughs on wooden bridges before reaching gravel Road 177 near a parking area. From the road, the Honker Lake Trail climbs the hillside past a small quarry to reach the southeast end of the parking area for the Woodlands Nature Station by a large sign.

The Woodland Nature Station includes the indoor Learning Center, which has displays about the plants and animals that live in LBL. The Backyard Area contains animals that cannot be returned to their natural habitat and so must remain in captivity. Birds in the Backyard area include red-tailed hawk, bald eagle, wild turkey, and several species of owl. There are also bobcat, coyote, white-tailed deer, fallow deer, and red wolf. Fallow deer are a Eurasian species that thrive in captivity and so have been transplanted across the globe. The Hillman Land Company brought them to the area in 1918. Fallow deer are smaller than whitetails and

have spots and a black tail. When excited, fallow deer run with a bouncy pogo-stick gait much like our western mule deer. Wild fallow deer can sometimes be seen near the Woodland Nature Station.

The Woodland Nature Station is also the site of part of the captive breeding program for the endangered red wolf. This close cousin of the timber wolf and coyote once roamed much of the southeast but nearly became extinct because of loss of habitat and hunting. But a small population was isolated and bred in captivity until the population was large enough to reintroduce back into the wild. A stable population of red wolves has now been established at Alligator National Wildlife Refuge in North Carolina on the Atlantic coast.

Other Hiking Options

1. Short and Sweet. The Center Furnace Trail is a 0.3-mile interpretive loop that highlights the history of iron mining and processing in the Land between the Lakes.

2. The Long Creek Trail is a 0.2 mile paved handicapped-accessible trail. The trail winds along Long Creek and is a good spot for watching wildlife or enjoying spring wildflowers.

3. Two other loop trails leave from the Woodland Nature Station. Hematite Lake Trail is a 2.2-mile loop featuring observation decks for wildlife watching and a photography blind. The Woodland Walk is a 1.0-mile loop leading to the boat dock on Honker Lake.

4. The Nature Station Connector leads 4.8 miles to the North/South Trail. A side trail to Token Trail Spring is located about halfway along this trail.

Appendix:
The Sheltowee Trace National Recreation Trail

The Sheltowee Trace Trail stretches nearly across the width of Kentucky, from Pickett State Park in Tennessee to the very northern tip of the Daniel Boone National Forest. On its journey across the state it visits many of premier hiking areas in the Kentucky Appalachians, such as the Big South Fork National River and Recreation Area, Cumberland Falls State Resort Park, Laurel River Lake, Natural Bridge State Resort Park, Red River Gorge Geological Area, Clifty Wilderness, and Cave Run Lake. There are other long trails in the region, but none are as long, as diverse, or as well suited to hikers.

The trail is named for Daniel Boone, who was given the name Sheltowee (Big Turtle) during his time with the Shawnee Indians. The route, which explores so much of the wild land remaining in Kentucky, is a fitting tribute to the state's most famous explorer. The trail is marked with white turtle-shaped blazes in addition to white diamonds used by the DBNF.

Despite the unparalleled opportunity for long-distance hiking that the Sheltowee Trace provides, only a modest number of hikers attempt to walk the entire trail each year. Instead, the trail serves as a main trunk line, linking together trail networks and providing opportunities for well-appreciated loop hikes.

But the Sheltowee Trace was not built just for hikers. Much of the trail is open to mountain bikes and horses. Some sections are open to off-highway vehicles (OHVs), and a few sections follow maintained roads.

If you look at a detailed map of the Daniel Boone National Forest you'll see that the forest service actually owns very little land in the middle third of the forest. For the trail to be continuous, many parts of it were located onto active or abandoned old roads so that the trail could cross areas where there is no public land. These sections mean that parts of the trail will be of little interest to hikers, except for those few who seek to walk the entire trail.

Management of the Sheltowee Trace is shared by the four forest districts that the trail passes through (the Stearns, London, Stanton, and Morehead), the three state parks (Pickett, in Tennessee, Cumberland Falls, and Natural Bridge) and the Big South Fork. These agencies control which trail sections are open to mountain bikes, horses, or motorized vehicles. In practice, closures for vehicles or horses are not often clear and may not be marked on the ground.

At least four OHV routes designated by the forest service use part of the STT. Just north of the Rockcastle Narrows hike, the Big Dog OHV route uses 2.7 miles of the STT between two intersections with DBNF Road 457. Near KY 80, the Pine Creek OHV (Off-Highway Vehicle) Route uses 2.9 miles of trail between DBNF 747 and KY 1956. The 9 miles south of the Turkey Foot Campground is the Turkey Foot OHV Route. The 9.5 miles north of S-Tree Campground is the S-Tree OHV Route. These last two areas sometimes receive heavy use.

The forest service issues a recreation guide for the Sheltowee Trace Trail

(R8-RG-229), which is helpful for a large-scale view of the trail. The best source of detailed information is the individual recreation guides for trails issued by the four ranger districts. The following table summarizes the recreation guide information into a single mileage table for the Sheltowee Trace. The table should help section hikers on the STT plan their trips and should be equally useful to any potential through-hikers. I used data from Dreaver et al. for the trail from Pickett to Cumberland Falls, since my measurements agreed well with theirs in other areas. Otherwise, I used mileages from the district recreation guides, unless I happened to wheel or drive a section myself. These new data indicate that at 279 miles the trail is 10 miles longer than previously measured. I've also tried to identify the trail sections that follow maintained roads and the trail sections that are open to ORVs.

Sheltowee Trace National Recreation Trail Mileage Table

From	To	Section	Total	Roads	Manager
TN 154	Double Falls Tr.	4.2	4.2		Pickett SP
Double Falls Tr.	Rock Cr. Tr.	0.8	5.0		BSF
Rock Cr. Tr.	John Muir Tr.	0.8	5.8		BSF
John Muir Tr.	Access Divide Road	3.6	9.4		BSF
Access Divide Road	TN line/Parker Mtn Tr.	0.5	9.9		BSF
TN line/Parker Mtn Tr.	Great Meadows CG	3.1	13.0		BSF
Great Meadows CG	Gobblers Arch Trail	1.9	14.9		Stearns RD
Gobblers Arch Trail	Mark Branch Trail	0.7	15.6		Stearns RD
Mark Branch Trail	Peters Mountain TH	1.5	17.6		Stearns RD
Peters Mountain TH	Off Laurel Ridge Road	5.6	22.7	★	Stearns RD
Off Laurel Ridge Road	DBNF 6308	3.0	25.7		Stearns RD
DBNF 6308	Devils Creek Road	2.7	28.4		Stearns RD
Devils Creek Road	Koger Arch Tr.	1.0	29.4		Stearns RD
Koger Arch Tr.	Kentucky Tr.	1.8	31.2		Stearns RD
Kentucky Tr.	KY 92/Yamacraw Bridge	1.4	32.6		Stearns RD
KY 92/Yamacraw Bridge	Lick Cr. Tr.	1.4	34.0		Stearns RD
Lick Cr. Tr.	Negro Creek Tr.	1.5	35.5		Stearns RD
Negro Creek Tr.	Alum Ford	3.5	39.0		Stearns RD
Alum Ford	Yahoo Falls Tr.	1.9	40.9		Stearns RD
Yahoo Falls Tr.	Big Creek	2.6	43.5		Stearns RD
Big Creek	US 27	4.2	47.7	part	Stearns RD
US 27	US 27 TH	1.1	48.8	part	Stearns RD

Sheltowee Trace National Recreation Trail Mileage Table

From	To	Section	Total	Roads	Manager
US 27 TH	4-way Jct	2.9	51.7		Stearns RD
4-way Jct	KY 700	5.0	56.7		Stearns RD
KY 700	Join KY 700	1.4	58.1		Stearns RD
Join KY 700	Leave KY 700	2.3	60.4	★	Stearns RD
Leave KY 700	McKee Bend	1.1	61.5		Stearns RD
McKee Bend	DBNF Boundary	2.5	64.0		Stearns RD
DBNF Boundary	KY 90	2.4	66.4		Cumberland Falls SP
KY 90	Cumberland Falls	0.2	66.6		Cumberland Falls SP
Cumberland Falls	Dog Slaughter Falls Tr.	2.9	69.5		London RD
Dog Slaughter Falls Tr.	Bark Camp Tr.	4.5	74.0		London RD
BarK Camp Tr.	Mouth of Laurel Boat Rmp	3.3	77.3		London RD
Mouth of Laurel Boat Rmp	Laurel Dam–S	2.4	79.7		London RD
Laurel Dam–S	Laurel Dam–N	0.5	80.2		London RD
Laurel Dam–S	Holly Bay Campground	4.2	84.4		London RD
Holly Bay Campground	KY 192	4.3	88.7		London RD
KY 192	Cane Creek	2.5	91.2		London RD
Cane Creek	Trail 401	1.1	92.3		London RD
Trail 401	DBNF Road 119	1.1	93.4		London RD
DBNF Road 119	DBNF Road 457–South	1.3	94.7	part	London RD
DBNF Road 457–South	DBNF Road 457–North	2.7	97.4	OHVs	London RD
DBNF Road 457–North	Sinking Creek	4.1	101.5	part	London RD
Sinking Creek	DBNF Road 747–N	1.6	103.1	part	London RD
DBNF Road 747–N	KY 80	2.9	106.0	part	London RD
KY 80	DBNF Road 1956	0.3	106.3	OHVs	London RD
DBNF Road 1956	Hawk Creek	1.7	108.0		London RD
Hawk Creek	DBNF Road 4095	1.5	109.5		London RD
DBNF Road 4095	I-75	3.5	113.0	★	London RD
I-75	DBNF Road 760–S	1.4	114.4	★	London RD
DBNF Road 760–S	DBNF Road 736	3.2	117.6	★	London RD
DBNF Road 736	DBNF Road 760–N	3.0	120.6	★	London RD

Sheltowee Trace National Recreation Trail Mileage Table

From	To	Section	Total	Roads	Manager
DBNF Road 760–N	Leave DBNF Road 4078	0.7	121.3	★	London RD
Leave DBNF Road 4078	KY 490	2.8	124.1		London RD
KY 490	Rockcastle River	1.5	125.6	★	London RD
Rockcastle River	On Road 489	3.3	128.9	★	London RD
On Road 489	Off Road 489	0.8	129.7	★	London RD
Off Road 489	Horse Lick Creek	1.3	131.0	★	London RD
Horse Lick Creek	Wolf Pen Branch	3.6	134.6	★	London RD
Wolf Pen Branch	S-Tree CG	4.5	139.1	★	London RD
S-Tree CG	DBNF Road 43	2.0	141.1	OHVs	London RD
DBNF Road 43	Leave DBNF Road 20	2.0	143.1	OHVs	London RD
Leave DBNF Road 20	DBNF Road 3062	2.2	145.3	OHVs	London RD
DBNF Road 3062	Leave DBNF Road 3062	1.0	146.3	OHVs	London RD
Leave DBNF Road 3062	US 421	2.3	148.6	OHVs	London RD
US 421	Road 443	1.3	149.9	★	London RD
Road 443	KY 89	4.7	154.6	OHVs	London RD
KY 89	DBNF Road 376	0.6	155.2	OHVs	London RD
DBNF Road 376	Turkeyfoot CG	3.7	158.9	OHVs	London RD
Turkeyfoot CG	War Fork	2.2	161.1		London RD
War Fork	KY 1209	7.2	168.3		London RD
KY 1209	Hale Ridge Road	0.5	168.8	★	London RD
Hale Ridge Road	DBNF Road 3047	1.6	170.4		London RD
DBNF Road 3047	Copperas Branch	2.6	173.0	part	London RD
Copperas Branch	Sturgeon Creek	0.3	173.3		London RD
Sturgeon Creek	Crestmont-Todds Road	2.6	175.9	★	London RD
Crestmont-Todds Road	KY 399	2.7	178.6	★	London RD
KY 399	Kentucky River	1.1	179.7	★	London RD
Kentucky River	KY 52	3.6	183.3	part	Stanton RD
KY 52	KY1036	6.4	189.7	★	Stanton RD
KY1036	Sand Gap Trail	3.7	193.4		Stanton RD
Sand Gap Trail	Balanced Rock Trail	1.5	194.9		Natural Bridge SP

Sheltowee Trace National Recreation Trail Mileage Table

From	To	Section	Total	Roads	Manager
Balanced Rock Trail	Lakeshore Trail	0.8	195.7		Natural Bridge SP
Lakeshore Trail	Whittleton Branch CG	0.5	196.2		Natural Bridge SP
Whittleton Branch CG	KY 15	2.3	198.5		Stanton RD
KY 15	Grays Arch TH	0.9	199.4		Stanton RD
Grays Arch TH	Jct Tr. 227	0.2	199.6		Stanton RD
Jct Tr. 227	Jct Tr. 226	1.4	201.0		Stanton RD
Jct Tr. 226	Join Tr. 221	0.4	201.4		Stanton RD
Join Tr. 221	Leave Tr. 221	1.3	202.7		Stanton RD
Leave Tr. 221	KY 715	1.3	204.0		Stanton RD
KY 715	Bison Way Trail	3.5	207.5		Stanton RD
Bison Way Trail	Lost Branch Trail	2.5	210.0		Stanton RD
Lost Branch Trail	Corner Ridge TH	2.0	212.0		Stanton RD
Corner Ridge TH	KY 77	1.0	213.0	★	Stanton RD
KY 77	US 460	2.8	215.8	★	Stanton RD
US 460	KY1274	5.4	221.2	★	Morehead RD
KY1274	Clear Lake TH	9.2	230.4		Morehead RD
Clear Lake TH	White Sulphur Horse Trail	1.5	231.9		Morehead RD
White Sulphur Horse Trail	Trail 113	3.0	234.9		Morehead RD
Trail 113	White Sulphur Horse Trail	0.5	235.4		Morehead RD
White Sulphur Horse Trail	Caney Loop Trail #226–W	1.5	236.9		Morehead RD
Caney Loop Trail #226–W	Caney Loop Trail #226–E	2.5	239.4		Morehead RD
Caney Loop Trail #226–E	KY 801	0.5	239.9		Morehead RD
KY 801	Big Limestone Trail	3.8	243.7		Morehead RD
Big Limestone Trail	US 60	1.7	245.4		Morehead RD
US 60	KY 32	6.8	252.2	★	Morehead RD
KY 32	Martin Branch Trail	5.9	258.1	part	Morehead RD
Martin Branch Trail	KY 799	6.1	264.2	★	Morehead RD
KY 799	Holly Fork Road #779	2.2	266.4		Morehead RD
Holly Fork Road #779	Dry Branch Road	2.3	268.7		Morehead RD
Dry Branch Road	N TH on KY 177	9.9	278.6		Morehead RD

Contact Information

U.S. Government Agencies

Abraham Lincoln Birthplace National Historic Site
2995 Lincoln Farm Road
Hodgenville, KY 42748
270-358-3137
www.nps.gov/abli

Big South Fork National River and Recreation Area
4564 Leatherwood Ford Road
Oneida, TN 37841
931-879-3625
www.nps.gov/biso

Cumberland Gap National Historic Park
Box 1848
Middlesboro, KY 40965-1848
606-248-2817
www.nps.gov/cuga

Land between the Lakes National Recreation Area
100 Van Morgan Drive
Golden Pond, KY 42211-9001
270-924-2000
www.lbl.org

Mammoth Cave National Park
P.O. Box 7
Mammoth Cave, KY 42259
270-758-2328
www.nps.gov/maca

Reelfoot National Wildlife Refuge
4343 Highway 157
Union City, TN 38261
731-287-0650
www.reelfoot.fws.gov

Daniel Boone National Forest
1700 Bypass Road
Winchester, KY 40391
859-745-3100
www.r8web.com/boone

Morehead Ranger District
2375 KY 801 South
Morehead, KY 40351
859-784-6428

Stanton Ranger District
705 W. College Avenue
Stanton, KY 40380
606-663-2852

London Ranger District
761 S. Laurel Road
London, KY 40744
606-864-4163

Somerset Ranger District
135 Realty Lane
Somerset, KY 42501
606-679-2010

Stearns Ranger District
US 27 North – P.O. Box 429
Whitley City, KY 42653
606-376-5323

Redbird Ranger District
HC 68, Box 65
Big Creek, KY 40914
606-598-2192

Kentucky State Agencies

Kentucky State Parks
500 Mero Street
Frankfort, KY 40601-1974
502-564-2172
www.kystateparks.com

Big Bone Lick State Park
3380 Beaver Road
Union, KY 41091-9627
859-384-3522

Carter Caves State Resort Park
344 Caveland Drive
Olive Hill, KY 41164-9032
606-286-4411

Cumberland Falls State Resort Park
7351 Highway 90
Corbin, KY 40701-8814
606-528-4121

Dale Hollow Lake State Resort Park
6371 State Park Road
Burkesville, KY 42717-9728
270-433-7431

Green River Lake State Park
179 Park Office Road
Campbellsville, KY 42718-9351
270-465-8255

Greenbo Lake State Resort Park
HC 60, Box 562
Greenup, KY 41144-9517
606-473-7324

Jenny Wiley State Resort Park
75 Theatre Court
Prestonburg, KY 41653-9799
606-886-2711

John James Audubon State Park
P.O. Box 576
Henderson, KY 42410-0576
270-826-2247

Lake Barkley State Resort Park
Box 790
Cadiz, KY 42211-0790
270-924-1131

Levi Jackson Wilderness Road State Park
998 Levi Jackson Mill Road
London, KY 40744-8944
606-878-8000

Natural Bridge State Resort Park
2135 Natural Bridge Road
Slade, KY 40376
606-663-2214

Pennyrile Forest State Resort Park
20781 Pennyrile Lodge Road
Dawson Springs, KY 42408-9212
270-797-3421

Pine Mountain State Resort Park
1050 State Park Road
Pineville, KY 40977-1712
606-337-3066

Breaks Interstate Park
P.O. Box 100
Breaks, VA 24067-0100
540-865-4413
1-800-982-5122 (outside Virginia)

*Kentucky State Nature Preserves
Commission*
801 Schenkel Lane
Frankfort, KY 40601
502-573-2886
www.kynaturepreserves.org

*Kentucky Department of Fish and
   Wildlife Resources*
#1 Game Farm Road
Frankfort, KY 40601
1-800-858-1549
www.kdfwr.state.ky.us

Contact Information

Kentucky Department of Fish and
  Wildlife Resources
Hunt Control Office, Building 112
Fort Knox, KY 40121
502-624-2712
www.knox.army.mil/fw

Kentucky Division of Forestry
627 Comanche Trail
Frankfort, KY 40601
502-564-4496
www.nr.state.ky.us/nrepc/dnr/forestry/dnrdof.html

Pennyrile State Forest
Box 465
Madisonville, KY 42431
270-824-7527

Tygarts State Forest
Box 255
Rodburn Hollow Road
Morehead, KY 40351
606-784-7504

Other Organizations

Berea College
Forestry Department
CPO 2144
Berea, KY 40404
859-985-3587
www.berea.edu

Bernheim Arboretum and Research Forest
Clermont, KY 40110
502-955-8512
www.bernheim.org

Jefferson County Memorial Forest
11311 Mitchell Hill Road
P.O. Box 467
Fairdale, KY 40118
502-368-5404
www.metro-parks.org

The Nature Conservancy,
  Kentucky Chapter
642 West Main Street
Lexington, KY 40508
859-259-9655
http://nature.org/states/kentucky/

Otter Creek Park
850 Otter Creek Park Road
Brandenburg, KY 40108
502-583-3361 (from Louisville)
502-942-3641 (outside Louisville)
www.ottercreekpark.org

Pine Mountain Trail Conference
c/o Letchner County Cooperative
Extension Service
P.O. Box 784
Whitesburg, KY 41858
606-633-2362
www.pinemountaintrailconference.org

Red River Gorge Trail Crew
www.gorgecrew.com

Robinson Forest
Department of Forestry
University of Kentucky
Lexington, KY 40546
859-257-7611
www.uky.edu/ag/forestry/robfor.com

References

Dreaver, B. G, J. A. Smith, and H. R. Duncan. *Hiking the Big South Fork.* Knoxville, Tennessee: University of Tennessee Press, 1999.

Kentucky Atlas and Gazetteer. Yarmouth, Maine: DeLorme Publishing, 1997.

Manning, Russ. *The Historic Cumberland Plateau: An Explorer's Guide.* Knoxville, Tennessee: University of Tennessee Press, 1999.

McDade, Arthur. *The Natural Arches of the Big South Fork: A Guide to Selected Landforms.* Knoxville, Tennessee: University of Tennessee Press, 2000.

National Geographic/Trails Illustrated. Big South Fork National River and Recreation Area Map #241. Evergreen, Colorado, 1998.

National Geographic/Trails Illustrated. Mammoth Cave National Park Map #234. Evergreen, Colorado, 1993.

Palmer, Arthur N. *A Geological Guide to Mammoth Cave National Park.* Teaneck, New Jersey: Zephyrus Press, 1995.

Pine Mountain Trail Conference. *Pine Mountain Trail Guide.* Whitesburg, Kentucky: Pine Mountain Trail Conference, 2001.

Ruchhoft, R. H. *Kentucky's Land of the Arches.* Cincinnati, Ohio: Pucelle Press, 1986.

Seymour, Randy. *Wildflowers of Mammoth Cave National Park.* Lexington, Kentucky: University Press of Kentucky, 1997.

Sides, S. D. *Guide to the Surface Trails of Mammoth Cave National Park.* St. Louis, Missouri: Cave Books, 1995.

Index

H

I

J

K

L

M

N

O

P

R

S

Let Backcountry Guides Take You There

Our experienced backcountry authors will lead you to the finest trails, parks, and back roads in the following areas:

50 Hikes Series
50 Hikes in the Adirondacks
50 Hikes in Connecticut
50 Hikes in Central Florida
50 Hikes in the Lower Hudson Valley
50 Hikes in Kentucky
50 Hikes in the Maine Mountains
50 Hikes in Coastal and Southern Maine
50 Hikes in Massachusetts
50 Hikes in Maryland
50 Hikes in Michigan
50 Hikes in the White Mountains
50 More Hikes in New Hampshire
50 Hikes in New Jersey
50 Hikes in Central New York
50 Hikes in Western New York
50 Hikes in the Mountains of North Carolina
50 More Hikes in Ohio
50 Hikes in Ohio
50 Hikes in Eastern Pennsylvania
50 Hikes in Central Pennsylvania
50 Hikes in Western Pennsylvania
50 Hikes in the Tennessee Mountains
50 Hikes in Vermont
50 Hikes in Northern Virginia
50 Hikes in Southern Virginia

Walks and Rambles Series
Walks and Rambles on Cape Cod and the Islands
Walks and Rambles on the Delmarva Peninsula
Walks and Rambles in the Western Hudson Valley
Walks and Rambles on Long Island
Walks and Rambles in Ohio's Western Reserve
Walks and Rambles in Rhode Island
Walks and Rambles in and around St. Louis

25 Bicycle Tours Series
25 Bicycle Tours in the Adirondacks
25 Bicycle Tours on Delmarva
25 Bicycle Tours in Savannah and the Carolina Low Country
25 Bicycle Tours in Maine
25 Bicycle Tours in Maryland
25 Bicycle Tours in the Twin Cities and Southeastern Minnesota
30 Bicycle Tours in New Jersey
30 Bicycle Tours in the Finger Lakes Region
25 Bicycle Tours in the Hudson Valley
25 Bicycle Tours in Maryland
25 Bicycle Tours in Ohio's Western Reserve
25 Bicycle Tours in the Texas Hill Country and West Texas
25 Bicycle Tours in Vermont
25 Bicycle Tours in and around Washington, D.C.
30 Bicycle Tours in Wisconsin
25 Mountain Bike Tours in the Adirondacks
25 Mountain Bike Tours in the Hudson Valley
25 Mountain Bike Tours in Massachusetts
25 Mountain Bike Tours in New Jersey
Backroad Bicycling in Connecticut
Backroad Bicycling on Cape Cod, Martha's Vineyard, and Nantucket
Backroad Bicycling in Eastern Pennsylvania
The Mountain Biker's Guide to Ski Resorts

Bicycling America's National Parks Series
Bicycling America's National Parks: Arizona & New Mexico
Bicycling America's National Parks: California
Bicycling America's National Parks: Oregon & Washington
Bicycling America's National Parks: Utah & Colorado

We offer many more books on hiking, fly-fishing, travel, nature, and other subjects. Our books are available at bookstores and outdoor stores everywhere. For more information or a free catalog, please call 1-800-245-4151 or write to us at The Countryman Press, P.O. Box 748, Woodstock, Vermont 05091. You can find us on the Internet at www.countrymanpress.com.